The conventional wisdom assumes a basic conflict between the voluntary sector and the state. The authors of this volume show that, far from competing with government, nonprofit organizations provide an alternative set of mechanisms through which to deliver publicly financed services. In many countries, for example, partnerships between local government and voluntary organizations are thriving.

The authors • put the current debate over the relative roles of government and the nonprofit sector into perspective by examining how the relationship between them has developed • evaluate the possibilities for cooperation between nonprofits and the state in coping with current social needs • assess the extent to which nonprofit organizations can assume new burdens, and • explore, in different national settings, the evolving relationship between the nonprofit sector and the state, which has come to be a central issue in the political discourse of our day.

GOVERNMENT AND THE THIRD SECTOR

Benjamin Gidron
Ralph M. Kramer
Lester M. Salamon
Editors

GOVERNMENT AND THE THIRD SECTOR

Emerging
Relationships
in Welfare
States

Jossey-Bass Publishers • San Francisco

Copyright © 1992 by Jossey-Bass Inc., Publishers, 350 Sansome Street, San Francisco, California 94104. Copyright under International, Pan American, and Universal Copyright Conventions. All rights reserved. No part of this book may be reproduced in any form—except for brief quotation (not to exceed 1,000 words) in a review or professional work—without permission in writing from the publishers.

For sales outside the United States contact Maxwell Macmillan International Publishing Group, 866 Third Avenue, New York, New York 10022

Printed on acid-free paper and manufactured in the United States of America

The paper used in this book meets the State of California requirements for recycled paper (50 percent recycled waste, including 10 percent postconsumer waste), which are the strictest guidelines for recycled paper currently in use in the United States.

Library of Congress Cataloging-in-Publication Data

Government and the third sector : emerging relationships in
  welfare states / Benjamin Gidron, Ralph M. Kramer, Lester M.
  Salamon, editors.
      p.   cm. — (Jossey-Bass nonprofit series) (Jossey-Bass
  public administration series)
    Includes bibliographical references and index.
    ISBN 1-55542-439-2
    1. Corporations, Nonprofit—Government policy.   2. Welfare state.
  I. Gidron, Benjamin.   II. Kramer, Ralph M.   III. Salamon, Lester M.
  IV. Series.   V. Series: Jossey-Bass public administration series.
  HD2769.15.G68   1992
  338.7'4—dc20   91-39144
                                                                 CIP

FIRST EDITION

HB Printing   10 9 8 7 6 5 4 3 2 1   Code 9238

A joint publication of

The
Jossey-Bass
Nonprofit Sector
Series

and

The
Jossey-Bass
Public Administration
Series

Contents

Preface — xi

Editors — xv

Contributors — xvii

1. Government and the Third Sector in Comparative Perspective: Allies or Adversaries? — 1
   Benjamin Gidron, Ralph M. Kramer, Lester M. Salamon

2. An Elaborate Network: Profiling the Third Sector in Germany — 31
   Helmut K. Anheier

3. A Partnership Between Government and Voluntary Organizations: Changing Relationships in Dutch Society   57
Herman J. Aquina

4. The Historical Precedent for Government-Nonprofit Cooperation in Norway   75
Stein Kuhnle, Per Selle

5. The Interrelationship Between the Public and Voluntary Sectors in Switzerland: Unmixing the Mixed-Up Economy   100
Antonin Wagner

6. The Voluntary Sector's Central Role in Managing Societal Instability in Northern Ireland   120
Arthur P. Williamson

7. The Changing Role of the Nonprofit Sector in Britain: Moving Toward the Market   147
Marilyn Taylor

8. A Resurgent Third Sector and Its Relationship to Government in Israel   176
Benjamin Gidron

9. Voluntary and Public Social Services in Italy   196
Sergio Pasquinelli

10. Building Welfare Systems Through Local Associations in France   215
Viviane Mizrahi-Tchernonog

Index   239

Preface

Since the mid 1970s, there has been a remarkable upsurge in public and scholarly attention in North America and Europe on the role of the nonprofit sector, particularly as an alternative provider of public services. Even in Eastern Europe, where former communist regimes are dissolving, there is tremendous interest in this "third sector" (between the market and the state), as a vehicle for public services and citizen participation.

While the relationship between the state and the voluntary associations of its citizens has been deeply rooted in history and in political theory since the seventeenth century, there has probably been more public discussion and research on this subject in the last decade than in the previous fifty years. For example, it is estimated that more than two hundred researchers in forty countries are now working in a new, interdisciplinary field of policy research, considered to be among the fastest growing and most dynamic areas in the social sciences. In the last decade, over twenty new research centers have been established in the United States and several have been established in Europe. Two new scholarly journals have been launched, and three international conferences of researchers on the nonprofit sector have taken place since 1987. Indeed, this book is a product of one such conference: "Voluntarism, Nongovernmental Organizations (NGOs), and Public Policy" held in Jerusalem in May 1989.

What accounts for all this activity? Developments in ideology and social policy pertaining to the "crisis of the welfare state" partly explain it — policies such as retrenchment in public spending, decentralization, debureaucratization, deregulation, and deinstitutionalization. The state has everywhere become a partner, a patron, or a purchaser of services from nonprofits, whose numbers increase each year.

The increased interdependence of government and the nonprofit sector — the major theme of this book — is implied in the widely used concept of a mixed economy, a pervasive mingling of public and private funds and functions, spawning quangos (quasi-nongovernmental organizations) and paragovernmental organizations, with the consequent blurring of the boundaries between the state, the market, the nonprofit sector, and the informal sector. Yet little of this is reflected in most comparative research on the welfare state, which generally conveys the misleading impression of government as a monolithic structure with no separation between the financing and the delivery of public services.

As the chapters in this book illustrate, welfare states vary greatly in the extent to which they rely on nonprofits. The Netherlands, where nonprofit organizations are the primary service-delivery system, and Sweden, where practically none are used, stand at either end of a continuum. Closer to the Netherlands is Germany, where over half of the social services are subsidized by government but provided by a diverse array of nonprofit organizations. Other countries with similar patterns are Belgium, Switzerland, and Austria. The United Kingdom and Norway are closer to Sweden because of the dominance of their statutory systems; France, Canada, and Australia stand between them and the United States, which is about in the middle.

Despite all the interest in nonprofit organizations, their relationship to government is still largely unexplored; thus there are no generally accepted concepts, models, theories, or paradigms for research. Instead, numerous metaphors are used: the new political economy, third-party government, nonprofit federalism, the enabling state, or the franchise state in the United States; indirect public administration in Finland, Germany, and Denmark; and the social economy in France.

The chapters in *Government and the Third Sector* seek to correct this shortcoming. Stripping away some of the rhetoric of the welfare state, the authors examine the actual realities of government-nonprofit relations in nine different national settings. In this way, the book differs from most previous descriptions of the modern welfare state; it brings into focus the little known but highly significant role performed by nonprofit organizations even in countries where the welfare state is well developed, such as in Norway, Switzerland, Germany, and the Netherlands. Similarly, the book differs from previous studies of the nonprofit sector by its explicit concentration on the relationship between the nonprofit sector and the state.

Except for the introductory overview, the chapters in this book were originally presented at three sessions we planned for the Second International Conference of Researchers on the Nonprofit Sector in 1989, which was hosted by the National Council for Research and Development of the Ministry of Science and Development in Israel. Benjamin Gidron of Ben Gurion University of the Negev served as chairman of the national organizing committee, and Ralph M. Kramer and Lester M. Salamon served on the international advisory committee. Fourteen researchers were commissioned to describe and analyze the relationship between government and the nonprofit sector, as well as to present the history, ideological background, legal character, roles, and relationships of the nonprofit sector in their country. The nine papers selected for publication in this volume serve as national case studies illustrating different patterns;

together they could ultimately lead to an empirically based theory of the role of nonprofits in welfare states and, at the same time, contribute to our understanding of social policy and the administration of voluntary nonprofit organizations. The results should be of interest to public policy makers and social scientists alike, as well as to board and staff members of nonprofit organizations in health, education, social service, the arts, and culture.

We want to acknowledge the skill and devotion of Rachel Lipski and Shulamit Kahana of the Ministry of Science and Development for their assistance in planning the Jerusalem conference in 1989.

February 1992　　　　　　　　　　　Benjamin Gidron
　　　　　　　　　　　　　　　　　　　Beer-Sheva, Israel

　　　　　　　　　　　　　　　　　　　Ralph M. Kramer
　　　　　　　　　　　　　　　　　　　Berkeley, California

　　　　　　　　　　　　　　　　　　　Lester M. Salamon
　　　　　　　　　　　　　　　　　　　Baltimore, Maryland

Editors

Benjamin Gidron is an associate professor and former chairman, Spitzer Department of Social Work, Ben Gurion University of the Negev, Israel. During 1990–91 he was a visiting associate professor at the School of Social Welfare, University of California, Los Angeles. Gidron has numerous publications on volunteer work, self-help groups and organizations, and nonprofit organizations. He organized the 1989 international conference on which this book is based and is active in international forums of researchers on the nonprofit sector.

Ralph M. Kramer is professor emeritus of social welfare at the University of California, Berkeley. He is the author of over seventy articles on citizen participation, social planning, and the voluntary sector in the United States and Europe. His books include *Voluntary Agencies in the Welfare State* (1981), *Participation* *of the Poor* (1969), *Readings in Community Organization Practice* (with H. Specht, 3rd ed., 1982), and *Community Development in Israel and the Netherlands* (1970). His books and articles in scholarly journals have been translated into Italian, Dutch, Spanish, French, Hebrew, and Hungarian.

Lester M. Salamon is a professor at The Johns Hopkins University and the director of its Institute for Policy Studies. Prior to this he was director of the Center for Governance and Management Research and of the Nonprofit Sector Project at The Urban Institute in Washington, D.C. Between 1977 and 1980, he served as deputy associate director for economic development of the U.S. Office of Management and Budget. Before that he was associate professor of policy sciences at Duke University. His most recent publications include *America's Nonprofit Sector: A Primer* (1992), *Human Capital and America's Future: An Economic Strategy for the 90s* (1991), *Beyond Privatization: The Tools of Government Action* (1989), *The Reagan Presidency and the Governing of America* (1985), and *The Federal Budget and the Nonprofit Sector* (1982).

Contributors

Helmut K. Anheier is a research associate in the Institute for Policy Studies of The Johns Hopkins University and an assistant professor in the department of sociology of Rutgers University. With Wolfgang Seibel he is coeditor of *The Third Sector: Comparative Studies of Nonprofit Organizations* (1990).

Herman J. Aquina is an associate professor in the department of policy sciences in the Catholic University of Nijmegen, the Netherlands. His work includes studies in policy analysis, political science, and the organization and dynamics of public decision making. His most recent research is in networks of governmental and other public organizations in social health care policies.

Stein Kuhnle has been a professor of comparative politics at the University of Bergen, Norway, since 1982. He is also the director of the Welfare State Research Program of the Norwegian Research Council for Applied Social Research. Kuhnle is the author of numerous books and articles on the development of the Scandinavian welfare states, social and political mobilization in Scandinavia, and political science in Norway.

Viviane Mizrahi-Tchernonog is an economist in the Centre de la Recherche Scientifique and a researcher in the Laboratoire d'Economie Sociale of the University of Paris.

Sergio Pasquinelli, research associate at the Istituto per la Ricerca Sociale in Milan, Italy, is a sociologist whose publications have appeared in U.S. and Italian journals. He is coauthor of a book on Italian voluntary action, *Identita e Servizio* (with C. Ranci and U. De Ambrogio, 1991).

Per Selle is an associate professor of comparative politics at the University of Bergen, Norway. He is affiliated with the Norwegian Center of Organization and Management in Bergen, where he is working on a study of the relationship between government and voluntary organizations.

Marilyn Taylor is a lecturer in the management of health and social care at the School for Advanced Urban Studies, Bristol University, England. She has worked as a policy analyst and researcher, and has published a range of work on community development, evaluation, and the role of the voluntary sector. She is chair of the editorial board of the *Community Development Journal.*

Antonin Wagner has been dean of the School of Social Work in Zurich, Switzerland, since 1976, and professor in public finance and social policy at the department of economics of the University of Zurich. In 1987, he was a visiting professor at the Florence Heller Graduate School for Advanced Studies in Social Welfare, Brandeis University. He has published widely in German, French, and English in the area of public finance and social policy.

Arthur P. Williamson is a senior lecturer in social administration and policy at the University of Ulster in Coleraine, Northern Ireland. His research interests include the role of voluntary organizations in social welfare and community development, with emphasis on their potential for bridging ethnic divisions in a society.

GOVERNMENT AND THE THIRD SECTOR

1

Government and the Third Sector in Comparative Perspective: Allies or Adversaries?

Benjamin Gidron
Ralph M. Kramer
Lester M. Salamon

A major assault on the concept of "the state" has been launched in recent years, not only in Eastern Europe but also in many parts of the West. Judging from the political rhetoric of our time, government has not only failed to live up to the promises that gave rise to the modern welfare state; it has actually made matters worse, undermining individual initiative and threatening economic prosperity as well. The upshot has been a widespread call for significant cutbacks in government expenditures and for the privatization or reprivatization of a host of social functions, from the delivery of electric power to the provision of social aid.

While most of the attention resulting from the critique of the modern state has focused on the need for greater reliance on the market and private business, increasingly attention has come to focus as well on voluntary citizen action and private, voluntary organizations. Such organizations, which are part neither of government nor of the private business sector, have played a critical role in virtually every part of the world. Yet for more than fifty years their role has been downplayed or ignored by both scholars and policymakers, who focused instead on the rise of the modern welfare state. As a consequence, we are in a poor position to assess the extent to which these organizations are able to assume the burdens that are now being thrust upon them or to evaluate the possibilities for cooperation between them and the state in coping with social needs.

The purpose of this book is to correct this situation. More specifically, it seeks to put the current debate over the relative roles of government and the nonprofit sector into perspective by examining how the relationship between them has functioned—and not simply in the United States, where this relationship has already attracted considerable attention (Filer Commission, 1975; Kramer, 1981; Salamon and Abramson, 1982a; Salamon, 1986, 1987), but in a number of other countries, including some where it has long been believed that the nonprofit sector has ceased to exist in significant form. The chapters that form the heart of the book were all originally presented at a research conference on "Voluntarism, Nongovernmental Organizations (NGOs), and Public Policy" held in Jerusalem, Israel, in May 1989. All explore, in different national settings, aspects of the evolving relationship between the nonprofit sector and the state, which has come to be a central issue in the political discourse of our day.

To lay the foundation for these analyses, this chapter looks a bit more closely at the premise that seems to underlie this political debate, suggests the basic rudiments of a framework for examining the relationship between the nonprofit sector and the state, and then shows how the national experiences examined in this volume relate to this framework. As background for the discussion, however, it is necessary to begin by defining somewhat more precisely what we mean by the nonprofit or voluntary sector and by the concept of institutional relationships.

Defining Terms

Because it has been overlooked for so long in scholarly research and public debate, the private, nonprofit sector is one of the least understood components of modern society. What is more, this set of institutions takes quite different forms in different national settings, reflecting differences in cultural traditions, legal structures, and political histories. These national differences also affect the relationships between nonprofit organizations and the state, producing wide variations in roles and responsibilities. In view of this diversity, it is important to be clear at the outset what our focus is here, particularly how we define the nonprofit sector and what dimensions of institutional relationships are primarily of concern.

The Third Sector

In the United States, the set of organizations that is the subject of this book is typically referred to as the "nonprofit sector." This is so because the organizations are defined primarily in terms of their eligibility for exemption from federal income taxes on grounds that they are not principally profit-seeking.

For comparative work, however, the term "nonprofit" is far less useful. For one thing, many nonprofit organizations, even in the American setting, do earn profits, though the profits do not inure to the benefit of the organizations' owners, as is the case with business enterprises. For another, tax laws and the definition of "profit" differ widely in different countries. For example, American nonprofits are taxed on so-called unrelated business income that would be treated as entirely appropriate and completely tax-exempt in many European countries.

For these and other reasons, it may be more useful to refer to this set of organizations as the "third sector," rather than the voluntary or nonprofit sector. This term is used widely in Europe as well as the United States to refer to an extraordinarily diverse set of organizations lying between the market and the state — organizations that are not strictly government agencies nor primarily profit-seeking enterprises. What distinguishes these organizations is that they are constitutionally separate from government, are not primarily commercial or profit-seeking in purpose (even though they may earn profits that are plowed back into the primary mission of the agency), have their own procedures for self-government, and serve some public purpose (Brenton, 1985;

Salamon, 1992). Some provide services such as health, education, personal social services, and arts and culture; but others have an essentially representational role, advocating for particular causes or groups. Included, therefore, are universities, symphony orchestras, adoption agencies, day-care centers, and hospitals, but also trade associations, labor unions, political parties, neighborhood organizations, self-help groups, and groups advocating for a wide variety of causes, from environmental protection to the preservation of civil rights.

The Concept of a Sector

Given the diversity of the organizations embraced within this third sector, there is reason to question whether it constitutes a distinctive sector at all. But this is true of the business sector as well. What this diversity suggests is the need to be aware that various attributes ascribed to the sector may in fact not apply equally to all its component parts. In fact, there are three quite distinctive, if interrelated, levels of analysis that can be used in discussions of the third sector.

One is the *sector level,* which embraces all, or almost all, the entities that meet the basic criteria outlined above. A second is the *field of service,* such as health, education, the environment, or the arts. Obviously, organizations in a particular field of service have more in common with one another than with organizations in another field. In fact, the third-sector organizations in a particular field of service may have more in common with government or business organizations in that same field than with nonprofits in a different field. Finally, there is the level of the *individual organization.* It is quite possible that an attribute that is generally true at the sector or field-of-service level may not hold for a particular organization.

Most of the chapters in this book focus on the sector level and attempt to conceptualize the relationship of the third sector and the state in different national contexts. It must be understood, however, that this level of analysis is not the only one that could be pursued, and that the relationships identified at the sector level still need to be verified at the levels of the field of service and the individual organization.

The Dominant Image: The Paradigm of Competition

Regrettably, little of the debate over the roles and relationships of the third sector and the state has taken account of the different dimensions that these relationships can take. Rather, the relationship has tended to be perceived in one-dimensional terms—as a choice between state dominance or third-sector dominance. Indeed, in much of the debate that has brought the voluntary sector to prominence in recent years, a dominant paradigm has monopolized the discussion. Simply put, this paradigm portrays the relationship between government and the nonprofit sector in terms that are close to what economists would call a zero-sum game—a competitive relationship in which one actor's gains are another's loss. The prevailing rhetoric thus posits a conflict between the nonprofit sector and the state. According to this view, the expansion of the welfare state over the past fifty years occurred largely at the expense of the voluntary sector. As Ronald Reagan put it in 1981: "We have let government take away those things that were once ours to do voluntarily" (quoted in Salamon and Abramson, 1982b).

This notion of a conflict between government and the voluntary sector is deeply rooted in "liberal" political philosophy stretching back to Locke and Mill, with its emphasis on individualism and political liberty. Conservative theorists like Edmund Burke refashioned these notions into a defense of the "little platoons" of family and social group that give structure to human existence, arguing that these "mediating structures" are needed to protect individuals from the overarching power of the state.

This view finds support as well within the Catholic tradition, which has favored a residual, last-resort role for the state and a preference for reliance on such institutions as the family, friends, neighbors, and the church as the first lines of defense in times of need. This view was codified in the 1891 papal encyclical, which endorsed the doctrine of "subsidiarity" as the preferred approach to solving social problems. Under this doctrine, the social unit closest to a person in need—family, friends, neighbors, the church—has the principal responsibility to respond. Only if these institutions are unable to perform their functions should responsibility be assumed by the next higher social level. The national government is thus an institution of last resort, to be used only when all other avenues have been exhausted. This philosophy of subsidiarity has been the basic operating principle of social policy in the Netherlands for almost the last one hundred years, and it is also important in other countries with a strong Catholic population, such as Germany, Austria, and Italy.

Although the notion of an inherent conflict between voluntary action and the state is deeply rooted in conservative political thought, it has taken modern form in the writings of a new group of neoconservative intellectuals such as Robert Nisbet (1953), Nathan Glazer (1971), and Peter Berger and Richard Neuhaus (1977). Using invidious stereotypes of oppressive, rigid state bureaucracies opposed to innovative, flexible, and humane voluntary organizations, these theorists have revived the concept of a fundamental conflict between the voluntary sector and the state. In this view, the rise of the modern welfare state has destroyed or seriously jeopardized the whole array of mediating institutions, including voluntary organizations, that were formerly available to buffer the individual from the impact of impersonal, macro-institutions such as the state and the large-scale corporation. The result, they contend, has been an alarming upsurge in anomie and despair.

If this concept of an inherent conflict between the voluntary sector and the state is rooted most clearly in conservative political thought, it also finds support on the left as well. While conservatives have faulted the state for undermining the position of more efficient voluntary efforts, those on the left have criticized blind faith in the capacities of ineffectual voluntary action as a barrier to the establishment of a truly effective system of public care available to all as a matter of right. To build a convincing case for public provision, liberals had to discredit the voluntary institutions that conservatives argued were sufficient to cope with community need. Sharp distinctions therefore had to be drawn between the capabilities and orientations of voluntary organizations and those of the state, distinctions that suggested a conflict between these two sets of institutions rather than a basis for joint action to cope with social needs.

With the decisive expansion of the welfare state in more recent times, moreover, a new theme has appeared in leftist thinking about the relationship between the voluntary sector and the state—a concern about the bureaucratization of the modern welfare state and its harmful effects on grass-roots organizations and the empowerment of the poor. In this view, the modern welfare state, however well intentioned, has come to be dominated by middle-class professionals and middle-class concerns, and has consequently lost touch with the needs of the truly disadvantaged. Positing a romanticized "golden age" in the past, when neighbors and family members assisted each other and local voluntary groups provided mechanisms for true empowerment, the New Left faults the modern welfare state with having sapped poor communities of whatever dignity and strength they retained and transforming indigenous voluntary organizations into extensions of the state apparatus (Janowitz, 1976; Hadley and Hatch, 1981; Pinker, 1985).

Finally, the concept of a zero-sum relationship between voluntary organizations and the state finds support in the dominant economic theory that has been used to explain the existence of the voluntary sector in a modern, market economy. This theory argues that nonprofit organizations exist because of inherent failures or limitations of both the market and government in providing public goods. According to this theory, the market is not sufficient to meet the demand for "public goods" because such goods can be enjoyed even by those who do not pay for them, creating a serious "free-rider" problem. In traditional economic theory, this limitation of the market serves as the theoretical rationale for government. But government too has inherent limitations as a provider of collective goods since, in a democracy, government action requires majority support. Where a significant minority wants a kind or level of public goods for which majority support is lacking, government is not available to help. It is to meet this "unsatisfied demand" for public goods, this theory holds, that nonprofit organizations exist (Weisbrod, 1977). But if nonprofit organizations exist only to do those things that government is *not* doing, it follows that the relationship between these two sectors is at best complementary, with one making up for the slack the other leaves. That the two could operate together to deal with social problems is something that this theory would find inappropriate at best and harmful at worst.

Limitations of the Competitive Paradigm

In short, political thinking on both the left and the right, as well as the major economic theory used to explain the existence of nonprofit or third-sector institutions, assumes a basic conflict between the voluntary sector and the state. Since the welfare state has expanded massively over the past generation, it was reasonable to expect, given this competitive paradigm, that the voluntary sector had largely ceased to exist. Yet the chapters in this book paint a far different picture. Far from withering away, the voluntary sector remains a vital force in much of the world.

Part of the reason, moreover, is that the presumed conflict between the voluntary sector and the state does not in fact exist. To the contrary, the relationship between the third sector and the state in most of the countries of the world has as many elements of cooperation as it does of conflict. Enshrined though it is in political rhetoric, in other words, the competitive paradigm does not seem to describe very well the actual realities of government-nonprofit relations. This is because the competitive paradigm glosses over a number of crucial issues that the chapters in this book identify as central themes. Six of these themes seem particularly important to note here.

Ideology Versus Reality

The notion of a conflict between government and the voluntary sector fails to hold up, in the first instance, because it was never intended as a description of reality. The notion arose, rather, as essentially an ideological construct, as a theory to explain a particular policy course. The fact that extensive cooperation existed between government and the voluntary sector did not alter the fact that opponents of state action preferred sole reliance on the voluntary sector instead. Under the circum-

Government and the Third Sector

stances, there was no reason to acknowledge, let al/ the cooperation that did exist. Similarly, those w/ establishment of governmental systems of aid had in.. tive to emphasize the important role that voluntary organiza tions seem to have played in helping government carry out its social functions.

What is more, this "conspiracy of silence" about the actual realities of government-nonprofit cooperation still persists. Thus when Ronald Reagan in the United States sought to justify significant cutbacks in government social spending, he did so by emphasizing the harm such spending had done to the nation's nonprofit sector, ignoring, or discrediting, the substantial support these organizations have received from the state (Salamon and Abramson 1982a). As Marilyn Taylor shows in Chapter Seven, Margaret Thatcher pursued a similar course in the United Kingdom, downplaying the joint action that existed between the voluntary sector and the state.

Unlike these ideological statements, the chapters in this book take a more empirical approach and examine the actual realities of government–third-sector interaction. What emerges is a picture not of inherent conflict, but of widespread cooperation and mutual support in virtually every country studied.

Level of Analysis

A second problem with the paradigm of conflict results from its failure to take sufficient account of the different levels at which the government–third-sector relationship can exist. Not only does the third sector take different forms depending on whether one is talking about the level of the sector, field of service, or individual organization, as we have already seen. The same is true of government; the nature of government's relationships with the third sector may differ widely depending on whether the national, regional, provincial, or local government is the subject of attention. Thus in Italy, as Sergio Pasquinelli shows in Chapter Nine, nonprofit organizations have little contact with government at the national level but work closely with public authorities in many local areas.

What is more, even within the central government there are numerous departments whose fiscal and regulatory relations with the third sector may vary quite dramatically. In Britain, for example, a recent Efficiency Scrutiny revealed that thirty-four different central government departments and agencies allocated grants for basic administrative expenses and special projects carried out by third-sector organizations. Also in Britain during the 1980s, there has been an extended and bitter struggle for power between central and local government in which voluntary organizations are caught in the middle. National policies of privatization and degovernmentalization have encouraged the contracting out of local-authority functions to nongovernmental organizations. But not all nongovernmental organizations are benefiting as a consequence. Rather, because of the requirements of grantsmanship and governmental accountability standards, it appears that large national agencies will be the principal beneficiaries and small community-based organizations the probable losers.

There are also important differences in the functions of the third sector on various levels; for example, advocacy is more likely to be promoted on the national level, and service provision in the locality. A shift from national to local control may therefore also involve shifting the function of the third sector from advocacy to service provision.

A similar decentralization of governmental power, and hence of government-nonprofit cooperation, is also underway in Holland and France, as the chapters by Aquina and Tchernonog in this volume suggest. In France, as in Italy, nongovernmental organizations have long had few ties to the national government, but a decentralization that began in 1982 has led municipal and regional authorities to rely increasingly on nongovernmental organizations to deliver services.

Because different roles can be played by the third sector in different fields of service and at different levels of government, great care must be taken in transferring generalizations from one level or field to another. Most of the national case studies that follow, like the rest of the literature on governmental-voluntary relationships, are focused on the sectoral level. Only

Government and the Third Sector 11

limited work has yet been done at the subsector level, mostly in the fields of education and health.

Different Functions

A further complication in characterizing government-nonprofit relations arises from the fact that there are not only differences in the level of analysis, but also in the kinds of functions that government and the voluntary sector perform, either separately or together. Most important, nonprofits have both service functions, social functions, and representational functions; government has financing, regulatory, and service functions. It is therefore quite possible for third-sector organizations to have one set of relationships with government with respect to their service functions and another with respect to their representational or advocacy functions. Indeed, tensions between these roles are almost inevitable since government policy is often the principal target of the advocacy activities of nonprofit agencies. Third-sector organizations are therefore often in the position of having to bite the hand that feeds them, attacking government agencies on which they are dependent for financial support. Similarly, government agencies sometimes find themselves having to enforce restrictions on organizations they need to carry out public missions. By focusing only on the conflictual side of these relationships, adherents to the conflict paradigm overlook the areas of cooperation that also exist.

Finance Versus Delivery of Services

A further challenge to the conflict paradigm results from the failure to recognize that the provision of public services itself involves at least two very different activities: first, the generation of resources to support the service; and second, the actual delivery of the service. The fact that government has assumed responsibility for the former does not mean that it also is monopolizing the latter. To the contrary, government finance can be combined with a wide assortment of delivery arrangements, from giving vouchers to consumers to negotiating service contracts with private nonprofit and for-profit organizations (Salamon, 1989). Adherents to the conflict paradigm too often leap from the fact of government finance to the conclusion that government is also delivering the services it is financing, a conclusion that the chapters here show is often seriously at odds with the facts.

The Impact of History

A further factor complicating the interpretation of relations between government and the third sector is the fact of change over time. A pattern of relationships that exists at one historical period may differ markedly from the situation that existed at an earlier period. What is more, current political disputes are read backward in time, so that the past comes to be viewed through the distorting prism of present issues. In the field of government-third-sector relations, this has often taken the form of imagining a pristine "golden era" of third-sector dominance and effectiveness in the past that was disrupted by the rise of the powerful welfare state.

If such a golden era ever existed, however, it finds little support in the record of the countries reported on in this book. Far from a new phenomenon, cooperative relations between government and the third sector turn out to have a long history in almost every country in which the topic has been examined.

The origins of social services in the United States, as in Great Britain and other countries, for example, are rooted in a combination of governmental and voluntary action. Private charity and the Poor Law coexisted side by side for hundreds of years in these countries, each developing at its own pace and with gradually increasing influence over the other. For example, the era of voluntary agency predominance in the United States lasted until the 1930s, when there was a massive expansion of governmental social welfare programs. But throughout the pre-1930s period there was an extensive pattern of government support to third-sector organizations. One estimate in the 1890s reported that two-thirds of the income of private charitable organizations in New York at that time came from governmental sources (Warner, 1894; Salamon, 1987). Despite the centrality of the public sector since the 1930s, moreover, a parallel, and to some extent commensurate, growth of voluntary organizations has occurred, producing a mixed economy in almost all fields.

A similar pattern prevailed in the United Kingdom. The development of the British welfare state can be viewed as two streams of statutory and voluntary initiative that occasionally intersected and, even when parallel, affected each other's courses. In the beginning, charity was sponsored by the church; later, because of the inability of private philanthropy to confront the ever-increasing scale and complexity of social problems, the government was forced to take increasing responsibility for the poor and disabled. By 1911 both sectors had developed sufficiently for Sidney and Beatrice Webb (1916), the well-known Fabians, to formulate a set of principles for a functional division of responsibility that is still regarded as valid, although the terminology has been modified. They rejected the 1869 "parallel bars" theory of two mutually exclusive sectors in which private charity was more highly valued and focused on aiding the deserving and the helpable, while the hopeless and undeserving were assigned to the local authorities. Instead, they proposed an "extension ladder" theory, in which voluntary organizations supplement the basic statutory services that provide a minimum standard of life for all. This became one of the major assumptions of the widely accepted "partnership" concept of statutory-voluntary relationships emphasized in the Wolfenden Report of 1978, but which the Thatcher government sought to reinterpret.

From a broader historical perspective, Paci (1987) has identified "long waves" of shifting governmental and voluntary responsibility, with one or the other dominant at a particular point in time but both involved in varying degrees. The work of Kuhnle and Selle in this volume is particularly revealing in this regard since it demonstrates a high level of cooperation between voluntary organizations and the state even in Norway, which has long been regarded as a case of clear state dominance in the provision of welfare services.

More recently, in most countries a rapid expansion of

third-sector organizations took place in unison with the "takeoff" in welfare state spending during the 1960s. This was followed by slowed growth since the 1970s, accompanied by trends toward self-help, community development, empowerment, and other forms of voluntarism.

Whatever the origins or recent history of government–third-sector relations, they have been altered significantly by the recent "crisis of the welfare state." This is most clearly apparent in the United States and the United Kingdom. In both, popular frustrations with the perceived excesses and inadequacies of the welfare state gave rise in the late 1970s and early 1980s to conservative regimes committed to reducing government spending. Although such moves were justified in terms of expanding the role of voluntary groups, they had the practical result, particularly in the United States, of reducing government support to third-sector organizations, thus limiting their ability to function (Salamon and Abramson, 1982a; Salamon, 1986). The cutbacks in government support to the voluntary sector appear to have been less severe in Great Britain, as Marilyn Taylor shows in Chapter Seven, but a significant shift in the character of this support did seem to take place; more emphasis was placed on specific service contracts, as opposed to direct support for the nonservice functions of third-sector organizations.

Elsewhere as well, the "crisis of the welfare state" produced significant challenges to the prevailing pattern of government–third-sector cooperation even as it elevated the visibility of the third sector in national policy debates. One of the more interesting examples of this is the Netherlands, probably the longest-lasting and most pervasive example of close government–third-sector cooperation. Confronted by budgetary pressures and aided by the declining influence of religious institutions and an increasingly secularized pattern of life, the Dutch government moved in the early 1980s to reduce the hammer hold that third-sector organizations, many of them religiously affiliated, held on social policy. Thus the central government reduced its direct support of service providers, shifted decision making to local governments, and struggled to reduce the multitude of nonprofit groups claiming state support. With respect to organizations serving the disabled, for example, the government was able to persuade three interest groups to merge into one "roof" organization, and ended funding of organizations dominated by professionals or concerned primarily with planning, coordination, or policy analysis. True to the country's "corporatist" tradition, with its extensive pattern of deference to organized group interests, this was done through extensive consultation with umbrella organizations representing various interest groups.

In short, the relationship between government and the nonprofit sector has not been static. To the contrary, it has changed significantly over time, reflecting the evolution of social policy more generally. Far from competing with the state, nonprofit organizations were more often significant advocates of expanded state responsibilities and in many cases have themselves benefited from the expansion of state action.

Different National Traditions

Finally, different national traditions and patterns with respect to the position of government and the market significantly shape the role that nonprofit organizations play. One major factor is the historic pattern of church-state relations. The strong role of the third sector in the Netherlands, for example, reflects the pillarized nature of the country's social structure, in which the state is subordinated to a plurality of interests originally rooted in religious differences.

Also important has been the type of legal system the society uses. Those countries based on civil or Roman law tend to be more state-oriented, while those rooted in the common law are more market-oriented (Anheier and Seibel, 1990, pp. 181-184).

A third factor influencing the patterns of relationship between government and the third sector is the degree of decentralization of state functions. Esping-Anderson (1990) and Anheier and Seibel (1990), among others, have identified three types of regimes in which rather consistent clusters of economic and sociopolitical variables are associated with specific patterns of governmental-voluntary relationships. The first of these is the liberal welfare states of the United States, Canada, Australia, and Britain, where market criteria still prevail in shaping the welfare system. A second cluster includes France, Germany, and Italy, which are characterized by considerably stronger state involvement, even though Germany and Italy delegate more to local authorities than is the case in France. Finally, there is the Scandinavian Social Democratic model, based on high taxes and a high level of governmentally provided social welfare with "no ideological space for voluntary organization" (Lorentzen, 1989, p. 11). Yet, even here, as Kuhnle and Selle show in Chapter Four, there is still a considerable third-sector presence.

In each country, policy issues relating to decentralization, to relations between health, education, and social care, and to privatization affect third-sector organizations in widely different ways. This occurs not only because of distinctive national trends, but also because these issues are perceived differently by organizations that differ widely because of their size, level of operations (national or local), scope, field of service, function (services or advocacy), degree of bureaucratization, professionalization, and so on. The multiple and sometimes conflicting interests of the third sector are thus an expression of its inherent diversity and of the wide differences in the circumstances it faces in different national settings.

Toward a Typology of Government-Nonprofit Relations

From what has been said, it should be clear that the relationship between government and third-sector organizations is far more complex than the rhetoric of current political debate would suggest. How, then, can we make sense of this complexity? What conceptual tools or models might be available to help sort through the variations that exist?

Although many possible answers to these questions might be imagined, we find it convenient to distinguish four basic "models" to depict the relationship between government and the voluntary sector in the modern welfare state. Central to these models is a distinction between two sets of activities that are involved in making human services available: first, the financing and authorizing of services; and second, the actual delivery of them. Too often these activities are treated as if they were one, when in fact they are quite distinct. Indeed, although the language commonly used in political discourse rarely acknowledges it, these two activities can be carried out by different institutions. This creates the possibility of four rather different patterns for handling the provision of human services, as shown in Figure 1.1.

Government-Dominant Model

In this model, government plays the dominant role in *both* the financing and delivery of human services. This is what most people have in mind when they think about the modern welfare state. We do not refer to it as the "welfare state model," however, because it is as consistent with a low level of welfare provision as a high level, and also because many supposed welfare states (such as Germany) turn out not to embody this model at all, as Anheier shows in Chapter Two. We therefore use the more descriptive term of *government-dominant model* to depict this approach. It essentially involves the government as *both* the principal financier *and* the principal provider of welfare services, using the tax system to raise funds for, and government employees to deliver, needed services.

Third-Sector–Dominant Model

At the opposite extreme is the situation in which *voluntary organizations* play the dominant role in both the financing and delivery of services. We call this the *third-sector–dominant* model. This model typically prevails where opposition to government involvement in social welfare provision is strong either for ideological or sectarian reasons, or where the need for such services has not yet been widely accepted.

Dual Model

In between these two extremes are two additional models in which financing and delivery of human services are in some sense

Figure 1.1. Models of Government–Third Sector Relations.

Function	Model			
	Government Dominant	Dual	Collaborative	Third Sector Dominant
Finance	Government	Government/third sector	Government	Third sector
Provision	Government	Government/third sector	Third sector	Third sector

shared between government and the third sector, albeit in significantly different configurations. In one of these hybrid models, *both* government and the nonprofit sector are extensively involved in *both* financing and delivering human services, but each in its own separately defined sphere. We refer to this as the *dual or parallel-track model*. This can take two different forms. First, nonprofits can *supplement* the services provided by the state, delivering the same kinds of services but to clients not reached by the state. Alternatively, the third sector can *complement* the offerings of government by filling needs not met by government activity. In either case the distinguishing feature is the existence of two sizable, but relatively autonomous, systems of service finance and delivery.

Collaborative Model

The other shared pattern also features significant action by both government and the third sector, but here they work together rather than separately. We therefore refer to this as the *collaborative model*. Typically, this takes the form of government providing the finance and third-sector organizations actually delivering the services, but the opposite is also theoretically possible. This collaborative model characterizes the system that is widespread in the United States.

Important differences can exist in the nature of the sharing that occurs, depending on the extent of discretion that the service provider retains in the bargain. On the one hand, nonprofits can simply function as agents of government program administrators, with little discretion or bargaining power. This might be termed the "collaborative-vendor" model. Alternatively, third-sector organizations can retain a considerable amount of discretion, either in managing programs or, through the political process, in developing them. Such a situation might be termed a "collaborative-partnership" model.

Because it is typically assumed that "who pays the piper calls the tune," many observers take for granted that the collaborative-vendor arrangement is the most common form of this model. The political clout of the third sector in many societies and the difficulty that large government agencies have in monitoring contractors, however, suggest that the collaborative-partnership model may actually be more common. That, at any rate, is the message of much recent research (Kramer, 1981; Salamon, 1981; de Hoog, 1984).

Obviously, the prevalence of these patterns may vary from subsector to subsector within a particular country and also from one period to another. There is also some sense in which the distribution of responsibilities is not wholly independent of the level of services that is available. Historically, the expansion of social welfare services has typically required the active involvement of the state, even though, as this framework implies, that involvement can take a number of different forms. What this means in practice is that the nonprofit-dominant model may not in practice be consistent with a high level of welfare provision. Thus, these models may differ to some extent in terms of the level of services provided and not simply in the allocation of responsibilities for finance and delivery between the public and private sectors.

Nevertheless, these models give us a language with which to discuss the differences in relative roles and responsibilities of government and the third sector among different societies and different subsectors. Using these models, what lessons emerge from the country analyses that form the heart of this book?

Lessons from the Field

Perhaps the central message that finds support in the country studies that follow is that the government-dominant model of social welfare provision, which has dominated the political rhetoric of the postwar era, turns out at best to be unstable, and at the very least to be overstated as a portrayal of the prevailing patterns of government–third-sector relations.

Germany—A Welfare State in Name Only

This point finds powerful support in Helmut K. Anheier's portrayal of the third sector in the Federal Republic of Germany

(Chapter Two). Bismarck's Germany is often taken, of course, as the classic example of the modern welfare state, in which an enlightened government has sought to bind workers to the social and economic status quo by using the state to guarantee a minimum level of social and economic protection. As Anheier shows, however, this government-dominated imagery obscures a reality that would more accurately be described in terms of our collaborative model. Far from a monolithic state-dominated welfare system, Germany boasts a very elaborate network of private, nonprofit organizations on which the public authorities rely heavily both to help shape and to implement social welfare policies.

The underlying principle of the division of responsibility between government and the third sector is subsidiarity, which evolved out of the historic conflicts between church and state in Germany. The essential feature of subsidiarity is the primary obligation of the state to assist smaller social units to accomplish their objectives. This has given these organizations a great deal of popular support as vehicles for coping with public problems. Indeed, in some fields (such as child care and youth institutions), third-sector organizations have a virtual monopoly on the actual provision (though not the financing) of care, and government is obliged to defer to them in structuring its programs.

The Netherlands — Institutionalized Sharing

A similar, and possibly more fully developed, system of cooperation between the third sector and the state is evident in the Netherlands. As Herman J. Aquina shows in Chapter Three, government finances the key services in the Netherlands, yet delivery is vested almost entirely in private, nonprofit hands. The relationship between government and third-sector organizations is not one of client to vendor, moreover. Rather, through a variety of umbrella organizations the nonprofit providers are able to exert considerable influence over the basic design of government programs, so that the shared action that exists takes on the character of a true partnership, with third-sector organizations functioning as full-fledged collaborators. Indeed, there is some concern that they may have the upper hand.

As Aquina shows, this pattern emerged as a solution to the intense religious conflict that threatened to rend Dutch society apart, particularly over the issue of religious education. By financing education through the public sector but delivering it through the private, nonprofit sector, the Netherlands was able to defuse a conflict that might otherwise have proved insoluble. Because it reflects prevailing social realities, therefore, this solution has been relatively durable and has been extended beyond the educational arena where it initially took root. In fact, Aquina suggests that it offers important lessons for other societies as a convenient arrangement to reduce conflict around issues where a single approach is not essential.

Norway—The Rich History of Government-Third-Sector Collaboration

In their analysis of the Norwegian case, Per Selle and Stein Kuhnle (Chapter Four) offer a slightly different perspective on the relationship between government and the third sector, but one with a similar message. To assess the extent to which the modern Norwegian welfare state represents the culmination of a conflict between the state and the third sector, Selle and Kuhnle went back to the historical record of early welfare policy. What they find directly refutes the conflict paradigm. Far from resisting the expansion of state involvement, voluntary health and welfare organizations were in the forefront of those demanding it. The rise of the welfare state did not, therefore, represent a historical discontinuity. Rather, cooperation and coordination between the voluntary and state sectors extended back well into the late nineteenth century. The differences between the eras before and after the welfare state is consequently not one of kind, but one of scope of cooperation. While the state has emerged as the dominant actor, it has done so with considerable complicity and involvement by the voluntary sector, even in the classic Scandinavian welfare state context.

Moreover, contrary to those theorists who argue that the voluntary sector remains strong only where extensive social heterogeneity and conflict exist, the Norwegian model suggests that it has a vital role to play even in circumstances of considerable social harmony. Rather than a situation of government usurpation of the position of voluntary groups, Selle and Kuhnle describe the Norwegian model as one of "coordination through shared goals rather than through forced hierarchical command." The relationships between government and the voluntary sector were blended into the history of the welfare state and did not change significantly over time because of a basic consensus over the goals of social policy in this society.

Switzerland—Decentralization Instead of Privatization

Unlike the three cases just discussed, where what appear to be classic government-dominated welfare states turn out on closer inspection to be collaborative patterns with extensive voluntary-sector involvement, in Switzerland the third sector is relatively underdeveloped. This is somewhat paradoxical, in view of the country's considerable ethnic and linguistic heterogeneity. According to the market-failure, government-failure theory of the voluntary sector, such heterogeneity is supposed to give rise to a vibrant voluntary sector since voluntary organizations are a vehicle through which minority views about desirable levels and kinds of public goods can be addressed.

As Antonin Wagner points out in Chapter Five, however, Switzerland has developed an alternate mechanism for meeting heterogeneous demands for public goods—namely, governmental decentralization. Through a federal system of cantons and municipalities, the public sector is able to tailor the provision of public services to the diverse demands of different ethnic and linguistic groups without having to resort to an extensive voluntary sector. Switzerland has thus been able to maintain a government-dominant model of social welfare provisions with a relatively small voluntary sector, despite the presence of extensive heterogeneity. The third sector in Switzerland performs at best a complementary function within a government-dominant system, filling in the holes left by the dominant system of decentralized government provision. Thus, Wagner suggests that the degree of centralization, not the diversity of demand, determines the extent to which the public sector is able to meet public needs.

Northern Ireland—A Government-Fostered Third Sector

A slightly different example of a stable government-dominant model is evident in the case of Northern Ireland, as portrayed in Chapter Six by Arthur P. Williamson. Focusing on the field of community relations and community development, Williamson shows how, in a society in a state of open conflict, government, far from usurping the position of the third sector, consciously fosters the creation of third-sector organizations to help it function in areas where it could not itself gain entry. Thus, the government has created a network of nonprofit mediating services and a trust jointly funded by the Irish Republic to finance them. In this way, the government is able to carry out through nonprofit institutions crucial functions that it cannot perform itself.

Great Britain—
A Government-Dominant System in Flux

The remaining four chapters portray government-dominant systems that are in the process of significant change, either toward decentralization, privatization, or both. Perhaps the fullest explication of these points is provided in Marilyn Taylor's description of the recent experience in Great Britain (Chapter Seven). As portrayed by Taylor, Britain prior to the Thatcher era was an essentially government-dominated social welfare system, though with significant third-sector involvement. The thrust of the Thatcher reforms was to move toward a market-oriented system in which both finance and provision were vested in private hands, both for-profit and nonprofit. The Thatcher ideology thus embraced the conflict paradigm of the relationship between the voluntary sector and the state and sought to strengthen the voluntary sector by reducing the role of the state.

The real result, Taylor argues, may well be rather different, however. With increasing stress on user fees and service charges, the welfare state may be replaced not by a system of privately based social care but by a system of "consumerism," in which the poor, lacking the means to purchase services, end up much worse off, and in which the voluntary sector surrenders much of the independence and concern for advocacy that makes it distinctive. She favors instead a movement toward a collaborative model, but one in which the advocacy and community-organizing roles of the voluntary sector are preserved with the help of public subsidization for these crucial functions. As Taylor puts it, government must not only fund services but also "take some financial responsibility for sustaining the health and vitality of the sector on which it depends for service delivery."

Israel—A Resurgent Third Sector

This emphasis on the advocacy role of the voluntary sector also finds reflection in Israel, which has been going through a slightly different process of change, as analyzed by Benjamin Gidron in Chapter Eight. Through much of its short history, Israel followed what we would term a collaborative pattern of social welfare provision, with active state support to voluntary organizations in a variety of fields, such as health and education. The government played a clearly dominant role in these relationships, however, controlling salaries paid by third-sector organizations and the fees they could charge for their services. In the terms we introduced earlier, Israel's collaborative pattern thus put the third sector in the position of a vendor rather than a real partner with government.

This reflected the felt need to create an "Israeli identity" for the many immigrants pouring into Israel, and the consequent need to suppress the pluralistic nature of the society. To the extent that third-sector organizations threatened to give expression to this pluralism, they had to be constrained and transformed into mere vendors for government-financed services. As Gidron shows, however, recent years have witnessed an upsurge of newly independent third-sector groups that are far less satisfied with this dependent position. Coupled with a reduction in government support, the result has been a more equal partnership between government and the third sector.

Italy — Groping Toward a Third Sector

A similar situation prevails in Italy, moreover, though here the third sector is beginning from a smaller base. As Sergio Pasquinelli shows in Chapter Nine, Italy exemplifies an essentially dual pattern of relationship between the third sector and government. Although religiously affiliated nonprofit organizations have long existed in the country, the rise of the welfare state left them with at best a complementary role vis-à-vis government. What is more, this role is exercised largely at the local level, where most of the responsibility for delivering, as opposed to financing, welfare services lies. The relationship between government and the nonprofit sector has hardly been one of conscious policy, however. Rather, it reflects ad hoc alliances and marriages of convenience that take shape as much for political as for policy reasons.

This pattern may be changing, however, as a result of a surge in formation of voluntary organizations in the late 1970s and 1980s. This surge reflects the emergence of environmental, women's rights, self-help, and other movements, and it could lead the way to more conscious national laws and policies on the role and rights of the voluntary sector.

France — Reshaping the State

A similar process of change also seems to be underway in France. As documented by Viviane Mizrahi-Tchernonog in Chapter Ten, France has long had a state-dominated social welfare system with most of the power vested in a centralized state apparatus. Voluntary organizations have been confined to a largely secondary role, filling gaps in the state's system of care.

In response to budget pressures and complaints about the rigidity of a centralized system, however, France in 1982 enacted legislation that significantly decentralized responsibility for social welfare. The result has been to stimulate a widespread pattern of experimentation in relations between government and nonprofit organizations at the local level. Called on to expand their social welfare responsibilities, but limited in personnel and experience, local authorities have begun turning actively to private "associations," to use the French term, in order to extend their reach and tailor their activities to the needs of particular groups.

In terms of the models identified earlier, France thus seems to be moving at the local level from a government-dominated or dual model to a collaborative model. In the process, local authorities have acquired a new function in the field of social welfare policy. In addition to their traditional police, and later administrative, functions, they have acquired the function of "animation, of organization, and of direction of the association life."

Conclusion

The nine case studies in this book thus make clear that the relationship between government and the welfare state is far more complex than the ideological rhetoric on the issue would suggest. The notion that an inherent conflict exists between government and the voluntary sector turns out to be a considerable exaggeration, if not a misstatement of the facts. The cases of Germany, Holland, and Norway in particular demonstrate that nonprofit organizations can function to satisfy differential demands for services in heterogeneous societies without undermining government's responsibility to provide basic services to all. Far from competing with government, nonprofit organizations have made it possible to build comprehensive social welfare systems in spite of unresolved conflicts between different factions in society. They do so by giving government an alternative set of mechanisms through which to deliver publicly financed services. Viewed historically, moreover, the voluntary sector has often been at the forefront of those advocating expansions in the state system of aid.

A second overarching theme that emerges from these nine case studies is that of change, and change in the direction of further elaborating collaborative partnerships between the third sector and the state. Where formerly it was taken for granted that the state was the appropriate vehicle for extending social welfare protection, increasingly emphasis is being placed on local government and private, voluntary involvement. This is the case most vividly in the United Kingdom, but it is also apparent in France, in Italy, and in Israel. The reasons for this range from the practical (the possibility of reducing costs by tapping voluntary effort) to the ideological (a preference for market-oriented systems over administered systems). Whatever the cause, the extent of experimentation with collaborative models of service provision is striking. Everywhere, governments are adopting the "animation" function vis-à-vis the nonprofit sector that Mizrahi-Tchernonog identifies in France.

This movement toward more active collaboration between government and the third sector brings with it, however, a series of concerns about the preservation of the distinctive characteristics of this sector. This third theme is explored most fully in Taylor's chapter on Great Britain, but it is evident in other chapters as well. As the third sector assumes a more prominent role in the provision of state-financed services, it inevitably finds itself drawn into the orbit of state regulation and requirements. Unless care is taken on both sides, this can lead to the diminution of the important advocacy and representational functions of these organizations and of their potential for innovativeness.

Finally, these chapters demonstrate the inadequacy of much of the traditional literature on the modern welfare state, which has tended to accept as given the prevailing ideology that left little room for a functioning private, nonprofit sector. In point of fact, significant third sectors continued to function within many supposedly state-dominated systems of social care. By failing to differentiate the state's role as the financier of services from its role as the deliverer of services, these accounts glossed over the significant role that nonprofit organizations actually played in many countries.

Whatever validity such treatment had in the past, moreover, it is becoming increasingly inadequate for the future. While it may be an exaggeration to say that the fate of the modern welfare state is now tied to the future of the voluntary sector, it is certainly the case that the two are increasingly closely connected. In such a climate, understanding the dynamics of the third sector and the patterns of interaction between it and the state have become urgent matters both for policy makers and those who seek to understand their decisions. Both groups should find the chapters in this book a good place to start.

References

Anheier, H., and Seibel, W. (eds.). *The Third Sector: Comparative Studies of Nonprofit Organizations.* Berlin: De Gruyter, 1990.

Berger, P. L., and Neuhaus, R. J. *To Empower People: The Role of Mediating Structures in Public Policy.* Washington, D.C.: American Enterprise Institute for Public Policy Research, 1977.

Brenton, M. *The Voluntary Sector in British Social Services.* London: Longman, 1985.

de Hoog, R. H. *Contracting Out for Human Services.* Albany: State University of New York Press, 1984.

Esping-Anderson, G. *The Three Worlds of Welfare Capitalism.* Cambridge, England: The Polity Press, 1990.

Filer Commission, *Giving in America.* Washington, D.C.: Commission on Private Philanthropy and Public Needs, 1975.

Glazer, N. "The Limits of Social Policy." *Commentary,* 1971, *52,* 51–58.

Hadley, R., and Hatch, S. *Social Welfare and the Failure of the State.* London: Allen & Unwin, 1981.

Janowitz, M. *Social Control of the Welfare State.* New York: Elsevier, 1976.

Johnson, N. *The Welfare State in Transition: The Theory and Practice of Welfare Pluralism.* Amherst; University of Massachusetts Press, 1987.

Kramer, R. M. *Voluntary Agencies in the Welfare State.* Berkeley: University of California Press, 1981.

Lorentzen, H. "The Welfare State and the Third Sector in Norway." Paper presented at the International Conference on Voluntarism, NGOs and Public Policy, Jerusalem, Israel, May 22–24, 1989.

Nisbet, R. A. *The Quest for Community: A Study in the Ethics of Order and Freedom.* New York: Oxford University Press, 1953.

Paci, M. "Long Waves in the Development of Welfare Systems." In C. S. Maier (ed.), *Changing Boundaries of the Political: Essays on the Evolving Balance Between the State and Society, Public and Private in Europe.* Cambridge, England: Cambridge University Press, 1987.

Pinker, R. "Social Policy and Social Care." In A. Yoder (ed.), *Support Networks in a Caring Community.* Dordrecht, the Netherlands: Martinus Nijhoff, 1985.

Salamon, L. M. "The Rise of Third-Party Government." *Washington Post,* June 29, 1980.

Salamon, L. M. "Rethinking Public Management: Third-Party Government and the Changing Forms of Government Action." *Public Policy,* 1981, *29*(3), 255–275.

Salamon, L. M. "Government and the Voluntary Sector in an Era of Retrenchment: The American Experience." *Journal of Public Policy,* 1986, *6*(1), 1–19.

Salamon, L. M. "Partners in Public Service: The Scope and Theory of Government-Nonprofit Relations." In W. W. Powell (ed.), *The Nonprofit Sector: A Research Handbook.* New Haven, Conn.: Yale University Press, 1987.

Salamon, L. M. "The Voluntary Sector and the Future of the Welfare State." *Nonprofit and Voluntary Sector Quarterly,* Spring 1989, *(1),* 11–24.

Salamon, L. M. *America's Nonprofit Sector: A Primer.* New York: Foundation Center, 1992.

Salamon, L. M., and Abramson, A. J. *The Federal Budget and the Nonprofit Sector.* Washington, D.C.: Urban Institute Press. 1982a.

Salamon, L. M., and Abramson, A. J. "The Nonprofit Sector." In J. L. Palmer and I. V. Sawhill (eds.), *The Reagan Experiment.* Washington, D.C.: Urban Institute Press, 1982b.

Warner, A. *American Charities: A Study in Philanthropy and Economics.* New York: Harper Collins, 1894.

Webb, S. and B. *The Prevention of Destitution.* London: Longmans, 1916.

Weisbrod, B. A. *The Voluntary Non-Profit Sector: An Economic Analysis.* Lexington, Mass.: Heath, 1977.

2

An Elaborate Network: Profiling the Third Sector in Germany

Helmut K. Anheier

This chapter, which analyzes the relationship between the nonprofit sector and the state in Germany, has two related purposes. The first is theoretical: contrary to conventional theories, which posit a conflict between the nonprofit sector and the state, in Germany a highly developed nonprofit sector *and* a highly developed welfare state coexist. As the welfare state developed, the nonprofit sector in Germany expanded—not contracted, as conventional theories would suggest. In fact, nonprofits operating in fields that are typical targets of welfare state activities expanded the most, and rank high among the top industries in terms of relative employment growth over the last twenty years.

Note: I would like to thank Lester M. Salamon for his comments and suggestions on earlier versions of this chapter, and Barbara Conrad for her assistance in its preparation.

The explanation for this lies in the relationship between the nonprofit sector and the state. In particular, the concept of "third-party government" (Salamon, 1981) is useful in helping explain this relationship. The term refers to the extensive pattern of government support given to nongovernmental entities to carry out governmental purposes, with significant discretion in financial and administrative matters vested in private, nonprofit providers (Salamon, 1987, p. 110).

This brings us to the second concern: the extent to which national circumstances affect the way third-party government actually operates. Salamon (1987) identified third-party government as the characteristic form of the government-nonprofit relationship in the United States. Although Germany shares with the United States a significant degree of public-private cooperation in the provision of social services, and nonprofit organizations that have considerable autonomy in the use of public funds, the underlying philosophy, principles, and orientations at work are somewhat different. Large parts of the nonprofit sector in Germany, the field of social services and welfare in particular, rest on the principle of subsidiarity. As we will see, subsidiarity is an extremely formalized and rigid version of third-party government; it leads to different and highly formalized types of public-private relationships, even though the form and extent of cooperation might seem similar.

To explore these points, this chapter is divided into several parts: first, we introduce the principle of subsidiarity and show how it relates to major characteristics of Germany. Then, we present a brief profile of the German third sector, to show some of the implications of subsidiarity, and focus on the free welfare associations as one of the clearest and most significant examples. Finally, we relate this discussion back to the comparison of third-party government and the principle of subsidiarity, and address several theoretical issues.

The Principle of Subsidiarity

In essence, subsidiarity means that the larger social unit (the state) should assist the smaller social unit (the family) only if the smaller unit can no longer rely on its own resources. In terms of social policy, it basically translates into a system whereby private provision of services takes precedence over public efforts, and local provision over nonlocal. Subsidiarity implies a hierarchy that begins with the individual, goes on to the immediate and extended family, the community, and the church, and ends with the state. At each step of the hierarchy, the higher level or unit is obliged to both protect and assist lower levels while respecting their independence.

The principle of subsidiarity is important to understanding the development of the relationship between the state and the nonprofit sector, and between the national government and the localities (see contributions in Bauer and Diessenbacher, 1984). One of the characteristics of the principle is that it is applicable to a wide range of institutional arrangements. Commentators remarked at the height of the economic recession in the early 1980s that when everybody was searching for a solution to the social and economic crisis, the principle of subsidiarity enjoyed such popularity that it was claimed by "alternative left movements," the Federal Employers Association, and virtually all political parties (Spieker, 1982, p. 15). With such a wide range of support coming from very different ideological camps, it seems useful to examine the origin of this principle.

Origins

The principle of subsidiarity originated in nineteenth-century Jesuit thinking and Catholic moral philosophy, and was meant to reconcile two developments that were seen as detrimental to the church: (1) greater individualism, which, outside the realm of the family and the local parish, coincided with an increased need for forms of social solidarity and nonfamily-based social services and welfare; and (2) the emergence of the secular nation-state, with its large-scale bureaucracy, which challenged the position of the Catholic church.

In its original formulation, the principle of subsidiarity advocated a static society with fixed, hierarchical relations among individual, family, local groups, occupational groups, and the state. In this system, a larger social unit may not assume responsibilities that can be achieved by a smaller unit. Moreover, the larger unit is obliged to assist the smaller unit if it is unable to meet its goals or objectives. Thus, the principle contained two essential elements: protection and obligation.

The principle of subsidiarity first came to prominence in Pope Pius XI's 1931 encyclical, *Quadragesimo anno* (*Forty Years*). The name of the encyclical recalls Pope Leo XIII's encyclical *Rerum Novarum* (1891) on social problems. *Rerum Novarum* advocated local solutions to social problems, albeit within a context of a preindustrial society. Some of this thinking is picked up again in *Quadragesimo anno,* which summarizes the Catholic attempt to find a position in the political conflict between liberal capitalism and collectivism (communism). Paragraph 79 contains the key passage: "Just as that which a single human being can achieve with his own will may not be taken from him and assigned to the realm of society, so is it equally against justice to demand from superior social entities what the smaller social community can bring to a good end; it is disadvantageous and confuses the entire social order" (translated from the German text in Plaschke, 1984, pp. 137–138).

The principle of subsidiarity has always been normative, even though subsequent legislation and practice changed much of its static, corporatist content. In the German case it has become a principle of division of labor between the public and the private nonprofit sector. To understand its form and significance today, it is important to see how the principle interacted with other characteristics of German history and society. Two examples should make clear how the principle of subsidiarity, in its basic formulation as a nineteenth-century expression of distrust in the centralized and secular nation-state, found its way into fundamental features of Germany's political system and legal structure.

The first is German federalism. Germany is now a federal republic in which the individual states (*Länder*) enjoy a relatively high degree of political power. This is particularly so in the fields of education and culture, the traditional domains of the third sector, which are almost exclusively a *Länder* matter.

Moreover, at the federal level, the *Länder* are represented in the Bundesrat (Federal Council). In the Bundesrat, the *Länder* enjoy veto power; all legislation from parliament addressing *Länder* matters must pass the Bundesrat.

That federalism took root in German soil after a long period of Prussian hegemony (1871-1933) and the centralization of national socialism is to a significant extent due to the churches' support for the principle of subsidiarity. Federalism was introduced by the Allies, the United States in particular, after World War II. While it could look back to no deep-seated democratic tradition, it could nonetheless take root in the ground provided by traditional regional differences between various parts of the country. Significantly, for some, *Länder* federalism became a welcome political system for the articulation and preservation of religious as well as regional privileges. For our purposes, it is important to note that federalism was soon brought into close ideological and political affinity to the principle of subsidiarity. The principle was advocated by both the churches and the ruling Christian Democratic Party throughout the 1950s and served as the basis for the division of labor between state and church in the field of social welfare. Thus, in terms of political history, the principle of subsidiarity was advanced by the same party that supported federalism. In contrast, the political opposition, the Social Democrats, at that time favored more direct state involvement—a secular, nondenominational welfare state and a more centralized, less federal political system.

Second, the principle of subsidiarity has also taken root in Germany's complex legal system. Germany is a civil-law country. The *Bürgerliches Gesetzbuch* (BGB, the civil code) came into effect only in 1900. The BGB, a late legal product of the Enlightenment, stands in the tradition of codification and legal abstraction. Codification assumes that a body of written law can, without contradiction, codify and regulate society. Legal abstraction implies that special laws (such as the stock corporation law, foundation law, the association code, and "lower-level" ordinances and procedural rules) all derive from a general body of law such as the BGB. While civil law regulates the relations among individuals and legal personalities, public law regulates the relations among state and public entities, and between the public and the private. It is important to note that the principle of subsidiarity is incorporated in the basic law (Constitution), and central public and private law codes, ranging from the tax code and the Social Code to the Federal Social Assistance Act, the Youth Welfare Act, and numerous *Länder* laws and municipal ordinances.

One of the most significant expressions of subsidiarity is the position of ecclesiastical law, which is constitutionally equivalent to public administrative law. Churches are established under not civil but public law, and they form corporations of public law. This legal privilege applies primarily to the member churches of the Rat der Evangelischen Kirchen Deutschlands (Council of Protestant Churches in Germany), whose congregations make up 41.5 percent of the population, the Roman Catholic church (43.3 percent of the population), and the Jewish community (less than 0.5 percent of the population). Other religious communities, in particular the nearly two million Moslems, form civil law organizations.

The reasons for the special treatment of the Catholic and Protestant churches are as historically complex as they are politically controversial. It seems best to approach the special status of the churches from Germany's political history and consider them together with other types of associations. Unlike in other countries (such as the French Loi de Chapelier of 1791 or the General Combination Act of 1799 in England), in Germany no legislation attacked the remains of late-medieval society, in particular the status groups (estates, *Stände*) and business associations of commerce and crafts. With a general democratic system of political representation lacking, these associations (*Verbände*) became influential economic and political instruments in the period of rapid economic development between 1850 and 1900. The social and political structure of Germany at that time did in fact share many aspects with the preindustrial, statist vision of subsidiarity.

The increased emergence of Prussian hegemony from the Vienna Congress to the proclamation of the Second Empire in 1871 culminated in the *Kulturkampf* (cultural struggle). This conflict between Bismarck and the Catholic regions of the country lasted from 1871 to 1891 and was, to a large extent, a political struggle between secular and religious powers over the division of labor as well as influence and responsibility in the areas of education, culture, and welfare. For the Catholic church and associations close to Catholicism, the principle of subsidiarity was a political expression against centralized secular power and, as some argue, against the notion of the sovereign and secular state as such (Herzog, 1975, p. 2595). The churches, the Catholic church in particular, lost much importance in the field of education, which became primarily a state matter not covered by subsidiarity, but they were able to maintain and strengthen the principle in the areas of social welfare services and health.

Application

Not only has the principle of subsidiarity been incorporated into basic features of German political structure and the system of federalism and basic law, but also it was incorporated in all relevant social legislation passed between 1950 and 1975, creating a protected, state-financed system of private service and assistance delivery that affords far-reaching autonomy to nonprofit organizations. This is apparent in three of the most significant bodies of legislation that pertain to private nonprofit providers in social services and welfare: the Social Code, the Federal Social Assistance Act, and the Youth Welfare Act.

Article 2 of the Social Code introduces the primacy of individual help and care over any other form of private or public social assistance and service provision. Article 3 mandates that the public sector and the nonprofit sector must work together in providing assistance and services: "In cooperating with non-profit-making, voluntary establishments and organizations, the [public] social assistance institutions seek to ensure that their activities and those of the [nonprofit and voluntary] establishments and organizations effectively complement one another for the benefit of those receiving assistance" (see Deutscher Verein, 1986).

The general concept of cooperation is further specified in the Social Assistance Act, a comprehensive piece of legislation on the public and private provision of welfare and social services. The act acknowledges that none of its provisions shall affect the position, functions, and activities of the public-law churches and the six private nonprofit social service agencies. Article 10 then reconfirms both the mandate of public-private cooperation and the independence of the churches and the free welfare associations, charging the public bodies responsible for social assistance to "collaborate with the public law churches and religious communities and with the free welfare associations, acknowledging in so doing their independence in the targeting and execution of their functions" (Article 10, Section 2).

Within the context of cooperation and independence, Section 3 requires the public sector to "support the free welfare associations appropriately in their activities in the field of social assistance." Section 4 establishes the principle that "if assistance in individual cases is ensured by free welfare associations, the [public] social assistance bodies shall refrain from implementing their own measures," except for "the provision of cash benefits."

While this section establishes the primacy of private delivery of social assistance over public assistance, irrespective of the mandate for public support (Section 3), Article 93 provides additional protection for the free welfare associations by forbidding government agencies from creating their own service providers at local levels "if suitable establishments of the free welfare associations . . . are available, or can be extended or provided." Similarly, Article 5 of the Youth Welfare Act states: "In so far as suitable establishments and arrangements provided by the free youth assistance associations are available or can be extended or provided, the [public] Youth Welfare Office shall not offer such establishments and arrangements of its own."

Resistance to the Concept

The principle of subsidiarity is thus more than a formula for public subvention; it is primarily an organizational principle for the division of labor between the public and the private sectors, creating no less than a protected, state-financed system of private service and assistance delivery. Such a far-reaching interpretation was politically controversial. It is beyond the scope of this chapter to give a full account of this still ongoing political debate, but some taste of its character may be useful. Among the numerous events, we will focus on the Supreme Court decision of 1967, which affirmed the constitutionality of the Youth Welfare Act.

In the early 1960s, several municipalities and the state of Hesse (at that time governed by the Social Democratic Party, which, in opposition in the Bundestag, had expressed reservations about Article 5 of the Youth Welfare Act) called on the Supreme Court to judge the constitutionality of the subsidiarity principle as formulated in the provisions of the Youth Welfare Act.

The case against the principle of subsidiarity can be summarized in several points. First, the law establishes privileges for the free welfare associations that amount to an embargo on public organizations in the field of social service delivery and assistance at the local level. Second, the law introduces a hierarchy among assistance and service providers whereby public organizations are devalued and put into a position of second choice. Together with the functional embargo, the principle of subsidiarity undermines the local right of self-administration by curtailing the powers of local authority.

Third, the principle of subsidiarity, based on Catholic moral philosophy and theology, stems from the idea of natural law and of a prestate social order. This, however, is a belief, a normative statement and ideology that might be acceptable to its followers but could not serve as a guiding principle of legislation affecting all citizens. Fourth, the privileges accorded to the free welfare associations, in particular their quasi-monopoly once established in a local area, lead to a restriction in the number of choices available to individuals seeking help. The relevant sections of the law violate Article 3 of the Social Assistance Act, which entitles citizens to select their preferred form of suitable assistance. Moreover, the law forces individuals to become clients of organizations they may not agree with.

In a controversial finding, the Supreme Court rejected

the charges, basing its ruling on several considerations. First, it argued that the translation of subsidiarity into a ranked system of providers does not imply a depreciation of public organizations. The Supreme Court emphasized the role of the public sector in the "overall responsibility" for provision of services at the local level. Second, the court observed that the language in which subsidiarity is described in the law does not imply any theological or natural law principle. It is primarily a principle dealing with the division of labor between the public sector and the free welfare associations.

Third, the court noted that neither the public nor the private nonprofit sector would be able to provide social services and assistance to all citizens, either financially or organizationally. This necessitates the cooperation and joint efforts that had characterized the relationship between sectors since the creation of the Federal Republic. The intent of the Youth Welfare Act and similar legislation, the court suggested, was to formalize and enhance such cooperation. Finally, the court pointed out that the right of choice of suitable and personal form of assistance (Article 3 of the Social Assistance Act) must coexist with the right to assist and the freedom of association for the free welfare associations in accordance with their own beliefs and convictions.

Since the ruling, the legal and practical implications of the principle of subsidiarity have continued to be subject to debate. Different implementations in the *Länder* have led to varying institutional arrangements in which the public sector and the free welfare organizations play slightly different roles and carry different weights in the areas of policy, finances, and programmatic activities. Nonetheless, we can identify a three-point political consensus that no major party contests:

1. The state assumes the overall political responsibility for the social welfare of society by providing a general policy framework.
2. The free welfare associations have the right to assume responsibilities and carry out activities within the general policy framework set by the state.

Profiling the Third Sector in Germany 41

3. The state is obligated to support the free welfare associations financially to ensure the adequate availability of social services to citizens in need of assistance.

The actual implementation and institutional setup varies by field and by *Länd*. In the case of personal social assistance, we find a system of public-private partnership which is schematically represented in Figure 2.1.

The Free Welfare Associations

Based on the preceding legal discussion, we can anticipate that the free welfare associations occupy an important position in social welfare and services in Germany. They are a prime example of the close relationship between the public sector and the private, nonprofit sector.

Organized in an umbrella organization called the Federal Consortium of Free Welfare, they run 68,466 institutions in the area of health care, youth and family services, and services for the handicapped, the elderly, and the poor (Bundesarbeitsgemeinschaft, 1990). They provide 70 percent of all family services, 60 percent of all services for the elderly, 40 percent of all hospital beds, and 90 percent of all employment for the handicapped. The free welfare associations employ 548,420 full-time and 202,706 part-time staff. The number of volunteers is estimated at 1.5 million, with a self-reported average number of 15.8 volunteer hours per month (Spiegelhalter, 1990). Operating independently but organizationally linked to some 60,000 institutions are the 27,362 self-help groups, clubs, and local voluntary associations.

To put the combined size and economic weight of the free welfare associations into perspective, it is useful to consider that the Catholic social service organization, CARITAS, alone employs more people than the industrial conglomerate Siemens, one of the largest employers in the Federal Republic. Together, the free welfare associations employ three times as many people as the federal post office.

While acknowledging the immense importance of the free

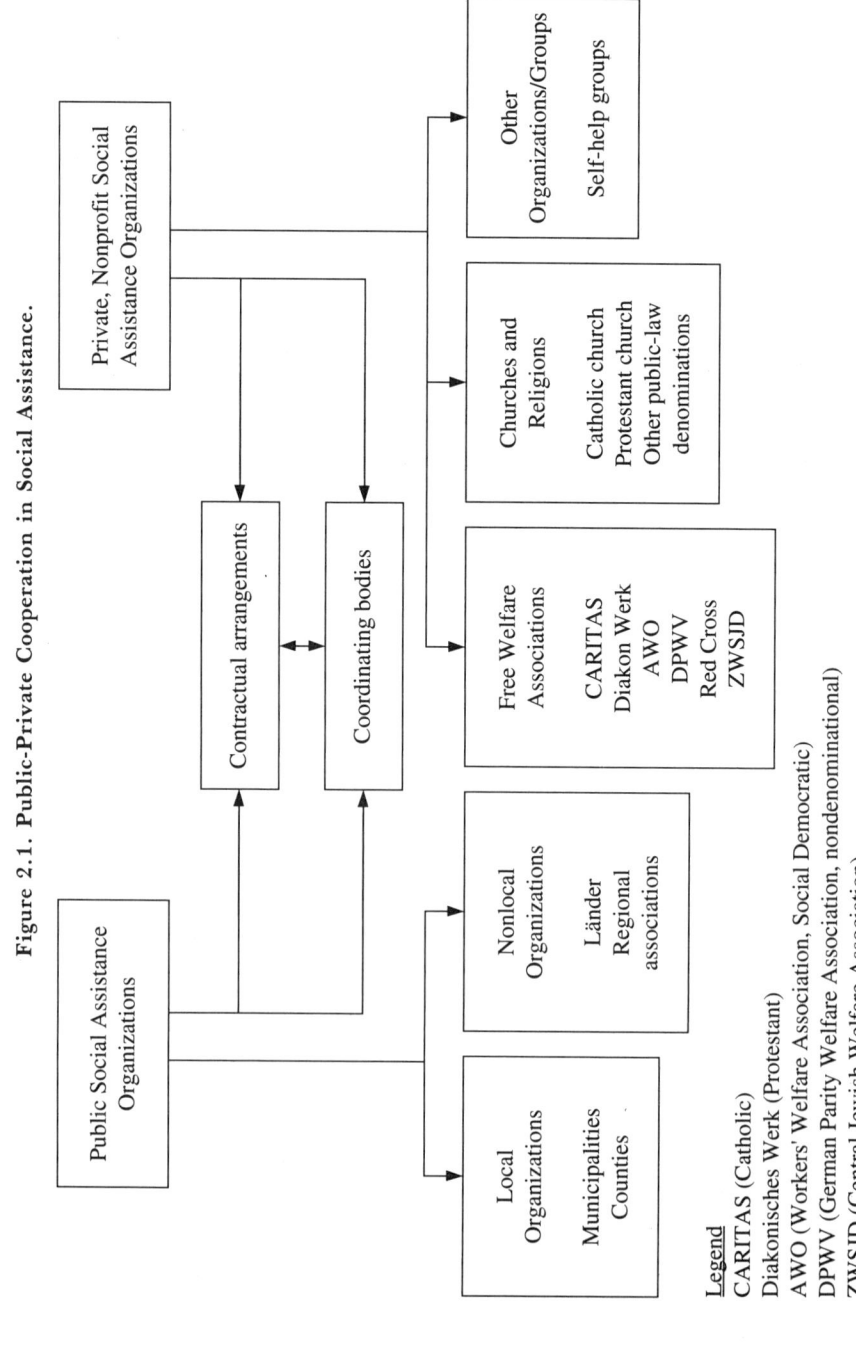

Figure 2.1. Public-Private Cooperation in Social Assistance.

welfare organizations, critics such as Thränhardt (1983) argue that their historical development is not the result of purposive collective decisions to provide welfare and to cater to the public good. Most of these peak associations originated primarily for political reasons; the legal and social policy rationales of the system were introduced afterward. They did not develop in a coherent fashion, but are largely unintended consequences of sometimes accidental policy decisions (Bauer and Diessenbacher, 1984; Sachse and Tennstedt, 1981). In general, however, each of the free welfare associations represents an institutional response to basic dilemmas (Bauer, 1978; Bauer and Diessenbacher, 1984; Heinze and Olk, 1981).

Diakonisches Werk (Protestant), founded as the *Innere Mission* (Inner Mission) in 1848–49, developed outside the official Protestant church structures. It began as a welfare-oriented evangelical movement, often in conflict with the secular political world. CARITAS, ideologically grounded in Catholic social ethics, developed within the Catholic church and is integrated into the religious hierarchy. CARITAS and Diakonisches Werk are the giants among the free welfare associations.

Arbeiterwohlfahrt (Workers' Welfare, secular), founded in 1919, has historically been linked to the Social Democratic Party. For the Social Democrats, who advocated public rather than private welfare provision, the Arbeiterwohlfahrt was created out of both political and economic necessity: political because all major parties at that time began to provide social services as a means of attracting and keeping members, and economic because public services were significantly reduced following World War I.

The Zentralwohlfahrtsstelle der Juden in Deutschland (Jewish) was created in 1917 to coordinate the numerous local welfare committees and activities at local levels. Dissolved by the Nazis, it was reestablished after World War II to provide assistance to concentration camp victims. In recent years, it has become increasingly involved in assisting Jews from Eastern Europe and the Soviet Union.

The Deutscher Paritätischer Wohlfahrtsverband, founded in 1920, is a consortium of nondenominational, nonpartisan private welfare organizations and hospitals. Like the Jewish welfare associations, the Deutscher Paritätischer Wohlfahrtsverband was in part an organizational response to the expansion of denominational and partisan welfare. It began as a close federation of independent hospitals, called the Fifth Welfare Association, and has grown in significance during the last two decades.

Finally, the Deutsches Rotes Kreuz (German Red Cross), international and humanistic in orientation, is both a relief organization (disaster aid, emergency assistance) and a social service organization. A federation of several local and regional Red Cross societies, it is perhaps the most politically autonomous of the welfare organizations.

In terms of services and finances, the state and the free welfare associations are closely interrelated. The clearest expression of this is in the area of financial support, though even here few financial data are available. The Arbeiterwohlfahrt had a total operating budget of about DM 100 million in 1984. According to the budget, it spent 40 percent of this sum on "participation in public tasks of the Federal Government" and received about 45 percent of its total budget in public subsidies. Similarly, 25 to 30 percent of Diakonisches Werk funds come from public subsidies; the figures for CARITAS are 25 to 40 percent. The Paritätischer Wohlfahrtsverband reports for 1987 that direct public support (subsidies) represented 15 percent of the revenue; private donations accounted for 10 percent; and fees and charges for 75 percent, including publicly subsidized payments. Since the Paritätischer Wohlfahrtsverband includes a disproportional share of hospitals, it is difficult to extrapolate to other free welfare associations.

The sparsity of data about the free welfare associations is truly surprising. What is more, classification systems used by the free welfare associations to report on employment and other basic economic data are incompatible with the classification system used in official government statistics. This complicates any direct comparison between the shares of nonprofit, commercial public-sector organizations in particular fields or areas. Nonetheless, we can assume that in the relevant fields, the free welfare associations constitute the great majority of the nonprofit providers.

Profiling the Third Sector in Germany

Table 2.1 present a detailed picture of the nonprofit sector; the areas in which the free welfare associations dominate are denoted with asterisks. The table shows that about every third nonprofit is classified as a church or religious association. This includes the Evangelical Church of Germany and the Roman Catholic church (including lay associations), Jewish congregations, the Islamic community, and also nonreligious associations like the Freemasons. About every fifth organization in the nonprofit sector is a kindergarten, which in Germany includes day-care centers and preschools. Together, religious organizations and kindergarten account for nearly half of all establishments in the nonprofit sector.

In terms of employment, we find that six fields—churches, hospitals, kindergartens, free welfare, homes for the handicapped, and homes for the frail elderly—account for 63.4 percent of all employment and 62.1 percent of the total wage bill in the nonprofit sector. This means that more than two-thirds of Germany's nonprofit sector is governed by the principle of subsidiarity.

The data allow for partial comparisons between 1970 and 1987. Several areas have enjoyed higher growth, whereas others grew at a less impressive rate. However, only one relatively small subsector, scientific libraries, suffered absolute decline; it is an area outside the realm of subsidiarity that experienced sharp cuts in government subsidies in the 1980s. Other fields show a concentration process, indicated by a decline in the number of establishments and an increase in the number of jobs. This is the case for unions and public-law business and professional associations, such as chambers of commerce, crafts associations, and bar associations.

The greatest expansion in both absolute and relative terms took place in social welfare, health, day care, and education—that is, fields governed by subsidiarity. In contrast, all forms of advocacy or interest representation expanded less between 1970 and 1987. Unions, political parties, employers associations, business and professional associations, and public-law professionals associations tend to have below-average growth rates. Overall, this seems to reflect a stronger emphasis on service delivery rather than interest representation.

Table 2.1. The Nonprofit Sector: Establishments, Employment, and Wage Bill.

	Establishments			Employment			Wage Bill 1987	
Organization/Industries	Number of establishments 1987	Percent of establishments 1987	Percent increase 1970-87	Number of jobs 1987	Percent of jobs 1987	Percent increase 1970-87	In million DM	Percent of total
Churches	25,005	31.5	21.8	116,367	13.4	64.0	4,040	11.2
Free welfare*	5,127	6.4	153.0	82,308	7.0	187.0	2,416	6.7
Free youth welfare*	1,311	1.6	6.0	11,193	0.9	20.7	346	1.0
Education and science	1,861	2.3	229.0	23,971	2.0	215.0	844	2.3
Sports and health	2,437	3.0	-	17,965	1.5	-	552	1.5
Unions	1,497	1.8	-2.8	12,178	1.0	29.7	591	1.6
Communal associations	61	0.1	-	1,562	0.1	-	62	0.2
Social security associations	50	0.1	-	1,887	0.1	-	85	0.2
Political parties	2,772	3.5	18.0	16,876	1.4	26.0	566	1.5
Employers associations	354	0.4	16.0	3,762	0.3	82.0	186	0.5
Business and professional assoc.	2,924	3.6	3.0	31,431	2.6	47.8	1,330	3.7
Public law business assoc.	1,329	1.6	-7.6	32,775	2.8	55.2	1,240	3.4
Hostels*	870	1.0	-	9,909	0.8	-	252	0.7
Recreational homes*	425	0.5	-	2,435	0.2	-	49	0.1
Canteens*	251	0.3	93.0	3,263	0.2	157.7	80	0.2
Homes: youth*	834	1.0	-	8,126	0.6	-	226	0.6
Homes: elderly*	1,512	1.9	-	45,394	3.9	-	1,197	3.3
Homes: nec*	455	0.6	-	4,820	0.4	-	149	0.4
Homes: children*	587	0.7	-	12,690	1.0	-	409	1.1
Homes: handicapped*	1,742	2.1	-	80,769	6.9	-	2,100	5.8
Homes: frail elderly*	1,778	2.2	-	81,007	6.9	-	2,251	6.3

Day care (other than child.)*	2,083	2.6	-	10,574	0.9	-	256	0.7
Universities	90	0.1	45.1	2,307	0.1	67.2	104	0.3
Scientific libraries	56	0.1	86.6	441	+	-22.6	15	+
Science institutions nec*	384	0.5	9.0	17,405	1.4	18.8	780	2.2
General schools	1,101	1.3	17.5	38,115	3.2	69.8	1,461	4.1
Vocational schools	1,738	2.2	116.4	43,546	3.7	221.3	1,095	3.0
Correctional schools*	271	0.3	66.2	6,964	0.5	29.0	222	0.6
Kindergartens*	14,577	18.3	87.5	97,076	8.3	190.5	2,359	6.6
Educational institutions nec*	486	0.6	-	6,896	0.5	-	151	0.4
Theater, opera	62	0.1	416.0	1,414	0.1	939.0	41	0.1
Orchestras and choirs	60	0.1	172.7	562	+	78.9	30	0.1
Museums and zoos	187	0.2	-	1,604	0.1	-	46	0.1
Adult education	657	0.8	-	9,559	0.8	-	267	0.7
General libraries	156	0.2	-	821	+	-	22	+
Sports institutions	255	0.3	72.2	1,604	0.1	114.2	26	+
Sport academies	48	0.1	-	550	+	-	15	+
Gardens and parks	14	0.1	-	56	+	-	1	+
Clinics and hospitals*	1,016	1.4	-16.9	246,866	21.1	21.1	9,166	25.5
Other health instit.*	2,977	4.0	156.0	33,131	2.9	2.9	931	2.6
							35,960	99.0**

* = includes establishments of the free welfare assocations
nec = not elsewhere classified
+ = less than .1%
** = errors due to rounding

Source: Statistisches Bundesamt: *Arbeitsstättenzählung 1987.*

There are two major reasons for this. First, higher growth of nonprofit industries in the area of service delivery appears as a consequence of demand factors caused by demographic shifts and changes in the labor force. The two most important factors are an increase in the number of elderly, which manifests itself in a higher demand for resident and ambulatory care, and an increased female participation in the labor market (a 27 percent increase between 1970 and 1987), which leads to a greater demand for services such as day care. Despite a declining and low birth rate throughout this period, the demand for day care seems to have increased substantially.

Second, we should recall that during the 1970s social welfare spending expanded to a very large degree. But given the principle of subsidiarity, this was less a matter of state actions alone; it involved the free welfare associations as implementers of welfare policies. Similar to the United States, but in contrast to many other welfare state countries, Scandinavia in particular, the German welfare state resulted less in an expansion of public service delivery and welfare administration than in an expansion of the nonprofit sector.

Table 2.2 presents the relative shares of employment for the for-profit, nonprofit, and public sectors in four industries, employing the German classification system of industries. Two general results can be obtained from the table. First, the nonprofit sector is more prominent in some areas than others. Prominent nonprofit industries are residential care and homes for infants, children, youth, elderly, the frail elderly and the handicapped, kindergartens, and correctional schools for youth. These tend to be industries in which the free welfare associations are prominent and where the principle of subsidiarity grants a privileged status to nonprofit providers.

Nonprofits are less prominent in areas covered not at all or to a much lesser extent by the principle of subsidiarity: higher education (universities), libraries, general schools, and most cultural and artistic areas. In all these cases, the public sector dominates. In the case of universities, the only full nonprofit university in the country is related to the Catholic church; other nonprofit establishments of higher learning tend to be seminaries

Table 2.2. The Share of Nonprofit, For-Profit, and
Public Employment: Sectoral Comparison of Selected Industries.

Industries	For-Profit Sector %	Nonprofit Sector %	Public Sector %	Total Employment in Industry
Homes				
Infants, children	9.4	73.1	17.5	17,368
Youth	9.5	72.6	17.9	11,198
Elderly	17.7	67.6	14.7	67,140
Handicapped	9.5	83.7	6.9	96,518
Frail elderly	20.2	63.0	16.8	128,510
Day care (not child)	5.4	46.4	48.1	22,766
Education and Research				
Universities	0.3	1.2	98.6	198,042
University hospitals	-	-	100.0	107,797
Libraries and archives	4.1	4.1	91.8	10,779
Scientific institutions nec	44.2	20.6	35.3	84,713
General schools	1.7	6.0	92.2	632,106
Vocational schools	17.6	21.5	60.9	202,898
Correctional schools	11.7	76.2	12.1	9,118
Kindergartens	1.0	62.3	36.7	155,874
Culture, Art, and Recreation				
Theater, opera	22.9	4.5	72.7	31,602
Orchestras and choirs	71.5	9.5	19.0	5,915
Museums and zoos	19.2	9.2	71.7	17,490
Adult education	-	100.0	-	9,559
General libraries	59.2	2.7	38.1	30,559
Sports institutions	52.0	3.1	45.6	63,408
Gardens and parks	-	0.6	99.5	10,146
Health				
Clinics and hospitals	14.2	34.2	51.0	722,734
Other health institutions	47.6	36.2	16.2	91,586

Source: Statistiches Bundesamt: *Arbeitsstättenzählung, 1987.*

and similar church-related institutions sometimes affiliated with public universities. In the case of primary and secondary schools, a major domain for nonprofits in other countries, we find that nonprofit organizations tend to occupy niches, like religious boarding schools and elite educational institutions.

Second, few fields show a pattern where all three sectors are significantly represented. This is the case for retirement homes and homes for the frail elderly, scientific institutions other than universities, vocational schools, correctional schools, educational institutions other than schools, and the health sector. These industries are either located next to an area dominated by the public sector, as is the case for scientific institutions and universities, or they represent fields that have experienced significant demand increases, as is the case for care for the elderly.

In short, the nonprofit sector is most prominent in areas covered by subsidiarity, least prominent in fields not covered by it; it occupies a significant though less dominant position in situations where demand increases brought about the entry of public and for-profit providers.

Subsidiarity and Third-Party Government

To some extent, the third sector in European societies is both the terrain and result of the conflict between organized religion, political opposition, and the state over the division of labor and spheres of influence. The German third sector is part of a society in which a weakened tradition of faith in the primacy of the state coexists with a strong tradition of economic liberalism. Both traditions have impressed their mark on the third sector and shaped its present form.

Within the legal and programmatic context of subsidiarity, the free welfare organizations are in a complex relationship with the state that goes well beyond monetary transfers. Depending on one's point of view, they are seen either as a corporatist arrangement where the state extends into the area of social services and welfare (Heinze and Olk, 1981), as tools of the churches and other "conservative" political forces to control a vital area of social welfare by creating quasimonopolies (Thränhardt, 1983), or as part of an efficient, responsive, and decentralized system in which the advantages of private and public involvement in the field of social services are realized to the benefit of all (Spiegelhalter, 1990).

In any case, the free welfare associations present a special and perhaps unique case, both in the field of social service delivery and in the area of interest mediation. Most welfare associations are closely linked to a religious or political belief, CARITAS to Catholicism, Diakonisches Werk to Protestantism, or Arbeiterwohlfahrt to social democracy. As interest associations they aggregate the interests of the social group they represent vis-à-vis the state; as instruments of government policy they participate in the formulation, financing, and implementation of public programs and activities. Thus, their role is inherently ambiguous.

Such inherent, fundamental ambiguity is absent from the U.S. case, but the role of the U.S. nonprofit sector is not free of ambiguity. In contrast to the German situation, the ambiguity here is the product of a multitude of changing and sometimes contradictory state and federal policies. In Germany, the ambiguity of the free welfare associations is enshrined in law, and is located in the core of nonprofit-sector–state relationships. It is not, as in the United States, a product of decentralized, less uniform, and less legalistic policy decisions.

There are other differences as well. First, there are differences in policy structure; nonprofits in Germany tend to be more integrated into the policy-making function of government than their American counterparts. Public authorities are required to consult the free welfare associations in matters of social policy; moreover, they are required by law to seek the endorsement of the associations when establishing public-sector organizations in the field of social welfare and assistance. In this case, the principle of subsidiarity resulted in what others called the neocorporatist welfare system (Heinze and C·lk, 1981).

Second, there are differences in structure and the market positions occupied by different types of providers in important areas of social services. Legal stipulations based on the principle of subsidiarity tend to protect the nonprofit organizations from both for-profit and public-sector competition. In this case, the principle of subsidiary leads to quasimonopolistic supply structures. The looser third-party government arrangement in the United States avoids this.

Third, there are differences in law and taxation. The public-law status of the Catholic and Protestant churches and the church tax system (a surcharge to income tax levied on the taxable income of all church members, to be collected by public tax authorities to the benefit of the churches) provide those parts of the nonprofit sector linked to the churches with a stable source of income. This makes church-related nonprofit organizations less dependent on the state in general, and on competitive grants, consumer fees, and charges in particular. Because the principle of subsidiarity is deeply imprinted in Germany's constitution and laws, it allows organizations access to sources of funds independent of both the state in general and current political incumbents in particular.

Fourth, there are differences in history. These include the factors and conditions in the political economy that are likely to lead to the emergence of forms of either third-party government or neocorporatism. The U.S. and the German nonprofit sector are the results of different historical development and rest on different deep-seated cultural and political perceptions about the state, society, and religion. Salamon (1987) suggests that third-party government has emerged as a way to reconcile two contradictory elements of American political thinking that expressed themselves in the conflict between the need for public services and hostility to the government bureaucracy that would be needed to provide them.

The nonprofit sectors in both the United States and Germany are, in part, formalized expressions of distrust of the state. In Germany, the distrust originated from the Catholic church and, in the immediate postwar era, the Allies. They favored and supported the rapid reestablishment of free welfare associations, which were regarded as politically less suspect than public welfare organizations. During the Christian Democratic administrations of the 1950s and 1960s, the free welfare associations were able to gain much ground vis-à-vis the state. The Christian Democrats fully institutionalized the principle of subsidiarity. Today, the free welfare associations occupy a quasi-monopolistic position: since 1961 municipalities or other potential suppliers are, for example, barred from establishing child-care and youth institutions if the free welfare associations are planning to do so. Alternative suppliers need the consent of the free welfare associations.

Finally, there are several theoretical issues. Presently, several promising developments exist at the theoretical level (Weisbrod, 1988; Douglas, 1983; Salamon, 1987; Hansmann, 1987; James, 1987), and, to varying degrees, they all face difficulties in explaining the size, scope, and importance of the German third sector. As we have argued elsewhere (Anheier, 1990), the German third sector is neither primarily the result of market or governmental failures (Weisbrod, 1988; Hansmann, 1987), nor of societal heterogeneity (James, 1987; Douglas, 1983), nor the direct reflection of other demand and supply factors.

This is not to say that theories based on institutional failures, societal heterogeneity, or excess demand and supply of ideological entrepreneurship are necessarily false. What is implied here is that they seem to make several assumptions that significantly restrict the scope of each theory both geographically and in terms of what types of organizations are covered. Based on Salamon (1987) we can list two of the most serious shortcomings of conventional theories that pertain to the relationship between the state and the nonprofit sector.

First, existing theories of nonprofit organizations assume a zero-sum situation between government and the nonprofit sector, and postulate a potentially competitive rather than a cooperative relation between both sectors. In other words, prevalent theories based on government failure (and related market failure) assume an antagonistic relationship between the nonprofit sector and the public sector. Neither the U.S. nor the German pattern of nonprofit-sector–government cooperation can be explained by these theories.

Second, conventional theories of the welfare state tend to neglect the role of private, nonprofit organizations altogether. The state is reified as *one* actor within the political economy of usually class-based interest groups, and little effort has been made to differentiate between the role of the state in policy formation, service provision, and financing. Once we realize that societies can develop different patterns of relationships between government and the nonprofit sector in each of these areas (policy, provision, financing), we begin to appreciate the greater empirical complexity and cross national variety of the division of labor between the sectors (DiMaggio and Anheier, 1990).

Conclusion

The German case provides evidence for the inadequacies of existing theories of the relationships between the nonprofit sector and the state. The third-party government thesis is much closer to accounting for German realities, but even this thesis has to be modified somewhat to do justice to the German case. The concept of subsidiarity has expanded, refined, and formalized the practice of third-party government. For comparative research, the relationship with the state is perhaps the most important factor in understanding the nonprofit sector cross nationally. The "state," however, is a shorthand term for both the regulatory regime and the institutional arrangement. Some authors (Anheier and Seibel, 1990; DiMaggio and Anheier, 1990) have argued that the political *and* organizational orientation of the nonprofit sector reflects the regulatory regime under which it operates. Thus, while the patterns or form of public-private cooperation might appear similar, their orientations may well be different. While both the German and the U.S. case reveal an extensive pattern of cooperation between the public and the nonprofit sector, they arrive at this result along significantly different routes.

References

Anheier, H. K. "A Profile of the Third Sector in West Germany." In H. K. Anheier and W. Seibel (eds.), *The Third Sector: Comparative Studies of Nonprofit Organizations.* Berlin: De Gruyter, 1990.

Anheier, H. K., and W. Seibel (eds.). *The Third Sector: Comparative Studies of Nonprofit Organizations.* Berlin: De Gruyter, 1990.

Bauer, R. *Wohlfahrtsverbände in der Bundesrepublik* (Welfare Associations in the Federal Republic). Weinheim, Basel: Beltz, 1978.

Bauer, R., and Diessenbacher, H. (eds.). *Organisierte Nächstenliebe: Wohlfahrtsverbände und Selbsthilfe in der Krise des Sozialstaats* (Organized Charity: Welfare Associations, Self-Help and the Crisis of the Welfare State). Opladen: Westdeutscher Verlag, 1984.

Bundesarbeitsgemeinschaft der Freien Wohlfahrtspflege. *Gesamtstatistik 1990* (Statistics 1990). Bonn, 1990.

Deutscher Verein für öffentliche und private Fürsorge. *Voluntary Welfare Services*. Frankfurt: Deutscher Verein, 1986.

DiMaggio, P., and Anheier, H. K. "The Sociology of Nonprofit Organizations and Sectors." *Annual Review of Sociology*, 1990, *16*, 137–159.

Douglas, J. *Why Charity? The Case for a Third Sector*. Newburg Park, Calif.: Sage, 1983.

Hansmann, H. "Economic Theories of Nonprofit Organizations." In W. W. Powell (ed.), *The Nonprofit Sector: A Research Handbook*. New Haven, Conn.: Yale University Press, 1987.

Heinze, R. G., and Olk, T. "Die Wohlfahrtsverbände im System sozialer Dienstleistungsproduktion: Zur Entstehung und Struktur der bundesrepublikanischen Verbändewohlfahrt" (The Welfare Associations in the System of Social Service Production: On the Emergence and Structure of Welfare Associations in the Federal Republic). *Kölner Zeitschrift für Soziologie und Sozialpsychologie*, 1981, *1*.

Herzog, R. "Subsidiaritätsprinzip (The Subsidiarity Principle). In *Evangelisches Staatslexikon* (Evangelical State Encyclopedia), 1975, 2591–2597.

James, E. "The Nonprofit Sector in Comparative Perspective." In W. W. Powell (ed.), *The Nonprofit Sector: A Research Handbook*. New Haven, Conn.: Yale University Press, 1987.

Plaschke, J. "Subsidiarität und Neue Subsidiarität. Wandel der Aktionsformen gesellschaftlicher Problembewältigung" (Subsidiarity and the New Subsidiarity: Changes in Social Forms of Solving Social Problems). In R. Bauer and H. Diessenbacher (eds.), *Organisierte Nächstenliebe: Wohlfahrtsverbände und Selbsthilfe in der Krise des Sozialstaats* (Organized Charity: Welfare Associations, Self-Help and the Crisis of the Welfare State). Opladen: Westdeutscher Verlag, 1984.

Sachse, C., and Tennstedt, F. (eds.) *Jahrbuch der Sozialarbeit 4* (Yearbook of Social Work 4). Reinbek: Rowohlt, 1981.
Sachse, C., and Tennstedt, F. (eds.) *Soziale Sicherheit und soziale Disziplinierung* (Social Security and Social Disciplining). Frankfurt: Suhrkamp, 1986.
Salamon, L. "Rethinking Public Management: Third-Party Government and the Changing Forms of Government Action." *Public Policy,* 1981, *29,* 255-275.
Salamon, L. "Partners in Public Service: The Scope and Theory of Government-Nonprofit Relations." In W. W. Powell (ed.), *The Nonprofit Sector: A Research Handbook.* New Haven, Conn.: Yale University Press, 1987.
Spiegelhalter, F. *Der dritte Sozialpartner* (The Third Social Partner). Bonn: Lambertus, 1990.
Spieker, M. "Sozialstaat und Subsidiaritätsprinzip" (Social State and the Principle of Subsidiarity). *Frankfurter Allgemeine Zeitung,* Nov. 13, 1982, p. 15.
Statistisches Bundesamt. *Unternehmen und Arbeitsstätten: Arbeitsstättenzählung vom 25 Mai 1987* (Enterprises and Work Places: Census of Work Places, May 25, 1987). Vols. 1, 2, 4, 5, 11. Stuttgart: Metzel-Poeschel, 1987.
Thränhardt, D. "Ausländer im Dickicht der Verbände: Ein Beispiel verbandsgerechter Klientelselektion und korporatistischer Politikformulierung" (Foreigners in the Jungle of Associations: An Example of Client Selection and Corporatist Policy Formulation). In F. Hamburger and others (eds.), *Sozialarbeit und Ausländerpolitik* (Social Work and Policy for Foreigners). Neuwied, Darmstadt: Luchterhand, 1983.
Weisbrod, B. *The Nonprofit Economy.* Cambridge, Mass.: Harvard University Press, 1988.

3

A Partnership Between Government and Voluntary Organizations: Changing Relationships in Dutch Society

Herman J. Aquina

In all societies the task of allocating goods and services is performed by various sectors. In Dutch society that task is performed by government, private business, nongovernmental organizations (NGOs) that are neither private nor public, and households. Currently, the relationships among these four sectors are undergoing change, as is government control. Throughout the West, governmental intervention has become so frequent and so intense that it is no longer efficient or effective. Since 1980, when the Netherlands Treasury asked explicitly how much government intervention would be appropriate in various policy fields if we were to start from scratch, the proper place of government in the welfare state has been a matter of open political debate. The question has become which goods and services will be supplied by the central government and NGOs, and who will be in control.

Core government in the Netherlands is not very large. Government allocates about 70 percent of the gross national product but directly controls only 10 percent. There is, however, an enormous collective sector in which government and more or less public organizations cooperate. Various terms have been used to refer to these public organizations: nongovernmental organizations (NGOs), paragovernmental organizations (PGOs), quasi-nongovernmental organizations (qua-NGOs, or quangos), and voluntary nongovernmental organizations (Hood and Schuppert, 1988). Not all NGOs are voluntary, or private initiative organizations as they are called in the Netherlands, and some may even have been created by core government.

So-called voluntary nongovernmental organizations traditionally played a very important role in the Netherlands, where they supply the major part of collective goods and services. While the role of NGOs may be changing in the Netherlands, their work is appreciated and their relative independence respected, especially in light of the fact that great expectations for government control of the welfare state could not be fulfilled.

This chapter discusses recent experiments to restructure the relationship between NGOs and government. It is based on empirical research conducted in the field of forensic health care, specifically psychiatric care in a correctional setting.

The Concept of NGOs

NGOs are neither public nor private. For the Netherlands, no formal definition can be given because no distinctive legal concept applies. Thus the legal status differs from one NGO to another, as do ownership, public powers, finance, administration, judicial supervision, and control by core government. The only element NGOs have in common is that they are neither public nor private.

For practical reasons, NGOs may be defined as alternative organizations for social action and characterized by their positions on continua whose opposite poles pose critical alternatives. Some examples are public versus private ownership, compulsion versus voluntarism, government grants versus private payments, centralization versus decentralization, public versus private law, and direct versus indirect government control (Dahl and Lindblom, 1953; Aquina, 1988). The Dutch Drivers License Bureau serves as an interesting example. Created by voluntary action and not by government, it is a nonprofit foundation with monopoly powers granted by public law. While it is financed by driver examination fees, its budget requires cabinet approval. Though members of the board are appointed by cabinet, they are nominated by designated private organizations. It is characterized as an NGO because, on balance, it is neither a public nor private organization.

According to Munnike and others (1983), there are 775 national NGOs in the Netherlands; 613 of these were autonomous administrative bodies, 57 NGOs *sui generis,* 73 foundations, and 342 public companies. These figures do not include regional or local NGOs, joint ventures, or other associations governed by private law. NGOs are very active and numerous in many policy fields in the Netherlands, including public housing, health, education, and welfare, and the mass media, all of which they dominate, and in social insurance, agriculture, public transport, and utilities, where nearly all of them have been established by core government. In other fields, like business and industry, NGOs are virtually nonexistent. Since the Netherlands is basically a free-enterprise society, government intervention operates mainly in matters of tax exemptions and other indirect incentives.

Voluntary NGOs are very prominent in the Dutch health care system, including forensic health care. Forensic health care is supplied mostly by nonprofit organizations, which operate special clinics that serve simultaneously as psychiatric hospitals and prisons. Netherlands courts may sentence adult criminals who need psychiatric treatment to imprisonment in such clinics. Inmates may refuse treatment, but they must remain in that clinic for a period determined by the court. Psychomedical treatment facilities for drug- or alcohol-addicted criminals are also run by nonprofit organizations, as are facilities for juvenile offenders and socially maladjusted youngsters.

The Dutch health care system, including forensic health

care, is financed primarily by nonprofit foundations, secondarily by private insurance companies, and to a lesser degree by households. Government is only minimally involved. Nor does government supply health care for itself, though the state finances university hospitals and state-owned psychiatric hospitals that house the most dangerous mentally disturbed criminals. Government regulation, on the other hand, is much more significant because the amount of the compulsory insurance premiums is determined by government. Government also sets ceilings on the income levels for members of the medical profession. Government also regulates prescriptions, planning for hospitals, and, to some extent, even medical treatment. Finally, there is a government planning system for hospitals and to some extent for medical treatment.

Government policy is formulated in cooperation with the so-called dome organizations, which represent all who are in the health care business. This cooperation is highly institutionalized in joint councils, where representatives of the dome organizations enjoy a majority. These dome organizations prepare government regulations with a goal of protecting their positions and the interests of the groups they represent. This pattern—dome organizations working in cooperation with government—is widespread. Indeed, in most policy fields the law requires the cabinet to ask dome organizations for advice in preparing its policy. In practice, this means that organized interest groups are given opportunities to do whatever they think is best, and these decisions are legitimized by the state.

Until recently, the prevailing pattern of collective decision making in the Netherlands could be described as corporatist (Schmitter, 1982; Scholten, 1987). Over the years, NGOs created a huge bureaucracy and an extremely complex web of decision making that has not necessarily resulted in efficient provision of services. As a consequence, there have been pressures for NGOs to become more democratic, accountable, and rational (Kramer, 1981). In the last decade, the cabinet tried to establish a new partnership with NGOs on the basis that, at least in theory, voluntary organizations can implement public policies, can provide diversified services against competitive prices,

Changing Relationships in Dutch Society

and can garner extensive public support because they are able to set priorities for collective expenditures through a political process that does not create a monstrous bureaucracy (Salamon, 1987).

Government has shown increasing concern about health care because demographic and technological developments have created a situation in which the old familiar network is no longer satisfactory. Costs of health care have risen so high so fast that fundamental political decisions are needed to solve the problem of how much society as a whole will spend for health care, who will get medical treatment, when, and how. Moreover, health care is no longer merely a technical matter that can be left solely to the medical profession, since the quality of health care has become a matter of widespread discussion. Finally, health care has encountered ethical difficulties, some of which can be solved on the political level only. All this does not mean that government must control the whole of the health care business, nor that government itself should supply health care. What it does mean is that existing NGOs must again legitimize their activities, even their existence, and that perhaps private firms or households can do the job better.

These considerations lead to basic questions of why there are NGOs in the Netherlands and what kind of future may lie ahead for them. As to the first question, there are technical, political, and ethical reasons.

Technical Rationale for NGOs

The legitimacy of NGOs rests on three technical grounds. In the first place, an NGO may be a more efficient allocation mechanism than a core government agency, a private firm, or households.

When the cabinet decided to ask voluntary organizations to supply forensic health care in 1929, it was expected that these organizations would be the most efficient alternative. It can be demonstrated that NGOs still are more efficient. However, this does not mean that NGOs in general are more efficient. Actually, many NGOs are blamed for wasting money, in many cases taxpayers' money. Regrettably, if a choice is to be made between public or other agencies to supply goods and services, hardly any reliable evidence about the relative efficiency of alternative allocation mechanisms is available.

Second, in principle, NGOs as a category are potentially more flexible than government agencies ever could be because the latter operate under tight bureaucratic rules that are not quickly changed. For example, an NGO that operates a psychiatric clinic for criminals is much more able than a state clinic to follow the latest developments in the criminal and psychiatric world.

The third reason why an NGO may be preferred over an alternative mechanism is that an NGO is reputed to have more know-how and experience. NGOs in the Netherlands very often have taken the initiative to supply collective goods and services because the central core government was either too weak or unwilling to do so. Initially, their performance was very amateurish, but it became more professional, and, over the years, knowledge and experience were accumulated that is not available anywhere else. This is especially true in fields like forensic health care, which in the beginning was a matter of good will by clergymen but is now highly professional.

NGOs may, of course, be legitimate instruments in government policy, and private voluntary organizations may welcome government intervention and eventually a transformation into NGOs as well. Private voluntary organizations such as public radio and television may need public support, including legal regulations and government funding, to provide their services. In the Netherlands, public media are operated by voluntary NGOs. Since radio and television programs are very much collective goods, they require public regulation. If a public system is preferred, funding must be secured to avoid free riding, a problem that simply does not exist if there is a state broadcasting system that can be as easily financed as any other core government agency. In the Netherlands, a core government agency collects a radio and television tax that is distributed among qualifying NGOs, which are almost completely free in determining both their programming and expenditure. Legally, these organizations are nonprofit foundations. In other sectors, such as health care, contributions are made compulsory by public law. In the case of social insurance, contributions are not only compulsory, they are collected in the same way as income taxes. Decisions regarding who receives an allowance are made by NGOs with discretionary powers in their field because NGOs know their clients best; they, in fact, laid the foundation for the social insurance system currently operating in the Netherlands.

Thus, there are not only technical reasons for legitimating NGOs, but government control of these NGOs might be advocated on technical grounds as well. The problem becomes which government, for there are many core government bureaucracies, a condition found in the area of forensic health care.

The problem for forensic health care is that it falls within the purview of two bureaucratic organizations whose concepts, goals, environments, and methods of utilizing policy instruments are entirely different. Since forensic health care is a law-and-order matter, it is managed by the Justice Department, which considers psychiatric clinics for convicts as social control facilities. With an emphasis on protection of society rather than treatment, Justice Department officials, known for their strict observance of rules, implement a very restrictive parole policy. However, since it is also a public health issue, forensic health care is also a matter for the Department of Health and Welfare, whose policies and activities are much more flexible than those of the Justice Department. Whereas the Justice Department operates psychiatric clinics in much the same way as it does prisons, the Department of Health and Welfare considers the inmate population of forensic health care clinics to be patients in need of care. This disparity in environment, between the humanistic perspective of a treatment-oriented Health and Welfare Department on the one hand and the social control-oriented perspective of the Justice Department on the other, creates a situation for forensic health care facilities that is far from ideal, resulting in unnecessary complexity, inconsistency, delays, and economic waste.

Were only one government bureau assigned the task of overseeing forensic health care, difficulties would still remain since social control is, in and of itself, a technically complex problem, and since health care, particularly forensic health care, is a highly professionalized area requiring more expertise than government is capable of exercising. With increasing pressure on government to control developments in health care because of rising costs, the need to address such issues as euthanasia, abortion, and proper psychiatric treatment, and the fact that the health care business is unwilling or unable to solve problems in a way that is acceptable for society as a whole, some new ideas have been introduced. In the areas of health care and postsecondary education, for example, these new ideas have resulted in a new budgeting system for forensic health care whereby government determines on an annual basis the amount of money a clinic may spend. Though these clinics are financed more by health insurance organizations than by government, the government is empowered to establish budget levels based on information that is provided by the clinics. The clinics, then, must establish policy programs that include estimated expenditures, and the details of program implementation are left to the discretion of the clinics' management. Basically, there are few restrictions as long as the goals of the program are realized. Such a system should enable government to determine beforehand if the clinics are socially worthwhile without having to address technical details about which it has no knowledge. It is also possible to determine afterward if the clinics did in fact supply the quality they had promised to deliver. The system thus becomes output- rather than input-oriented, as had previously been the case. Formerly, clinics received as much money as they had inmates, and the quality of treatment was not taken into account. While a clinic was required to meet certain standards to qualify for funding, effective treatment was not financially rewarded.

A major technical problem then becomes how to operationalize the concept of quality. This problem can be solved by experts only if technical criteria play a role. In the university system, for example, the quality of research is assessed by independent committees of experts who are regarded as peers by the scientific community. Forensic health care clinics have refused to adopt such a system; in fact, in their unwillingness to relinquish any power, they have even tried to withhold data about therapies and their effectiveness from one another and from government whenever possible. Unlike the universities, these clinics are strong enough to maintain autonomy because both the division of labor between government and NGOs (like clinics) and other allocation mechanisms, and government control of these organizations, are to some degree the result of politics.

Political Considerations

Some authors conclude that the Dutch have a natural feeling for NGOs (Daalder, 1981). They may have a point, but it cannot be denied that there always has been a strong *étatist* movement in the Netherlands that has at the same time been centralistic. Though this movement was very influential around 1800, its proponents did not succeed in getting full control of the two most important fields of public concern in the nineteenth century—the educational system and the system of social security and relief for the poor. Implicit in the solution to these two problems is a very intricate government-NGO partnership that shaped the main pattern of the twentieth-century welfare state.

The *étatists* were initially very successful in exercising control over the educational system, mainly because the enlightened Protestant bourgeois class was in power at that time. This group was interested in high-quality education for its children, which church schools and local government schools could not provide. In the middle of the nineteenth century, however, the lower Protestant classes began to claim schools of their own in order to educate their children in the spirit of their belief, funded by government. Very soon, the Catholics followed, because they saw Catholic schools as a perfect means to emancipate. After about half a century of bitter fighting, the *étatists* had to give in, mainly because of the spread of the democratic franchise that gave the lower Protestant and Catholic classes their share in political power. What finally emerged was a very intricate NGO-government partnership. Now about half of the educational institutes are NGOs, and the other half are state-operated schools.

But there is some state control in technical educational and managerial affairs about which the government is advised by dome organizations of schoolteachers and administrators. More than anything else, this so-called school struggle has helped to shape the basic features of the Dutch collective sector in which NGOs play such a dominant role.

By the end of the nineteenth century, political power in the Netherlands was divided somewhat equally between Catholic and Protestant parties, the socialist democrats and the conservatives, and this pattern that still exists. For ideological reasons discussed in the next section, confessional (religious or sectarian) parties are strongly in favor of completely independent NGOs, while socialists and conservatives prefer either a state-controlled supply of goods and services or reliance on private business under some form of state control. Since none of these parties can ever hope to win a political majority, the end result will be a compromise in which there are many NGOs under some state control. In the Netherlands, given the distribution of power, this is the only workable structure that secures the supply of collective goods and services.

One might get the impression that NGOs are confessional organizations since confessional parties favor this kind of arrangement, but this is not necessarily so (Schendelen, 1984). Many NGOs in the Netherlands are not confessional organizations. There is a Protestant clinic for prisoners who need psychiatric treatment, but there is also a nongovernmental clinic for the same purpose founded on the British notion of charity. And most public housing construction associations are voluntary organizations with no religious or political background. Confessional groups employ the concept of NGOs to serve their needs and interests, to keep their flocks together. On the other hand, they advocate NGOs per se because these arrangements reinforce their political philosophy of subsidiarity. Thus, it is no surprise that the other major issue in nineteenth-century politics—the problem of poor relief and social security—was solved in the same way as the school struggle. It also helped to establish a tradition of government-NGO partnership. The implementation and, to a certain degree, the formulation of social security programs is a matter for NGOs, and these programs have very little to do with confessional organizations.

In the first half of the twentieth century, the pattern of relationships between core government and NGOs was firmly established in most policy fields. Most core government bureaus involve the active participation of all kinds of NGOs. Each of these organizations has struggled to achieve its place in the system, and none is willing to relinquish it voluntarily. And even though NGOs have succeeded in the past in getting firm control of core government itself, they are currently in danger.

One reason is overregulation, which tends to make NGOs like core government agencies. Because each organization was anxious to protect its own position, a good deal of government regulation was sought. The outcome is a paradox: NGOs complain about too much government regulation, which they themselves had requested in the first place. This same situation exists in the area of fundraising. Over the years, NGOs have continually asked for more government funding because it provides a solid financial foundation, but now they are among the first to face budget cutbacks because of government's mandate of fiscal austerity.

In sectors where there has traditionally been an elaborate network between government and powerful NGOs, it is difficult to make changes in policy. Government may be in a better position because of growing discrepancies between institutionalized NGOs and social groups, which means loss of social and political support for existing NGOs. The changing social position of NGOs is a second reason that they are currently in danger.

NGOs use of professionals to represent them tends to isolate association leaders from what the memberships perceive as their immediate interests. As Schmitter (1982) suggests, these organization have increasingly become service agencies, like private business firms, and less often the focus of political and social identity.

A third social development taking place in the Netherlands that endangers NGOs is the emergence on the social and political agenda of new substantive citizen concerns. Previously less important groups such as taxpayers, tenants, and women have become more significant (Offe, 1984). Schmitter holds that groups such as these will threaten existing arrangements only if they succeed in getting the sponsorship and support of public authorities. Such a situation actually occurs in the Netherlands. For example, the cabinet successfully withstands pressures of health care directors interested in the quality and quantity of health care, no matter what the social cost. Instead, the cabinet sponsors groups whose interests are not yet represented by existing NGOs. The cabinet is somewhat uncertainly followed by Parliament and political parties seeking electoral success. Since many party officials have political power because they have been educated in nongovernment organizations and may still be affiliated with them, their actions are not surprising. For the cabinet, such connections between officials and NGOs can be viewed as an opportunity to protect the common good against a demanding coalition of interest groups, as represented in Parliament.

This is not to say that NGOs face a dismal future. After a series of central government planning experiments in the 1970s, the government acknowledged that core government should leave some more or less public affairs to NGOs, and not merely for technical reasons. NGOs are supposedly countervailing powers balancing excessive government control. Even a perfect democratic welfare state has not, by definition, solved the problem of power (Offe, 1987). Wherever there is power, there is a chance that power will be abused without the presence of a strong countervailing force. A pluralist democracy may be defined by the principle of equality among organizations as well as by the principle of voting equality among individual citizens (Dahl, 1982). The federalists realized that the latter may result in an elective despotism. On the other hand, NGOs themselves have been blamed for having monopoly powers since in practice they have usually called the tune that government will sing.

Ethical Rationale

We have seen that political ideology played a major part in making NGOs such highly valued arrangements in the Netherlands.

Changing Relationships in Dutch Society

The four most important political ideologies in the Netherlands — Catholicism, Calvinism, social democracy, and conservatism — are ethical systems that eventually generate such institutions (Couwenberg, 1953). Since in the Netherlands there is an enormous diversity in political and other ideologies, NGOs become the only viable alternative arrangement for supplying collective goods because no majority could be formed to achieve consensus on substantive policies for society as a whole. Since each NGO takes care of its own business as much as possible, NGOs collectively can hold Dutch society together because social and political conflicts are minimized. In fact, diversity is seen as a major cultural characteristic of Dutch society, one that should be protected as a value in itself.

The Catholics always have been advocates of subsidiarity. They claim that social tasks must be performed at the lowest possible level, the autonomy of the organizations on various levels must be respected as long as they do well, and only if they fail may the state intervene. Otherwise, the state's role is to preserve the social order on a subsidiarity basis; in no case may it deprive individuals of their natural right to form a cohesive group and take care of themselves as a group. Such a point of view does not, of course, leave much room for core government; on the contrary, it favors NGOs.

The majority of Protestants in the Netherlands are Calvinists. While their ideas about government may be theoretically different from the Catholics, in terms of practical politics they are the same: the only function of the state is to maintain the social order according to the will of God. Thus, independent groups can take care of themselves.

While the Social Democrats and the conservatives may not have a theological basis, their political ideology is very much an ethical system. Conservatives in the Netherlands are extremely afraid of the abuse of power. They have tried to prevent it by inventing procedures and institutions that have resulted in a system of countervailing powers and checks and balances. It is possible to defend NGOs on such grounds. Even Social Democrats could accept NGOs, though they may be less anxious to prevent the abuse of power than to promote constructive use of power. No central government can do without more or less independent social organizations, since in certain circumstances they know best how to get the job done. According to Social Democratic reasoning, government has to be functionally decentralized; within such a system, NGOs can perform tasks and at the same time promote social and political democratization.

The proper place for government in society is not just a structural or institutional problem that can be discussed only in general terms. What government should do depends on substantial social issues as well. Any social group in the Netherlands has its own ideas about policy programs like education, housing, mass media, or forensic health care. Because there is a wide range of preferences, it is not always possible to reconcile opposing views. In democracies, a way to resolve conflicts requiring a collective decision is to adopt the alternative preferred by the majority. However, most conflicts do not require a collective decision. It is possible to reduce or eliminate conflicts between a majority and a minority (or between minorities, as is very often the case in the Netherlands) by forming associations of co-believers or consensual associations (Dahl, 1970). Do not all citizens possess the fundamental right to have their interests taken equally into account as long as the well-being of others is not disproportionately affected by the exercise of that right? The problem of proportions is, of course, a matter of political debate, but the Netherlands is rightly known for its tolerance.

Government policy explicitly promotes pluralism wherever possible. The Dutch mass media system, for example, is very complex because the law requires that public broadcasting shall reflect our cultural, religious, or social diversity. NGOs are thought to represent this diversity better than a core government agency could ever do. For the same reason, alternative private forensic health care clinics are subsidized by government. Health care in general, forensic health care in particular, is not just a technical, medical activity, but one involving moral judgments about the quality of life.

NGOs make it possible for core government to escape the necessity of making political decisions that might result in severe political and social unrest for which it would otherwise be held accountable. NGOs can accomplish tasks without strict core government control over every detail. Some matters can be left to groups of co-believers, and others requiring central regulation can be dealt with by dome organizations in which the antagonists are given their share in power.

Some authors, such as Bernard Crick (1962), even hold that politics simply can be defined as the activity by which differing interests within a given unit of rule are conciliated by giving them a share in power in proportion to their importance to the welfare and the survival of the whole community. For Crick, the moral consensus of a free state is precisely the activity of politics itself and nothing else. Politics will fail if it cannot maintain that order. This idea of politics deserves some discussion.

First of all, it is not always possible to reconcile conflicting opinions. What should we do if a private school does not appoint lesbian teachers when this was one of the purposes for establishing the school as an NGO? The Dutch constitution explicitly forbids sexual discrimination as well as government intervention in the school's internal affairs. A solution for problems like this is not easily found. Forensic health care was a very urgent problem in the 1970s, when the antipsychiatric movement's ideas led to experiments that the Netherlands as a society could not tolerate. Some clinics invented therapies that might have been beneficial for their inmates but not for their environment, including the population of neighboring villages. Eventually, the police had to come in to restore order in the clinics. The question remains, however, what exactly constitutes the limits of government intervention.

Second, the aggregate provision of services by NGOs may not meet all social needs, since NGOs can be deliberately paternalistic. Government is in the better position to distribute resources equitably. For most of us, modern society should honor the fundamental right of every citizen to a decent standard of living. This idea can be realized by core government only if we make care not just a duty, as the NGOs do, but a right for all citizens. According to this philosophy, there would be public schools in any community where there are a qualified number of people requesting it, even if there is an NGO-operated school. Moreover, public schools would pay attention to all aspects of Dutch culture, including its Christian and humanistic tradition, without exception.

Paternalism in public radio and television is balanced in about the same way. There is an independent channel that is not affiliated with any social group; it provides programs of a general character such as news not supplied by other organizations. It is not a voluntary organization, since it has been created by government, but it is an NGO, independent from government in its actual program design, that ensures the freedom of the press from both government and pressure groups as represented in voluntary NGOs. The introduction of privately owned commercial radio and television may provide another check on paternalism.

Third, while NGOs may agree on a policy, the aggregate result of agreements may not be what the Dutch society as a whole has asked for. Power may be disproportionately distributed even among NGOs, with powerful interest groups getting the larger part. Specialized psychiatric institutes are in a minority position in health care dome organizations, which means that their interests are underrepresented. It could be demonstrated that health care programs adopted by dome organizations and government are less favorable for these institutes than they are for powerful segments of the health care business. Schmitter (1982) discussed some sources of contradictions and types of responses in what he called "societal corporatist arrangements," a concept that is very much akin to our concept of nongovernmental organizations. In the final analysis, he wonders: "Might these civil servants not find that devolution of authority to neo-corporatist intermediaries and their internal presence in state agencies could deprive them from their historical status of authoritative decision makers and care takers of the general interest?" It is doubtful that Dutch civil servants ever had that historical status. It cannot be denied, however, that Schmitter's conclusion might be as true for the Netherlands as it is for other comparable countries. There is some recognition of the need for core government involvement to guarantee public priority setting and accountability.

Conclusion

The political debate about NGOs concerns the legitimacy of these organizations compared with alternative allocation mechanisms like core government agencies, private business, and households. It is also about the degree of government control. Under some circumstances, NGOs may be preferable allocation mechanisms because of technical, political, and ethical considerations. Under other circumstances, government control may be preferred. The present political climate is favorable for deregulation and privatization, on the one hand, and for better quality control, on the other. The first claim may require more independent nongovernment organizations, the second, more governmental intervention. While this seems to be a paradox, it is one that can be solved. Government may be held responsible for the general welfare, which includes the equitable allocation of diverse collective goods and services. Therefore, the government must raise money, while the public should be able to set priorities. On the other hand, the actual supply of collective goods and services and even public control of output levels and quality could be left to NGOs. Since the implementation of programs can never be separated from the formulation of these same programs, there may also be some role for NGOs in setting priorities. In the 1970s, it was thought that central core government could do anything. Since then there has been a growing awareness that core government needs more or less independent nongovernmental organizations that should become more accountable to the public.

References

Aquina, H. J. "PGOs in the Netherlands." In C. Hood and G. Schuppert (eds.), *Delivering Public Services in Western Europe.* London: Sage, 1988.

Couwenberg, S. *Het Particuliere Stelsel.* (The Voluntary Nonprofit System.) Unpublished doctoral dissertation, University of Leiden, 1953.

Crick, B. *In Defence of Politics.* Chicago: University of Chicago Press, 1962.

Daalder, H. "Consociationalism, Center and Periphery in the Netherlands." In P. Torsvik (ed.), *Mobilization, Center and Periphery Structures and Nation-Building.* Oslo: 1981.

Dahl, R. A. *After the Revolution?* New Haven, Conn.: Yale University Press, 1970.

Dahl, R. A. *Dilemmas of Pluralist Democracy.* New Haven, Conn.: Yale University Press, 1982.

Dahl, R. A., and Lindblom, C. E. *Politics, Economics, and Welfare.* New York: Harper Collins, 1953.

Hood, C., and Schuppert, G. F. (eds.). *Delivering Public Services in Western Europe.* London: Sage, 1988.

Kramer, R. M. *Voluntary Agencies in the Welfare State.* Berkeley: University of California Press, 1981.

Munnike, H. F., and others. *Organen en Rechtspersonen Rond de Centrale Overheid.* (Organizational Structures and Corporate Entities in Central Government). Den Haag, 1983.

Offe, C. *Contradictions of the Welfare State.* London: Hutchinson, 1984.

Offe, C. "Democracy Against the Welfare State?" *Political Theory,* Nov. 1987, *15*(4), 501–537.

Salamon, L. M. "Of Market Failure, Voluntary Failure, and Third-Party Government: Toward a Theory of Government-Nonprofit Relations in the Modern Welfare State." *Journal of Voluntary Action Research,* 1987, *16*(1), 29–49.

Schendelen, M. (ed.) "Consociationalism, Pillarization and Conflict Management in the Low Countries." *Acta Politica,* Jan. 1984, 19.

Schmitter, P. C. "Reflections on Where the Theory of Neo-Corporatism Has Gone and Where the Praxis of Neo-Corporatism May Be Going." In G. Lehmbruch and P. Schmitter (eds.), *Patterns of Corporatist Policy-making.* London: Sage, 1982.

Scholten, I. (ed.) *Political Stability and Neo-corporatism: Corporatist Integration and Social Countries in Western Europe.* London: Sage, 1987.

Streeck, W., and Schmitter, P. "Community, Market, State— and Associations?" In W. Streeck and P. Schmitter (eds.) *Private Interest Government: Beyond Market and the State.* London: Sage, 1985.

4

The Historical Precedent for Government-Nonprofit Cooperation in Norway

Stein Kuhnle
Per Selle

The study of voluntary organizations has been almost completely missing from the literature on the history and growth of welfare states that has been written in the last twenty years. Instead, dubious myths about the relationship between government and voluntary organizations have evolved. Two examples from quite different contexts (Sweden and the United States) illustrate a perspective about the welfare state that seems to prevail among the general public. Burenstam (1983) claims that the welfare state is heartless because it has destroyed the alternative social security net in society; Nisbet (1962) argues that government is much to blame for the weakening of voluntary institutions and the resulting rise of alienation and anomie in the modern world.

Salamon (1987) has found this theme expressed in many other accounts of the voluntary sector. At the same time, he

75

has also shown that the portrayal of a "golden age" of voluntary sector purity corrupted by government funds simply does not correspond with the actual development of relations between government and voluntary institutions in the United States.

But what about Norway—a country, like Sweden, with a much stronger tradition of legitimacy of state intervention, and where the welfare state has become more comprehensive? Has the Norwegian state actively destroyed and weakened alternative social security nets such as voluntary organizations? Has the voluntary sector been in continuous conflict with government? In a period when the third sector receives renewed public attention all over Europe, these questions are important.

Norway and other Scandinavian countries were set early on a route leading to universal, citizen-based welfare institutions. The idea of "people's" or universal social insurance was firmly on the political agenda from the 1890s, long before social democracy gained political strength (Kuhnle, 1981; Seip, 1984). Sweden introduced the world's first universal old-age pension in 1913. Compared with other modern welfare states, the Scandinavian model is characterized by universal benefits, a large state role in organization and financing, and a unified organization of social security (Kuhnle, 1986; Erikson, 1987).

Norway has a long history of state, provincial, and local government institutional solutions in the welfare area, but this does not imply that there has not been room for other institutions. Voluntary organizations of various kinds emerged in the last century, but both mutual aid societies and philanthropic organizations were sparsely developed and unable to cope with the many new needs that arose rapidly during the last decades of the nineteenth century. In Norway, voluntary welfare provision did not really represent an alternative to state-sponsored welfare.

However, in spite of the state's dominant role in the welfare state in Norway and Scandinavia, room for voluntary organizations has always existed. Between 1900 and 1940, many such organizations developed. We question the common belief that government and voluntary organizations represent two different worlds and thus, implicitly, have been in a state of

Government-Nonprofit Cooperation in Norway 77

conflict. This chapter attempts to develop a deeper and more general theoretical understanding of the dynamic relationships between the state and organizations.

Norway 1900-1940

A New Typology[1]

A number of problems arise when we try to interpret historical developments, because the concepts used are frequently broad and imprecise. However, we consider two dimensions especially important in developing a perspective on past events. The first dimension relates to how close organizations are to the state with respect to the scope, frequency, and ease of communication and contact. Organizations may be either near (and hence integrated with the state) or distant (and hence separate from it). The second dimension is the organizations' degree of dependence on the state, in terms of financing and control; they may be either autonomous or dependent.

Taking the two dimensions together, we have developed the typology shown in Figure 4.1. What we define as a voluntary organization could conceivably be any of the four types.

Most analytical approaches to the study of the development of the voluntary sector and the welfare state fail to capture the dynamics of the relations between the two sectors. Either they assume the state is imperialistic or that the sectors remain static. Many analyses of modern politics begin with an ideal state and completely autonomous voluntary organizations. A more dynamic perspective would argue that to understand the characteristics of voluntary organizations at a given point, we must simultaneously understand government; we cannot understand the one without the other. In different countries or in the same country at different periods, both the state and voluntary organizations would be described quite differently.

Many analysts have argued that because of changes in public policies, voluntary organizations have moved from box 4 (which advocates of a minimal state consider ideal) toward box 1 and box 2, where their freedom of action is severely limited.

Figure 4.1. Relations Between the Public and Voluntary Sectors.

	Nearness	Distance
	(in communication and contact)	
Dependence	(1) Integrated dependence	(2) Separate dependence
(in finances and control)		
Independence	(3) Integrated autonomy	(4) Separate autonomy

Box 3 supposedly constitutes the ideal of pluralism: groups of people organize themselves and try to make an impact on public policy on issues that affect them, without becoming integrated into the decision-making or implementation processes.

The complexity of relations between the state and voluntary organizations in Norway becomes apparent when we consider examples of the three major types of organizations operating in the health and welfare sector in the first decades of this century.

1. Organizations for the welfare of the general public (Nasjonalforeninqen for Folkehelsen; Norske Kvinners Sanitetsforening; Norges Rode Kors). These were large charitable organizations with broadly defined objectives.
2. Organizations for the care and treatment of what was perceived as a self-inflicted problem, such as alcoholism (Bla Kors, Hvite Band). These more specialized temperance organizations, based on Christian values, not only tried to fight the spread of the "evil" of alcohol, but they also owned and operated large-scale institutions.

Government-Nonprofit Cooperation in Norway 79

3. Special organizations for the care of people whose problems were perceived as undeserved, such as the blind, the deaf, and the physically handicapped (Norges Blindeforbund, Norske Doves Landsforbund, Norges Vanforelag).[2]

Organizations in the first two categories worked for the welfare of the general public, and not primarily for their own members.[3] There is, however, an important difference between the two types. Those in the second group had a specific philosophy; we would expect them to be more concerned with their organizational autonomy than the first group. The second group can help us understand how much autonomy government is willing to grant voluntary organizations as producers of public services. Organizations in the third group, however, worked primarily for the welfare of their own members, although the original initiatives to organize depended on people without handicaps. This distinction—general public or members only—turns out to be important in this period when welfare was becoming a public, rather than a private, responsibility.

The three large charitable organizations in category 1 were active in the fight against tuberculosis, the greatest epidemic in Norway since the Black Death. In fact, this was the sole mission of Nasjonalforeninqen, which was set up in close cooperation with the medical association (Laegeforeninqen) and the government. These organizations illustrate the typical mixed system that came to dominate Norway from the turn of the century, a system of cooperation between government and private voluntary agents that moved steadily toward increased public responsibility. In 1900, new legislation on tuberculosis asserted the superior responsibility of the government and challenged traditional attitudes on the division between society and the individual citizen. By providing for forced hospitalization, the legislation acknowledged that the disease was no longer a purely private matter. There was, however, no realistic alternative to the state assuming responsibility; the other sectors did not have the capacity to perform tasks on the scale required.

Norske Kvinners Sanitetsforening, established in 1896, was the first to take on the problem of tuberculosis. Nasjonalforeninqen for Folkehelsen entered the arena from 1910. Starting about 1920, the Norges Rode Kors (Red Cross) also became involved in the epidemic, transforming itself from an organization for victims of war to a more general welfare organization. Competition among the three organizations at the local level led in 1925 to an agreement that new local associations would not be established where the three already operated. In 1947, they joined with the newest charitable organization, Norsk Folkehielp (established in 1939), in a Council of Cooperation to coordinate with the government and one another, and to prevent other organizations from entering the field. These organizations came to play a major role in disseminating health information and operating institutions. After 1945, in contrast to many other countries, no broad charitable health organization based on individual membership and local associations was established.

In the fight against tuberculosis, these four organizations received major funding from a state lottery and from the state monopoly on the sale of liquor and wine, illustrating the close relationship between the sectors. The state also defined its responsibility by financing expenditures to institutions providing care in accordance with the laws on tuberculosis (1900) and health insurance (1909), and through general appropriations over the government budget; by guaranteeing the operation of institutions by paying deficits on operational costs; and by taking over the management and sometimes ownership of nonpublic institutions. The picture that emerges is one of close contact and coordination. Because of this mutual dependence, the three organizations active in the fight against tuberculosis seem to belong in box 1 of Figure 4.1.

Organizations in the second category do not easily fit into Figure 4.1. The temperance movement was one of the largest mass movements in Norway. At the turn of the century, the predominant public view toward drinking was one of moral denunciation; it was believed that the state should punish alcoholics who caused public disturbances. This attitude toward alcoholics was part of a puritan morality that made a distinction between the deserving and the undeserving poor; the will to help was usually missing. On the other hand, the first temperance institutions, Bla Kors and Det Hvite Band, were marked by Christian charity and went beyond preventive efforts. They believed that alcoholism was a vice and that overindulgence in alcohol gradually developed into an illness. These organizations became the most important actors in the early development of institutions for the care of alcoholics.

The first attempt through legislation to establish a special relief scheme for compulsive drinkers, morphine addicts, and other victims of intoxicants dates from 1898, when the law recognized the right to have a person declared incapacitated with the possibility of commitment to a sanatorium. However, few such institutions were available. The first known sanatorium was created on private initiative in 1882, and members of the temperance movement and medical practitioners served on the board. Most people in the temperance movement considered treatment and care a public responsibility because the state earned income from the sale of alcohol; these people wanted to concentrate on preventive efforts (Bones, 1978). Before the turn of the century, some private medical sanatoriums were established by the wealthy, but none survived for long (Fuglum, 1972). Improvement came only when the two organizations began to build and operate sanatoriums in 1908 and 1913; later sanatoriums received state subsidies.

The evolution of care for alcoholics was strongly influenced by morality. Religious and medical professional interests shaped a system of institutional care based on financial support from the government; the government was expected to assume responsibility for chronic drinkers. During the years between the world wars, public expenditures in general diminished and state subsidies to the organizations were sharply reduced. Private sanatoriums accepted only voluntary patients; committals were left to the government.

Voluntary organizations pioneered, and still dominate, institutional care for alcoholics. State institutions for the most difficult cases developed only as a supplement to the voluntary effort. The voluntary organizations develped their role as the major service provider in close cooperation with the government and are completely dependent on public subsidies. They are an important and integrated part of a system of care in which public responsibility has been manifest.

The close cooperation between the Christian temperance organizations and the state is also noteworthy from an ideological perspective. These organizations have always believed that care for alcoholics, which they consider a public task, could best be established in cooperation with government. Thus they were quite willing to receive public support. At the same time, they sought to maintain their autonomy. Increased public support was not perceived as an indication of weakness, but rather as a sign of growing public understanding of the tasks performed by the organizations.

Today these institutions are still privately owned, with their own boards and administration, but they are fully integrated elements of the public care system. Operating expenses and patient care are publicly financed. The organizations are not obsessed by the idea of autonomy; they look upon themselves as important opinion makers and agents of influence in public affairs. These organizations are not easily placed in our typology because they did not have a period of separate autonomy; even if they were important welfare pioneers, they were closely linked to public policy.

In the third category, organizations for the physically handicapped were established to reduce the extent of personal isolation. In the second half of the nineteenth century, private citizens and the government established schools and supported charitable enterprises of a religious nature. Many, but not all, were later dissolved as new organizations, not exclusively for the handicapped, developed. Initially, the fundamental aim of these earlier organizations was to change public attitudes about the dependency of the handicapped and to develop self-help. The primary objectives were providing information and services, and the principle of autonomy from the state was explicit. In general, though, these organizations have shifted the use of their donated income from the provision of welfare services and information to more emphasis on advocacy.

These voluntary organizations are welfare pioneers. A

school law in 1881 concerning the mentally deficient and institutions for the physically handicapped involved the state early on, but overall the scope of public subsidies was very limited. However, the real pioneers were private citizens who, beginning in the early nineteenth century, created a number of schools before either government or organizations entered the arena.

Organizations soon contacted the government on policies where the state had already demonstrated some interest, such as subsidies to private institutions and contributions to organizational initiatives. Apart from schools, public services for the handicapped through financial support for private charity supplemented those provided by government in the interwar period. An official committee in 1924 even endorsed the principle of "government-supported private management." In summary, the period until 1940 was one in which good relationships with government prevailed, while at the same time voluntary organizations retained a high degree of freedom of action. Lines of communication were simpler. There was nearness in the sense of easy access, although this did not necessarily translate into immediate and substantial support for the aims of the organizations.

Organizations of this type are also not easy to place in our typology. Historically, these organizations have been more concerned with autonomy than those in the first or second group. If any organization at all can be placed in box 4, it must be the organization for the deaf, which from its inception was the most introverted. But generally, all three moved gradually toward a position in between box 1 and box 3, with a further development toward box 1 after 1945.

The activity of the organizations in category 3 was strongly linked to the prevailing ideologies. Seeking to improve the quality of life of their own members, these organizations promoted social activities for people who had difficulty participating in everyday life. They also provided schooling and financial support for individuals who were outside the reach of government and hence suffered severe deprivation. In the beginning, they were self-help organizations. A central objective was that their members should not inconvenience the public, and therefore increase of personal autonomy was the goal. Although they first wanted to separate themselves from government, as popular views on public responsibility changed, the organizations began to explore the possibility of obtaining public funds. In this process there is a development from "internal" to "external" activity but without organizations giving up their role in welfare provision.

The Deeper Meaning of the Relationship

The relations between the three types of voluntary organizations and the state in Norway are not easily assigned to existing theoretical approaches. We have seen that, from the very beginning, organizations cooperated closely with public authorities. Sometimes organizations were pioneers, and sometimes the government may have been reluctant to take on certain tasks, but generally it is not possible to discern a pattern of visionary organizations and a reactionary public bureaucracy. Cooperation rather than conflict has been the rule.

The period leading up to 1940 represented an open situation; the ultimate shape of the welfare system was still unsettled. (The system assumed a definite, if not necessarily final, form in the 1950s and 1960s.) The strengthening of the state model was not mainly a consequence of ideological compulsion but rather of internal organizational processes in a system with a high degree of consensus on ideology and goals. Gradually a consensus developed that the state should have the primary responsibility, whether executed directly or indirectly, for health, social insurance, and social policy in general.

This does not mean that the state took over tasks from the other sectors; rather, new social needs were uncovered and new rights were acknowledged. It was realized that only through comprehensive public efforts could the necessary resources for an adequate, rational, and equitable supply of welfare services be provided. In this sense, the system developed in a vacuum with little competition from the other sectors. Public solutions did not come about as a result of failure in the other sectors; the voluntary sector was a cooperative driving force in the process of ideological and organizational transformation toward increased public responsibility. It is incorrect to depict the state forcing itself into areas previously occupied by voluntary organizations. Nor have public service provision and responsibility increased at the expense of the voluntary sector, although the scope and type of public activity have obviously changed the potential for voluntary action.

How should we characterize the relations between sectors in the period up to World War II? During this time voluntary organizations both mobilized and emphasized member activity, and they also tried to influence the political culture in favor of greater welfare and democracy (Engberg, 1986). Very early on, they emphasized cooperation because a consensus existed about goals and means of social development. Reflecting the organizational and ideological climate of the time, charitable organizations sought public solutions rather than private ones.

We have said that the organizations in categories 1 and 2 embodied a cooperative attitude from the outset. Cooperation meant that an understanding about the tasks to be done had priority over organizational demands and autonomy. The concepts of common interests and the general will seem appropriate in this case. The organizations work for the good of all; they consider the results more important than the demarcation between sectors, and thus they do not perceive a clash of interests with government.

In the literature on pluralism and corporatism, and by implication in the theories of democracy, we find the view that special-interest representation has increased at the expense of popular representation. This has been regarded as the major problem in weaving together public and private interests. We argue that health and social welfare organizations, especially those that work for others rather than their own members, have developed characteristics that resemble those found in the system of popular representation. This means that such organizations are very different from most special-interest organizations, especially trade unions and economic interest organizations, which became integrated parts of public policy after World War II. The problems for democratic procedures that arise when special-interest organizations gain significant access to public policy making are therefore different from those we outline here.

In different periods, different aspects of social life become a public interest. When new policy areas take form, this process is always part of important ideological change, such as a change in the way of looking at society. It means that a new problem area has been "discovered" (even if it existed for a long time) and that it is now possible to do something about it. In the interwar period, health and social welfare became a new policy area, implying a special set of relations between government and society.

The process of integration between government and voluntary organizations has a long history. Voluntary organizations as far back as the 1820s received public subsidies; in the 1840s, the emissaries of the teetotalers received government subsidies. From the 1860s, private schools for the handicapped, rifle clubs, and sports groups all obtained state subsidies. After 1875, public subsidies were increasingly offered to night schools, workers' academies, and similar enterprises. In other words, organizations were, from very early on, parts of public policy.

Participation by organizations in official committees is not new either. Temperance organizations participated in the national council for temperance education (Landsradet for Edruska Psundervisning), which was already established in 1902. The close cooperation resulted in the creation of a government council of temperance (Statens Edruskapsrad) in 1936, giving the temperance movement a role on a permanent, national-level committee. The movement was even more integrated in public policy in 1969, when the Directorate for Sobriety was established, although it had lost much of its mobilizing potential in the meantime.

Another area of early contact between organizations and government was the cultural, especially popular academies (folkeakademiene). This began as early as 1899, when the state offered a grant to a committee with representatives of the government and the academies to appraise and recommend lectures. In the period of economic stagnation in the 1920s, the public grants were reduced, but they again increased in the 1930s. The cooperation was formally institutionalized when the government council for enlightenment of the people (Statens Folkeopplysningsrad) was established in 1946.

In the field of health, we have already mentioned the role of government as initiator of the establishment of Nasjonalforeningen in the fight against tuberculosis. The director of public health (*Medisinal-direktoren*) had a permanent seat on the board, and a number of municipalities became members of the voluntary organization. Another example is the central board for care of the handicapped (Centralstyre for Vanforeomsorqen), which was created in 1916 with representatives from the organizations. This model of integrated participation was used in 1923, when the central board for centers of remedial measures (Sentralstyre for Hjelpestasjonsvirksomhet) was formed.

Pressure-group activity was obviously not a postwar phenomenon either. Voluntary organizations have always tried to influence public authorities on issues that affect them, and not least on legislative matters. The temperance movement and the linguistic movement for New Norwegian, *landsmal,* are examples from before World War II. A similar process took place after the war, when the perceptions of public responsibility for sports, nature preservation, the position of women, the environment, and developmental aid changed.[4] Government has been much less controlling in the field of culture than in the health and social welfare area, perhaps because the idea of rights is less obvious and the consequences of inadequate provision are less concrete and dramatic.

Nothing Lasts Forever:
New Roles for Voluntary Organizations

The idea of public responsibility for welfare grew particularly strong and explicit during the postwar expansion period, but a trend to revise this perspective began to emerge in the second half of the 1970s. In the 1980s, these tendencies have materialized in the creation of modernization programs for the public sector in Norway, other Nordic countries, and in the Organization for Economic Cooperation and Development (OECD) area generally (Olsen, 1988). New values — decentralization, self-help, and "consumer democracy" (the participation of users of social services in decisions regarding the location and extent of the service) — are emerging and new possibilities for voluntary organizations are open.

As we have seen, cooperative relations between some types of voluntary organizations and government have a long tradition, and many new relations have been developed and formalized since 1945. In spite of this, for almost forty years after World War II, the role of voluntary organizations in the welfare sector was hardly taken into account in political discussions. If organizations were mentioned, it would mostly be in the influential radical-liberal press as examples of welfare providers who had outlived themselves. Charity in any form was obsolete and reactionary because welfare services were expected to be provided by the state and by professionally educated persons. Nor did voluntary organizations attract the interest of social scientists. The 1950s, and especially the 1960s, were decades of rapid and extensive expansion of the welfare state. Social insurance programs were finally made universal, new programs for special groups such as orphans and single mothers were established, and benefits were, on the whole, made much more generous (Kuhnle, 1986).

The striking "invisibility" of voluntary welfare organizations in politics, social research, and public debate does not necessarily imply that their activity and importance declined during the period of welfare state expansion. On the contrary, a recent analysis indicates that increases in the scope and range of state, voluntary, and commercial welfare occurred simultaneously (Kolberg, 1984). This happened over a period of unequalled, continuous economic growth and overall consensus among political parties on the strengthening of welfare state programs until the end of the 1970s. The growth in state welfare seems to have gone hand in hand with growth in voluntary and commercial welfare. The number of members in the broad voluntary organizations (our categories 1 and 2) has decreased since the mid 1970s, while the number of specialized "handicap organizations" has grown tremendously. Furthermore, the health and welfare organizations have become more professional, have increased the number of employees, and have increased their service activity (Selle and Hestetun, 1990). The extent of nonpaid voluntary work has declined, making it more necessary to distinguish between voluntary work and voluntary organizations.

The state has never reigned supreme in the welfare field. In the study of welfare provision, it is important to distinguish between the three public functions of financing, producing, and controlling welfare provision. Even if public authorities today fund almost all expenditures for operating welfare institutions, this does not imply that the institutions must be publicly owned. In Norway in 1985, 14 percent of all beds put in somatic hospitals, 21 percent of the places in psychiatric institutions, and as much as 35 percent of all places for the mentally retarded were owned by voluntary organizations. Voluntary organizations own 60 percent of all beds in institutions for alcoholics, and 32 percent of the beds in institutions for child and youth care (NOU, 1988). About 75 percent of all welfare service centers for the elderly were run by voluntary organizations but publicly financed. In the field of noninstitutional work, which is subject to fewer legal regulations, voluntary organizations perform more extensive tasks than the public sector.

The welfare state was under critical scrutiny from left-oriented social scientists during its most expansionary period (Lingas, 1970; Lochen, 1965; Midre, 1973; Oyen, 1974). Generally, they claimed that realities did not correspond to ideals set. The welfare state created "clients"; basic social problems remained unsolved. However, economic growth was strong, unemployment extremely low, and the rate of inflation bearable, although this changed around 1980. The international oil crises of 1973 and 1979–80 triggered analyses of the size and growth of the public sector and debates about the "crises"—financial, social, political—of the welfare state. Earlier critics of the welfare state became defenders of what had been achieved through state-sponsored social intervention (Ringen and Waerness, 1982; Kolberg, 1983; Brox, 1988). From neoconservative and European liberals, the welfare state came under attack for being inefficient and overregulated; individual freedom was claimed to be constrained. A greater role for the market was advocated by the political right, which wanted to limit public-sector growth and to permit more private solutions in the welfare field. The answer of the political left to persistent social problems and the mismatch between needs and resources has been to demand decentralization of political decision-making responsibility and to increase citizen participation in welfare matters.

These strategies for a change in welfare policies obviously have different consequences for people and for the role of politics in society. One common implication of the various critical perspectives on the welfare state has been the development of a more unified look at the role of voluntary organizations. Intermediary structures and voluntary organizations have been "rediscovered" across the left-right political spectrum (NOU, 1988; Lorentzen, 1984; Offe, 1984).

The changed political setting in Norway is not unique, and international sources have almost certainly influenced ideological trends in Norway. There has been a growing attention to debureaucratization and to the welfare role played by family and voluntary organizations in Western Europe (Paci, 1987). The OECD publication *The Welfare State in Crisis* (1981) described, or perhaps even inaugurated, the changing political atmosphere among the richer nations. Due to the growing importance of the oil sector in the Norwegian economy, Norway steered clear of the second international oil crisis but not the internationally dominant views on the assumed crises of the welfare state.

During the political debate of the 1980s, voluntary organizations were rediscovered. All three long-term (four-year) governmental programs produced in Norway in the 1980s—two by Social Democratic governments (Stortingsmelding 79, 1980–81; Stortingsmelding 4, 1988–89), one by a three-party nonsocialist government (Stortingsmelding 83, 1984–85)—have been marked by a new and strong emphasis on the "civil society" and "the third sector." References to the importance of social networks began to appear in these regular government programs from the mid 1970s, but the text has been much elaborated and expanded in the 1980s. The general ideological, if not always empirical, tendency to individualize, privatize, and decentralize welfare responsibility in Norway seems to have been a conscious strategy to upgrade the importance of voluntary organizations and informal social networks, although one may assume that public money saving is the hidden agenda of this ideological facade. The most recent long-term governmental program (Stortingsmelding 4, 1988–89), produced by the Social Democratic government, notes: "In the effort to develop the *welfare society* [our translation] it is important to improve the cooperation between public authorities and voluntary organizations, self-help groups, and local cooperative initiatives. To solve important tasks, and in order to make everyday life easier, many people find it to their advantage to work together. Others feel that life becomes more meaningful when they can do something for others on a voluntary basis. This kind of activity deepens and strengthens welfare, it creates solidarity, nearness and community."

The quotation signals a much more modest ambition on the part of the state compared to statements in the 1960s. Voluntary organizations are now regarded as useful partly because they offer the opportunity for personal engagement and meaningful activity, for cultural realization, and for recreation; partly because they perform socially useful work within the health and welfare sector and create social networks; and partly because they function as schools in democracy. There is suddenly no limit to their progressive role. The activity of many organizations is perceived as a direct and practical expression of values such as togetherness and solidarity.

The belief that the voluntary sector rather than the state can solve future welfare needs gained particular strength in the 1980s, but the modern belief is ideological, politically opportune, and more rhetorical than empirically based. The belief has been advocated in the long-term governmental programs and in general political debates without supporting documentation. In fact, regular and detailed official statistics on the scope and activities of voluntary organizations, and on their cooperative interaction with local government, have not been collected in Norway. It was perhaps partly this obvious need for data that in 1985 gave the nonsocialist government the incentive to establish a public investigatory committee on voluntary organizations. But the creation of this committee could also be interpreted as an opportune political tool for many voluntary organizations and their spokesmen in government.

It was the first public investigatory committee ever in

Norwegian political history to deal with the subject of voluntary organizations. Its report (NOU, 1988) was published in 1988 when the Social Democratic party had recaptured governmental power. However, after the general election of September 1989, the three nonsocialist parties formed another government and nothing came of the committee's proposals. One explanation may be that the report uncovered a variety of priorities, not only between representatives of the government and voluntary organizations but also among representatives of different types of voluntary organizations. Although the committee submitted few concrete proposals, it did convey the opinion that voluntary organizations should take on more tasks in the health and welfare sector, especially in the field of "open" (noninstitutional) care for the elderly, but also in kindergartens, education, and development aid. The committee did not, however, propose solutions that in any decisive way would affect the general conditions for organized voluntary activity. No major change in the boundaries between the public and private spheres was suggested. The committee described the relationship between the state and organizations as harmonious. From the perspective of the state, voluntary organizations are collaborators in the solutions of practical tasks. The report fosters a positive, even romantic view of the voluntary sector in contrast to the public sector.

The development toward "consumer democracy" and decentralization can, however, offer new possibilities for voluntary organizations that could lead to changes in the demarcations between sectors. If we use the concepts of the British sociologist Richard Titmuss, who distinguished between social, fiscal, and occupational welfare, it is obvious that the importance of fiscal and occupational welfare has recently increased (Titmuss, 1974). Larger groups of income earners have benefited from tax deductions (mortgages, private pension insurance) on their income declaration in the 1980s (Gloppen and Kuhnle, 1989), and the scope of various types of occupational welfare (pension schemes, health services, day-care institutions for children, and so on) has expanded (Hippe and Pedersen, 1988).

Besides this internal pressure on the Scandinavian welfare model, the trends toward stronger political and economic integration among European nation-states will surely imply an element of external pressure on the model. An international system where the free flow of capital, goods, services and people is permitted will certainly open opportunities for crossnational, nonpublic welfare providers of different sorts. It is quite possible that the market alternative is much stronger today than in the past, both in ideology and resources, and that a similar case can be made for the voluntary sector. Ideologically, there seems to have been a shift toward a view of the public and voluntary sectors as alternatives. Whether sufficient energy and resources exist to take on new tasks is another matter (Brenton, 1985; Grindheim and Selle, 1989). In any case, there appears to be pressure on the Scandinavian welfare model connected to problems of efficiency and legitimacy. The pressure is not only in the direction of changes from the central to the local level, but also to changes in the boundary between sectors.

The situation now has two characteristics in common with the period between 1900 and 1940: uncertainty and experimentation. New forms of organization are tried out without a clear picture as to what might develop overall. The contrast is also striking because in the period leading up to 1940, there was a development toward increased public responsibility that did not exclude the possibility of voluntary organizations. In the 1950s and 1960s, the expansion of the public sector — caused by its own dynamics, political consensus, and a consistently growing economy — was so comprehensive that in spite of the fact that extensive tasks were performed in the voluntary sector, they were almost invisible in official documents and public debate. The recent problems of efficiency and legitimacy of the Scandinavian model from the end of the 1970s have contributed to the realization that other products and suppliers of welfare have been operating all the time. Furthermore, this realization has prompted debates about the appropriate roles for old and new actors in the voluntary sector. A major ideological change seems to be taking place.

Lessons from History and Prospects for the Future

Historically the relationship between voluntary organizations and government in the welfare area in Norway has been one of extensive cooperation and integration rather than of conflict. This is corroborated by a systematic look at such relationships between major organizations and the state in the 1900-1940 period. In the period after World War II cooperative relations have been extended, but the structuring of cooperation and integration is basically unchanged. These conclusions lead us to question key assumptions in pluralist and corporatist theories on what constitutes "public" or "private." We have observed coordination through shared goals more than through either forced hierarchical command or coordination of a corporative-pluralist type where the state is involved in a political struggle between self-interested, powerful, organized actors. Furthermore, we believe this symbiosis has been more comprehensive for the broad general welfare organizations working for others than for the specialized organizations that work mainly for their own members. Rather than expressing important distinctive values and being in conflict with government, the voluntary organizations have been cooperative driving forces in the ideological and organizational transformation toward increased public responsibility. They have sought public solutions rather than private ones. Which values voluntary organizations express and which organizational solutions they prefer depends, however, on the context and on the structuring of the relationship between the different sectors.

The ideological climate of the 1980s is very different from that of the 1900s and 1950s, and the relative size of the government sector and of an affluent middle class is much larger. The Scandinavian model characterized by universal social policy schemes, a large role for the state in organization and financing, and a unified organization of social security, may come under pressure for significant structural change, for both domestic and external reasons. Domestically, pressure has slowly (and "invisibly") built up over the last fifteen to twenty years, because of the growth of occupational welfare of different kinds, the effects of fiscal welfare on the growth of private, individual insurance, and the decentralization of responsibility for some health and social services. The Norwegian welfare state is becoming organizationally more fragmented and faces the danger of becoming socially more segmented.

External pressures increase as a consequence of the greater internationalization of politics and the economy, sparked in particular by the development toward a truly common market in the European Community (EC). Adjustment to the EC development may lead to a reduction of value-added tax levels and of other indirect taxes, and thus to a loss of public revenues not easily compensated. Freer movement of capital, goods, services, and people across countries in Europe may encourage crossnational, nonpublic health and social security schemes, and the nation-state may on the whole lose some political importance.

To these structural factors putting pressure on the welfare state must be added the 1980s' strengthened ideological belief in nongovernmental solutions to welfare and other needs. With less consensus on public responsibility in the welfare area, and with greater ideological and economic strength of the nonpublic sectors, voluntary organizations could become an important force in a move away from public responsibility. We may also anticipate more conflicts between various types of voluntary organizations representing different values.

Notes

1. This section, which partly overlaps with Kuhnle and Selle (1990), is largely based on three dissertations in comparative politics written under our guidance: Hestetun (1985), Grindheim (1986), Onarheim (1988); and on historical overviews by Raaum (1988) and Seip (1984).
2. Since World War II, there has been an enormous increase in this third group; only these three organizations existed before 1940, while currently there are forty-eight.
3. Organizations in categories 1 and 2 work with specific problems and therefore specific groups of people, but they would be oriented toward the welfare of others.
4. After World War II new policy areas appeared, reflecting new interest areas without at all decreasing the importance of health and social welfare questions. A number of new permanent committees of cooperation were established. In 1946, a government bureau of athletics (Statens Idrettskontor) was set up, soon to become the government bureau

for youth and sports (Statens Ungdoms og Idrettskontor). In 1953, a government council for youth (Statens Ungdomsrad) was created; in 1957 a council for sports; and in 1979 for cultural history (kulturminne). Sports were increasingly regarded as important in preventative public health and in providing social outlets for children and youth (Selle and Svasand, 1987). From the 1950s we also find increasing government cooperation with organizations for the environment, but the council of cooperation for outdoor life (Samarbeidsradet for Friluftsliv) was not established until 1986. In the 1990s environmental and women's issues will become main public policy areas, where a new type of relationship between government and voluntary organizations will develop.

References

Bones, B. *Alkoholomsorq i Norge* (The Care of Alcoholics in Norway). Oslo: Statens Institutt for Alkoholforskning, 1978.
Brenton, M. *The Voluntary Sector in British Social Services.* London: Longman, 1985.
Brox, O. *Ta Vare pa Norge* (Take Care of Norway). Oslo: Gyldendal, 1988.
Burenstam, L. S. *Den Hjartolosa Valfardsstaten.* (The Heartless Welfare State). Stockholm: Timbro, 1983.
Engberg, J. *Folkerorelserna i Velferdssamhallet* (People Movements in the Welfare Society). Unpublished dissertation, University of Umea, 1986.
Erikson, R., and others (eds.). *The Scandinavian Model: Welfare States and Welfare Research.* New York: M. E. Sharpe, 1987.
Fuglum, P. *Kampen om Alkoholen i Norge 1816-1904* (The Norwegian Battle of Alcohol 1816-1904). Oslo: Universitetsforlaget, 1972.
Gloppen, S. and Kuhnle, S. "Velferd og Skatteutgifter" (Welfare and Tax Expenses"). *Aftenposten*, Aug. 29, 1989.
Grindheim, J. E. *Velferd Eller Veldediqhet? En Analyse av Frivillige Organisasioners Rolle i Utviklinqen av Alko-holistomsorgen i Norge* (Welfare or Charity? An Analysis of the Voluntary Organization's Role in the Development of the "Care for Alcoholics"

Issue in Norway). Unpublished dissertation, Department of Comparative Politics, University of Bergen, 1986.
Grindheim, J. E., and Selle, P. "The Role of Voluntary Social Welfare Organizations in Norway: A Democratic Alternative to a Bureaucratic Welfare State?" Norwegian Centre for Organization and Management (LOSsenter), University of Bergen, May 1989.
Hestetun, P. A. *Velferdsekspansion og Organisasjonsendring: Ei Analyse av Frivillige Orqanisasionar si Rolle i Arbeidet mot Tuberkulosen* (Welfare Expansion and Organizational Changes: An Analysis of Voluntary Organizations' Role in the Struggle Against Tuberculosis). Unpublished dissertation, Department of Comparative Politics, University of Bergen, 1985.
Hippe, J. M., and Pedersen, A. W. *"For Lang og Tro Tjeneste?"* (For Long and Loyal Service?). *FAFO-Rapport 084.* Oslo: 1988.
Kolberg, J. E. *Farvel til Velferdsstaten?* (Can We Wish the Welfare State Goodbye?) Oslo: Cappelen, 1983.
Kolberg, J. E. "Private og Offentlige Velferdskomponenter" (Private and Public Components of Welfare). In H. Lorentzen (ed.), *Privat Eller Offentliq Velferd?* (Private or Public Welfare?). Oslo: Universitetsforlaget, 1984.
Kramer, R. *Voluntary Agencies in the Welfare State.* Berkeley: University of California Press, 1981.
Kuhnle, S. "The Growth of Social Insurance Programs in Scandinavia: Outside Influence and Internal Forces." In P. Flora and A. J. Heidenheimer (eds.), *The Development of Welfare States.* New Brunswick, N.J.: Transaction Books, 1981.
Kuhnle, S. "Norway." In P. Flora (ed.), *Growth to Limits: The Western European Welfare States Since World War II,* vol. I. Berlin: De Gruyter, 1986.
Kuhnle, S., and Selle, P. "Meeting Needs in a Welfare State: Relations Between Government and Voluntary Organizations in Norway." In A. Ware and R. Goodin (eds.), *Needs and Welfare.* London: Sage, 1990.
Lingas, L. G. (ed.). *Myten om Velferdsstaten* (The Myth of the Welfare State). Oslo: Pax, 1970.
Lochen, Y. *Idealer og Realiteter i et Psykiatrisk Sykehus* (Ideals and Realities in Psychiatric Hospitals). Oslo: Universitetsforlaget, 1965.

Lorentzen, H. (ed.). *Privat Eller Offentliq Velferd?* (Private or Public Welfare?) Oslo: Universitetsforlaget, 1984.
Midre, G. (ed.) *Samfunnsendring og Sosialpolitikk (Societal Change and Social Policy)*. Oslo: Gyldendal, 1973.
Nisbet, R. *Power and Community*. (2nd ed.) New York, Oxford University Press, 1962.
NOU (Norwegian Public Reports). *17 Frivillige Organisasjoner* (Voluntary Organizations). Oslo: Statens Trykningskontor, 1988.
Offe, C. *Contradictions of the Welfare State*. London: Hutchinson, 1984.
Olsen, J. P. "The Dilemmas of Organizational Integration in Government." In J. P. Olsen, *Organized Democracy*. Bergen: Universitetsforlaget, 1983.
Olsen, J. P. "The Modernization of Public Administration in the Nordic Countries: Some Research Questions." *Administrative Studies*, 1988, *7*, 2-17.
Onarheim, G. *Ein Analyse av Frivillige Organisasionar sitt Arbeid for Funksionshemmma* (An Analysis of Voluntary Organizations' Work for Disabled Persons Issues). Unpublished dissertation, Department of Comparative Politics, University of Bergen, 1988.
Organization for Economic Cooperation and Development (OECD). *The Welfare State in Crisis*. Paris: OECD, 1981.
Organization for Economic Cooperation and Development (OECD). *Social Expenditure 1960-1990*. Paris: OECD, 1985.
Oyen, E. *Sosialomsorgen og dens Forvaltere (Social Welfare and Its Administrators)*. Bergen: Universitetsforlaget, 1974.
Paci, M. "Long Waves in the Development of Welfare Systems." In C. Maier (ed.), *Changing Boundaries of the Political*. Cambridge, Cambridge University Press, 1987.
Raaum, J. "De Frivillige Organisasjonenes Framvekst og Utvikling i Norge" (The Emergence and Growth of Voluntary Organizations in Norway). In NOU (Norwegian Public Reports), 1988, *17* 239-355.
Ringen, S., and Waerness, K. (eds.). *Sosialpolitikk i 1980-ara* (Social Policy in the 1980s). Oslo: Gyldendal, 1982.
Salamon, L. M. "Partners in Public Service: The Scope and

Theory of Government-Nonprofit Relations." In W. W. Powell (ed.), *The Nonprofit Sector: A Research Handbook.* New Haven, Conn.: Yale University Press, 1987.

Seip, A. *Sosialhielpstaten Blir Til.* Oslo: Gyldendal, 1984.

Selle, P., and Hestetun, P. A. *Fylkes og Krinsnivaet i Organisasionssamfunnet* (The Making of the Social Assistance State). Oslo: TANO Publishers, 1990.

Selle, P., and Svasand, L. "Cultural Policy, Leisure and Voluntary Organizations in Norway." *Leisure Studies,* 1987, *4,* 347-364.

Stortingsmelding 79. *Langtidsprogrammet 1982-85* (The Long-Term Program 1982-1985). Oslo: 1980-1981.

Stortingsmelding 83. *Langtidsprogrammet 1986-89* (The Long-Term Program 1986-1989). Oslo: 1984-1985.

Stortingsmelding 4. *Langtidsprogrammet 1990-93* (The Long-Term Program 1990-1993). Oslo: 1988-1989.

Titmuss, R. M. *Social Policy.* London: Allen & Unwin, 1974.

5

The Interrelationship Between the Public and Voluntary Sectors in Switzerland: Unmixing the Mixed-Up Economy

Antonin Wagner

Almost fifty years ago, the American sociologist C. W. Mills published a stimulating essay entitled "Collectivism and the 'Mixed-up' Economy" (1942). In Mills's opinion, the "mixed" economy appears to be a "mixed-up" economy in which the respective weights of the state and private enterprise and the distribution of power between these two sectors are left undetermined. Therefore, more precise and realistic criteria are needed "of what is to be left in private hands and what is to be collectivized" (p. 183).

Since Mills wrote his essay, economists have developed the well-known theory of market failure. This theory emphasizes the existence of both "public" and "collective-consumption" goods for which the private sector is an unsatisfactory provider, likely to produce suboptimal quantities. This insight contributed — if not in practice, at least in theory — to determining the

The Public and Voluntary Sectors in Switzerland 101

respective weights of the state and private enterprise and to unmixing the "mixed-up economy."

In the meantime, however, it has come to be recognized that some goods and services are provided neither governmentally nor privately and that a third or "voluntary" sector of production has developed. In a three-sector economy with for-profit, governmental, and nonprofit sectors, the problem of institutional choice has two aspects. One is the choice between for-profit organizations and the other institutional forms. This choice hinges on the nature of the commodity produced—whether it is essentially a private good or has collective-good qualities. The second choice is between governmental and private nonprofit institutions. So far, few theoretical approaches have been developed to help us to understand this second part of the choice problem and to predict the circumstances under which the voluntary sector will develop or decline. In this context Weisbrod's seminal article "Toward a Theory of the Voluntary Nonprofit Sector in a Three-Sector Economy" (1986) represents a useful theoretical model.

Weisbrod's model sees voluntary provision of collective goods as a response to government failure. The public sector is the institution of choice when consumer demands are homogeneous. On the other hand, nonprofit organizations are meant to meet heterogeneous demands from minorities willing to pay for higher levels of service, thereby overcoming some of the problems of over- and undersatisfaction in the public sector. Nonprofits are useful in providing collective goods when consumer demand is heterogeneous (Weisbrod, 1988, p. 25).

In essence, Weisbrod's demand-diversity model predicts that the private nonprofit sector will be prevalent in a country of unusual diversity, like Switzerland. The first section of this chapter intends to verify this hypothesis. The finding, however, is that the size of the Swiss nonprofit sector in no way corresponds to what the demand-diversity model seems to predict. In the second section I argue that the size of Switzerland's nonprofit sector reflects its federal constitutional structure, rather than demand diversity. It seems that the degree of decentralization determines the extent to which the public sector is able to satisfy diverse demand. Therefore, the nonprofit sector does not function so much to correct governmental failures associated with unsatisfied demand, as it does to supplement government provision of collective goods. This problem is dealt with in the third section, which shows that the Swiss nonprofit sector, as an extragovernmental provider of goods and services, has to be seen as a supplement to, rather than a substitute for, public activities.

In conclusion, the fourth section goes into the system of incentives that, given the typical function of nonprofits in Switzerland, has been set up to encourage consumers to reveal their demands and to enable voluntary organizations to assume their task in providing collective-consumption goods. Income tax deductibility of donations to nonprofits and special treatment of voluntary organizations under tax laws (indirect subsidization) are used, in a rather restrictive way, as carrots. The Swiss idea of militia creates a societal pressure of its own and provides the "stick" for undersatisfied demanders to reveal their true preferences and their willingness to pay.

The Size of the Nonprofit Sector in Switzerland

If government responds to the demands of the majority and the nonprofit sector responds to the demands of the undersatisfied, then we can predict that the greater the diversity of demand, the larger the size of the nonprofit sector will be. Greater variance in consumers' demands is supposed to lead to relatively greater extragovernmental provision of collective goods and a relatively smaller role for the public sector. On the other hand, it can be expected that the variation in individual demands (and hence the degree of dissatisfaction with the politically determined level of output of public goods) will be smaller the greater the homogeneity is within a political unit.

The question then arises as to what socioeconomic characteristics influence the demand for collective-consumption goods and what are the most appropriate proxies for heterogeneity of both the quantities and qualities of collective goods demanded. Weisbrod (1986, p. 26) correctly assumed that diversity of income and wealth would be a less satisfactory proxy for heterogeneity of collective goods demanded than the diversity of other characteristics. Demand for collective goods is likely to vary with income and wealth, as are tax rates, which, under an income tax system, are typically a function of income and wealth. If we postulate that heterogeneity of demand at the same tax rate could be offset by heterogeneity of tax rates, then income and wealth distribution appear not to be a satisfactory proxy for the degree of demand heterogeneity of a given population. As explained below, other population characteristics highly correlated with the demand for public goods but not highly correlated with tax rates are therefore better proxies for the diversity of quantities demanded.

If our assumption with respect to satisfactory proxies for demand diversity is correct, Switzerland would qualify as a country with a high degree of heterogeneity despite a Gini coefficient of income inequality (0.284) that is more typical of a country with a relatively homogeneous income distribution (Leu, Brigitte, and Frey, 1986, p. 124). As far as other socioeconomic characteristics are concerned, Switzerland is a country of unusual diversity. A population of 6.6 million people lives on 41,293 square kilometers, 40 percent of which is concentrated in nine urban areas (Zurich, Geneva, Basel, Bern, Lucerne, St. Gallen, Winterthur, and Bienne). The population density (people per square kilometer) varies regionally between 5,237 (Basel-Stadt) and 25 (Grisons). About half the resident population participates in the work force. Six and a half percent of the active population is employed in the agrarian sector, 38.0 percent in the industrial sector, and 55.5 percent in the service sector. Forty-eight percent of the population is Roman Catholic, 44 percent Protestant, and 8 percent belongs to other religious groups. Sixty-five percent are German speaking, 18 percent French speaking, 10 percent Italian speaking, and 1 percent speaks the Raeto-Romantsch language. Twenty-four percent of the population is under nineteen, and 14 percent is over sixty-five (*Volkswirtschaft*, 1989, Vol. 1, pp. 1–47). If in the framework of a demand-diversity model variances in age and sectoral employment on the one hand, and such measures of heterogeneity as religion, language group or cultural identity, and urbanness on the other hand are used as explanatory variables, one might expect to find Switzerland among the countries that make a more extensive use of nonprofits than those with a relatively homogeneous demand structure. In order to test this hypothesis, we need certain quantitative data about the size of the nonprofit sector relative to other economic sectors.

However, in Switzerland as elsewhere, the state of quantitative knowledge of the nonprofit sector is affected by the hodgepodge of definitions (Weisbrod, 1988, p. 62) and accordingly is very poor. The nonprofit sector represents a mixture of heterogenous organizations engaged in a variety of activities (Fragniere, 1987). Tax regulations do not answer the question of definition because an organization can qualify as nonprofit and not belong strictly to the voluntary sector, and vice versa.

As explained elsewhere (Wagner, 1990), the taxonomy used by the System of National Accounts (SNA) is helpful in analyzing quantitative aspects of the voluntary sector. According to this taxonomy, there is, in addition to the government and the business sectors, a third sector of production, which includes private, nonprofit organizations serving households by providing social, educational, health, cultural, recreational, and other community services free of charge or below cost. Unlike those in the first sector, these organizations are not mainly financed and controlled by central, state, or local government. Unlike the second sector, third-sector goods and services being offered free or below cost are not produced for the market. If we follow Weisbrod (1988, p. 59), third-sector organizations can be divided into two general categories: "commercial"-type nonprofits (especially membership organizations such as trade unions, clubs, and associations), providing services to their own members; and "public"-type nonprofits, providing services to persons who do not contribute to the organizations' activities through contributions or membership fees.

Based on this classification, a list of nonprofits could be established as a first quantitative criterion reflecting the relative size of the third sector of production. Such a list would show that Swiss nonprofits mainly perform a variety of social services, although they are less widespread in the area of health, educational, and recreational services. Forty-nine percent of the twenty-seven hundred social organizations registered in the canton of Zurich, for example, are voluntary (Geiser and Sporri, 1987, p. 301). In the same canton, some two thousand organizations—engaged in a variety of social, educational, and cultural activities—are designated tax exempt by the cantonal tax administration (Kantonales Steueramt Zurich, 1987).

The number of nonprofit organizations, however, does not reflect the true size and significance of the voluntary sector. The role assumed by the nonprofit economy must therefore be measured by other means. Financial resources at the disposal of nonprofit organizations represent a more accurate measure of the relative size of a nonprofit economy than the mere number of institutions involved. The expenses of voluntary organizations providing social services—minus government subsidies—have been estimated at a total of 250 million Swiss francs for the year 1984 (Wagner, 1990, p. 8), or 10 percent of the expenses of all three levels of government for social services. To these service-type nonprofits an important number of social security organizations in the area of income transfers (especially pension plans and health insurance companies) has to be added, because social security funds are, to a large extent, organized privately. In 1984, they spent 6.5 billion Swiss francs (minus government subsidies). This means that approximately 20 percent of the total income transfers have been effected by private social security institutions.

The relative size of the nonprofit economy can also be measured by the sector's contribution to the gross domestic product (GDP). In 1985, the contribution of nonprofit organizations (Private Organisationen ohne Erwerbscharakter) to Switzerland's GDP was about 4.2 billion Swiss francs, or 1.8 percent, measured at market prices (*Volkswirtschaft*, 1988, Vol. 10, p. 31). This figure gives the most accurate picture of the relative size of Switzerland's nonprofit economy because it includes all nonprofits, not just nonprofits of the social-service type. Weisbrod (1988, p. 172) has calculated the percentage of national income originating in the nonprofit sector of the U.S. economy as ranging between 1.9 percent in 1943 and 4.4 percent in 1985. This comparison therefore indicates that in relative terms the nonprofit sector in Switzerland today is smaller than in the United States, a country with a comparable degree of demand diversity.

In addition, the nonprofit sector should be quantified not only on its contribution to national output but also on its function as an employer. In fact, because nonprofits are typically labor intensive, their contribution as employers is far more important. A calculation based on the same data used above (for estimating the contribution to GDP) shows that in 1985 the Swiss nonprofit sector employed about 3 percent of the entire national labor force. This is less than the 5 percent calculated by Weisbrod (1988, p. 64) for the United States economy. The estimated total of 85,000 paid workers in Switzerland's nonprofit sector is clearly an understatement, however. The total labor amount is considerably greater because of the large numbers of unpaid volunteers (mostly women) supplying millions of hours annually. A recent estimate for some of the most important voluntary providers of social services puts the amount of unpaid volunteers at the equivalent of 126,000 persons (Geiser and Sporri, 1987, p. 336). A more detailed analysis, focusing on thirty-five organizations providing health and social services in the canton of Zurich, shows that 9,000 volunteers are "employed" in addition to 37,850 paid staff members (Informationsstelle des Zurcher Sozialwesens, 1985, p. 7). These figures underline the gigantic addition to the paid labor force that volunteer labor constitutes in the social and health services area.

In summary, some quantitative knowledge of the nonprofit sector in Switzerland has been assembled. The findings should corroborate our hypothesis that in a country with a heterogeneous demand structure there is a strong tendency to transfer various service-provision functions to nonprofit and nongovernmental organizations. However, when compared to the United States—a country with a similar degree of demand diversity—none of the Swiss quantitative criteria indicates such a tendency. The role assumed by the nonprofit economy in Switzerland does not correspond to the predictions based on the demand-diversity model. The possible reasons for this are explained in the next section.

The Public and Voluntary Sectors in Switzerland 107

Adjustment Possibilities for Dissatisfied Consumers

In a country such as Switzerland with a heterogeneous demand structure, dissatisfied consumers might be expected to turn to voluntary organizations and other elements of the nonprofit sector as the nongovernmental providers of collective-consumption goods. However, several other adjustment possibilities are also generally available: migration to other governmental units, utilization of private market alternatives, or formation of lower-level governmental units (Weisbrod, 1986, p. 26). Given this range of options, dissatisfied Swiss consumers tend to prefer migration to other governmental units or formation of lower-level governments.

Migration

Migration to other governmental units is available as an option only if the public sector of the country in question consists of different government levels. In the federation of Switzerland, governmental functions are shared between one national, twenty-six cantonal, and approximately three thousand local governments. As shown in Table 5.1, the significance of cantonal and local governments (expressed as a percentage of GDP) is quite sizable and, what is more significant, has not declined since World War II. This contradicts the so-called Law of Popitz, which predicts that in a modern society more and more tasks will have to be assumed by central government, so that the relative size of local governments is likely to decline.

Not only did the relative size of cantonal and local governments in Switzerland not decline, but the division of tasks in the Swiss public sector is such that cantonal and local governments have continued to be the main providers of public goods and services in areas where dissatisfaction on the part of consumers is most likely to occur: educational, social, health, and cultural and recreational services (see Table 5.2).

The tax structure of local and cantonal governments in Switzerland assures that they are able to finance and sustain a high level of service provision. Income taxes constitute a very important source of revenue for both cantonal and local governments (see Table 5.3). In addition, this form of taxation offers

Table 5.1. Relative Size of Different Government Levels in Switzerland.

Year	Expenditures as Percent of GDP		
	Federal	Cantonal	Local
1950	8.4	7.6	6.4
1955	7.2	6.8	5.5
1960	7.0	7.7	5.5
1965	8.1	9.5	6.6
1970	8.6	10.5	7.5
1975	9.8	13.2	9.6
1980	10.3	12.9	9.7
1985	10.0	12.8	9.7

Source: "Oeffentliche Finanzen der Schweiz," 1986, p. 3.

Table 5.2. Cantonal and Local Governments as Service Providers (1984).

Services	Federal Government	Cantonal Governments	Local Governments
Educational	15.2	52.8	32.0
Cultural and recreational	7.7	24.5	67.8
Health	0.5	66.1	33.4
Social	0.2	41.8	58.0

Source: Oeffentliche Finanzen der Schweiz, 1986, p. 15.

Table 5.3. Tax Base of Cantonal and Local Governments in Switzerland (1984).

Type of Revenue	Percentage of Total Revenue		
	Federal level	Cantonal level	Local level
All taxes (100%)	42.4	32.8	24.8
Income taxes (100%)	24.7	41.6	33.7

Source: Oeffentliche Finanzen der Schweiz, 1986, p. 132.

the advantage of having a flexible tax base with the ability to increase with overall economic growth.

Given the qualitative and quantitative structure of the public sector in Switzerland, adjustment by migration within and between regions becomes an attractive alternative for dissatisfied consumers. As Tiebout (1956) would say, people have the option to vote with their feet. More than in other countries with a similar degree of heterogeneity in demand but a less well structured federal system, people in Switzerland seem to move to other governmental units where their demands are better met, instead of resorting to voluntary organizations. Local and cantonal governments as the primary service providers seem to form a valuable alternative to the kind of "nonprofit federalism" (Salamon, 1987, p. 43) existing in other countries with a diverse demand structure.

New Governmental Units

Forming new governmental units constitutes a second option of adjustment available to consumers dissatisfied with a less than optimal provision of collective-consumption goods, provided that they are willing to pay for added output. In cases like Switzerland, where governments exist at three hierarchical levels (central, cantonal, and local), the new governmental units most probably will not be territorially based but rather functionally based. Functional governments are organized on the territory of one (or more) local governments, to provide a specific collective good not offered by the local governments in question, or to improve the provision of a commodity where demand is undersatisfied. This form of public service supplementation seems to play an important role in Switzerland, as can be illustrated by the existence of a multitude of Zweckverbande (special-purpose governmental organizations) and the legal status of the Catholic and Protestant churches as quasipublic governments.

Zweckverbande come into existence when territorial governments are too small (mainly because of technical reasons) to provide collective-consumption goods. In 1985, in the canton of Zurich alone, a total of 164 special-purpose governmental organizations providing a wide range of services were registered (see Table 5.4). They spent a total of 249.1 million Swiss francs (current expenditures and amortization). A little over half (56.6 percent) of their revenue resulted from their business activities; another 41.3 percent was generated by cantonal (17 percent) and communal (24.3 percent) subsidies (Zurcher Gemeindefinanzen, 1987, p. 118).

Table 5.4. Special-Purpose Governments in the Canton of Zurich.

Purpose	Number of Special-Purpose Governmental Units in 1960	in 1985
Social services	7	2
Burial services	17	16
Educational services	2	11
Hospitals	4	9
Nursing homes	—	14
Alcoholism prevention	2	7
Drinking water	3	13
Sewage treatment	15	34
Garbage disposal	1	8
Recreational services	1	9

Source: Statistisches Amt des Kantons Zurich, 1988.

A similar function is assumed by the churches, in most cases the Catholic and Protestant churches. In Switzerland, church and state generally are not separated. In most cantons a church tax is levied (as a percentage of the state income tax), and churches are organized as territorial local governments, overlapping partly or completely with the political government units, depending on the size of the population and its religious characteristics. In the canton of Zurich alone, the local Catholic and Protestant churches in 1985 spent a total of 260 million Swiss francs, or 6 percent of the expenditures of the local governments of this canton (Zurcher Gemeindefinanzen, 1987, p. 60). To a sizable extent, these churches provide social, health, and educational services and therefore supplement the public provision of collective-consumption goods. They represent an attractive alternative for undersatisfied consumers and play an important role in their adjustment process.

The range of options other than resorting to voluntary organizations available for dissatisfied consumers in Switzerland explains why in this country the relative size of the nonprofit sector is smaller than one would expect, given the high degree of demand diversity. It seems that the relative size of the nonprofit sector is not so much a function of the heterogeneity of demand as it is the degree to which the public sector is able to satisfy the diverse demands of its constituents. The federal

The Public and Voluntary Sectors in Switzerland 111

constitutional structure of Switzerland, the role played by special-purpose governmental organizations, and the high level of governmentally provided services reduce the significance of voluntary organizations. From this point of view the degree of decentralization and other structural elements of the public sector seem to be at least as appropriate as explanatory variables for the size of the voluntary sector as demand diversity.

Nonprofit Institutions: Supplements or Substitutes?

The reasoning in the preceding section suggests that in a country like Switzerland with a hierarchically structured government, the voluntary sector might be smaller than in countries with a monolithic public sector. But even in a federalist context, nonprofit institutions might come into existence as extragovernmental providers of collective-consumption goods, albeit with different functions than they might perform in a more centralized system.

In principle, nonprofit institutions tend to engage mainly in two kinds of activities. First, some organizations specialize in providing collective-type goods, either identical to the governmentally provided goods, such as a nonprofit university, or complementary, such as a nonprofit research laboratory. Second, some nonprofit organizations engage in activities of a completely different nature, mainly providing private-good substitutes for collective goods. Private goods (like books sold or classes offered by private adult education centers) may have a substitutive character for the corresponding public good (education).

In addition to voluntary organizations, some private enterprises may also engage in activities supplementing or substituting for the governmental provision of collective goods. For-profit enterprises not only produce "ordinary" private goods; their output sometimes also includes collective-consumption goods. However, this is not the rule. In most cases the exclusion principle is not applicable and technological or cost constraints are serious obstacles for profit-seeking organizations engaging in the provision of collection goods. Should they, nonetheless, proceed to do this, it would still be necessary for government, from an allocative-efficiency standpoint, to play an important role, because private markets tend to produce suboptimal quantities of collective-consumption goods. All in all, it seems that private business is more likely to be a provider of private-good substitutes than a provider of collective-good supplements.

The assumption now is that the function of voluntary organizations varies from country to country, depending on the different modes of adjustment available for undersatisfied consumers. In Switzerland, resorting to voluntary organizations is not a first-choice option. Territorial governments and quasi-governmental units offer a wide range of collective-consumption goods. In this context, we expect that nonprofits specialize in the complementary provision of collective-type goods, rather than in either activities with substitutive character or activities aimed at providing collective goods identical to the ones produced in the public sector. In other words, nonprofit institutions have a supplemental, rather than a substitutive, function with respect to the public sector. There is little incentive for them to compete with a multitude of public and quasipublic organizations and to engage in the provision of identical collective goods.

With respect to private-good substitutes, the for-profit sector is a more likely alternative provider than the voluntary sector. Private-good substitutes have the advantage over collective-consumption goods that they do not require sharing and therefore are fully under the individual's control, as car drivers resisting the use of public transportation know. The demand for private-good substitutes (relative to the demand for collective goods) should therefore increase with the growth of per capita income, and provision of these goods becomes an attractive field of activity for classical profit-seeking firms with which nonprofit institutions would have to compete.

In Switzerland, voluntary organizations seem to be less inclined to participate in this competition and to conquer private markets than are their counterparts in the United States. Cutbacks in U.S. government funding force nonprofits to resort to new measures of raising revenues and to compete with private business, moving away from charitable and collective-type

The Public and Voluntary Sectors in Switzerland 113

services into the sale of private-type goods (ordinary private goods and substitutes to collective goods) (Weisbrod, 1988, p. 108). Because nonprofits in Switzerland are subsidized more generously than elsewhere, they are less prompted to sell private output and to "cross-subsidize" their charitable activities.

A description of the situation in Zurich with respect to typical collective-good "industries" such as cultural and recreational services may offer some examples. Recreational and cultural facilities and services are, to a large extent, either provided directly or subsidized by the city of Zurich (Horlacher, 1984). In addition Pro Juventute, the local section of a voluntary umbrella organization specializing in social services for children and youth, offers services that are complementary to the publicly financed cultural and recreational services, by maintaining a system of community centers situated in different neighborhoods. On the other hand, as an alternative to recreational activities that require sharing, for-profit enterprises offer a whole range of private-good substitutes to collective services, like private dance classes or language courses. Among the organizations involved in this kind of activity is Migros, originally a food distributor and supermarket chain and more recently the fifth largest of Switzerland's private firms. A similar structure of voluntary provision of collective goods is detectable in such areas as hospital services, higher education, day-care facilities, and libraries.

Incentives Used to Encourage Voluntarism in Switzerland

Although voluntary organizations are less important in Switzerland than in similar countries, and their function seems to be reduced to supplementing governments and quasigovernments in providing collective-consumption goods, they too face financial problems, as elsewhere. Because they do not have the coercive and compulsive powers of governments to levy taxes, voluntary organizations must face the free-rider problem associated with providing collective goods. If nonprofit institutions are to correct governmental failures associated with undersatisfied demand, they must overcome the free-rider problem by determining the true demands for collective goods and obtaining information on individuals' willingness to pay. In principle, nonprofits use two instruments to overcome their handicap of a lack of coercive power. One is a stick, some kind of societal pressure put on undersatisfied consumers to reveal their greater willingness to pay for collective goods by making a donation; the other is a carrot—direct and indirect subsidies to voluntary organizations to overcome their lack of adequate financing (Weisbrod, 1988, p. 28).

In Switzerland, as in most other countries, government support is probably the most common strategy to help voluntary organizations face their financial problems. Tax exemptions, mainly in the form of income tax deductions granted to nonprofits, are used as indirect subsidization. Organizations eligible to receive favorable tax treatment have to be specified in special tax regulations. As far as Switzerland is concerned, all three government levels have to be taken into consideration. In addition to the federal income tax law, twenty-six different cantonal tax laws are involved.

The tax-exemption regulations spelled out in a recently proposed federal income tax law will, when enacted, be used as a skeleton for the cantonal tax laws. It suggests how the Swiss tax laws deal with the tax exemption of nonprofits. Article 26 enumerates all institutions that will be considered income tax-exempt; in addition to the federal, cantonal, and local governments, and the social security and religious organizations, all institutions serving exclusively public and common-interest purposes are declared tax-exempt. This regulation reflects perfectly well the "supplemental" character of nonprofit institutions in Switzerland. The rationale for singling out voluntary organizations as tax-exempt under the income tax law is that they are engaged in providing goods usually provided by governments. Exemption from income taxation is exclusively based on the common interest served and not on specific services or goods provided.

However, some cantonal tax laws, in addition to this common-interest rationale, enumerate special domains of public good provision in which organizations may qualify for tax

The Public and Voluntary Sectors in Switzerland 115

exemption. This is the case in the canton of Zurich, where institutions serving educational purposes are mentioned separately (paragraph 16, lit. b of the cantonal tax law). Because in this cantonal law tax exemption is defined more extensively than in the federal regulation, a great number of nonprofit institutions qualify as tax-exempt. There are more than two thousand in the canton of Zurich. They belong to both the commercial-type nonprofits—membership organizations like the Frauenverein (women's club) or AkademischeSportverband (academic sport club)—and the public-type nonprofits providing services to the whole community (like the zoological garden). Despite the large number of institutions qualifying for tax exemption, indirect subsidies probably do not amount to a huge sum.

Government not only stimulates voluntary organizations indirectly by tax subsidies, but more importantly supports nonprofits through outright cash grants. In 1984, according to *Oeffentliche Finanzen der Schweiz* (1986, p. 15), in Switzerland the so-called transfers to third parties (not other governments and not public enterprises) amounted to over 10 billion Swiss francs, up from something over 2 billion twenty years earlier. About 20 percent of these transfers went to farming and have nothing to do with the nonprofit sector. Most of the rest, however, was used to subsidize nonprofits, 33.2 percent in social welfare, 12.6 percent in education, and 6 percent in cultural and educational services, the classic domains of Swiss voluntarism.

The size of these subsidies to third parties could suggest that the voluntary sector in Switzerland by far exceeds our estimates presented earlier in this chapter. A clear line has to be drawn, therefore, between the legal status of nongovernmental organizations (NGOs) and their economic function. Very often Swiss NGOs are financed almost exclusively by government grants. Economically speaking, these are cases of public service provision, meaning provision via government purchase and contracting out, not only via government production. This can best be illustrated by schools of social work operated as private institutions in Switzerland. In 1986, out of a total of 22.8 million Swiss francs of expenses, 36 percent was financed by federal subsidies, 46 percent by cantonal subsidies, 9 percent by subsidies of local governments or quasigovernments (like churches), and only 9 percent by tuition.

A second instrument used by nonprofits to overcome their lack of coercive power in generating revenues is social pressure. Undersatisfied consumers are forced to reveal their true preferences and their greater willingness to pay for collective goods. Each individual society may rely on its own mechanism in this respect. Switzerland's political system, with its grass-roots democracy and its emphasis on citizen participation, creates its own kind of societal pressure to contribute to voluntary organizations. The idea of militia, which is at the root of Switzerland's political system, prepares the ground for donations and in-kind contributions to voluntary organizations by stipulating that every citizen has an obligation to assist in the defense of the country. Giving is, so to speak, part of the social fabric, part of the rules and norms of the social system.

This explains why income tax deductibility is not used as extensively as in the United States to encourage donations. Most cantonal tax laws are quite restrictive in this respect. As far as the corporation income tax is concerned, many cantons limit tax deductibility for charitable donations to nonprofits to a percentage of taxable income. As for the personal income taxes, deductibility of donations is restricted by a fixed ceiling. The lower these limits, the higher are the private costs to the donor of transferring one unit of income to a charitable organization. The negative effects of restrictive tax-deductibility regulations on the income-generating capacity of nonprofits to some extent are compensated by the fact in a federal democracy that citizens are less tax resistant and private philanthropy does not need to be stimulated to the same extent through tax incentives as in a more centralized political system.

Summary

This chapter is not meant to give a mere description of the nonprofit sector in Switzerland. Nor does it attempt to develop or prove a positive theory of voluntarism. The intention, rather,

The Public and Voluntary Sectors in Switzerland 117

has been to provide some evidence for assessing the validity of the demand-diversity model developed by Weisbrod (1986). The analysis suggests the type of arguments that help to explain the role of voluntary organizations in a three-sector economy from an institutional perspective of a specific country.

We found that under the circumstances prevalent in Switzerland, structural elements of the public sector constitute at least as good an explanatory variable for the size of the voluntary sector as demand diversity. A federally structured public sector with strong local governments and the existence of quasipublic service providers present to the dissatisfied consumer a wide range of options for adjustment other than dependence on the voluntary sector. In this context, nonprofit organizations function mainly as providers of collective-good complements, rather than goods that are identical to the publicly provided goods or private-good substitutes. Nonprofits assume therefore a more supplemental role with respect to the public service providers, as opposed to the substitutive role they play elsewhere. Accordingly, tax incentives either for donators or for nonprofits are of lesser importance. Giving and volunteering are deeply embodied in the Swiss social fabric, and income tax exemption is granted only when nonprofits fulfill a common interest. Direct subsidies, however, are used extensively, so that many nonprofits become quasipublic service providers.

References

Fragniere, J. "Action Sociale et Benevolat Social" (Social Action and Voluntarism). In *Rapport à l'Intention du Conseil Suisse de la Science sur les Problèmes de Recherche dans le Domaine du Travail Social Non-marchand et de l'Action Benevole*. Lausanne: Ecole d'Etudes Sociales et Pédagogiques (EESP), 1987.

Geiser, K., and Sporri, D. "Strukturmerkmale des Ambulanten Sozialwesens" (Structural Features of the Welfare System). In M. Fehlmann, C. Haefeli, and A. Wagner (eds.), *Handbuch Sozialwesen Schweiz*. Zurich: Verlag Pro Juventute, 1987.

Horlacher, F. *Kultursubventionen: Begrundung Offentlicher Kulturforderung und Zielgerichtete Ausgestaltung von Kultursubventionen, mit*

Besonderer Berucksichtigung der Zurcher Kulturpolitik (Government Subsidies for Cultural Activities, with Special Reference to the Situation in Zurich). Frankfurt: Verlag Peter Lang, 1984.

Informationsstelle des Zurcher Sozialwesens. "Arbeitsmarktstudie Sozial und Gesundheitswesen" (Analysis of the Labor Market in Social Welfare and Public Health Institutions). Zurich: Informationsstelle des Zurcher Sozialwesens, 1985.

Kantonales Steueramt Zurich. "Verzeichnis der Selbstandigen Anstalten Sowie Koerperschaften und Anstalten mit Gemeinnuetzigen Zwecken" (List of Public Enterprises, Local Communities, and Nonprofit Institutions). Zurich: Rechtsabteilung des Kantonalen Steueramtes, 1987.

Leu, R. E., Brigitte, B., and Frey, R. L. "Die Personelle Einkommens und Vermogensverteilung in der Schweiz" (Distribution of Personal Income and Wealth in Switzerland). *Schweizerische Zeitschrift fur Volkswirtschaft und Statistik,* June 1986, *122,* 111-141.

Mills, C. W. *Power, Politics, and People.* New York: Ballantine Books, 1942.

Oeffentliche Finanzen der Schweiz (Public Finance Statistics of Switzerland). Bern: Bundesamt fur Statistik, 1986.

Salamon, L. M. "Of Market Failure, Voluntary Failure, and Third Party Government: Toward a Theory of Government-Nonprofit Relations in the Modern Welfare State." *Journal of Voluntary Action Research,* 1987, *16*(1), 29-49.

Statistisches Amt des Kantons Zurich. *Statistische Berichte des Kantons Zurich* (Statistical Report of the Canton of Zurich). Zurich: Statistisches Amt des Kantons Zurich, 28. Jahrgang, Heft 2, 1988.

Tester, E. "Die Steuerbefreiung von Gemeinnutz igen Institutionen im Kanton Zurich" (Preferential Tax Treatment of Nonprofit Institutions in the Canton of Zurich). Zurich: University of Zurich (mimeographed), 1988.

Tiebout, C. "A Pure Theory of Local Government Expenditure." *Journal of Political Economy,* Oct. 1956, 416-424.

Volkswirtschaft, Die (The Current Year). Bern: Eidgenossisches Volkswirtschaftsdepartment, 1988.

Volkswirtschaft, Die (The Current Year). Bern: Eidgenossisches Volkswirtschaftsdepartment, 1989.

Wagner, A. "The Nonprofit Sector in Switzerland: Taxonomy and Dimensions." In H. Anheier and W. Seibel (eds.), *The Third Sector: Comparative Studies of Nonprofit Organizations*. Berlin: De Gruyter, 1990.

Weisbrod, B. A. "Toward a Theory of the Voluntary Nonprofit Sector in a Three-Sector Economy." In R. Ackerman (ed.), *The Economics of Nonprofit Institutions*. New York and Oxford: Oxford University Press, 1986.

Weisbrod, B. A. *The Nonprofit Economy*. Cambridge, Mass.: Harvard University Press, 1988.

"Zurcher Gemeindefianzen 1984 und 1985" (Financial Statistics of the Local Communities of Zurich, 1984 and 1985). In *Statistische Mitteilungen des Kantons Zurich*, Heft 118. Zurich: Statistisches Amt des Kantons Zurich, 1987.

6

The Voluntary Sector's Central Role in Managing Societal Instability in Northern Ireland

Arthur P. Williamson

International visitors to Northern Ireland are often surprised by the region's vigorous voluntary sector and by the buoyant community activity that has prospered and developed during two decades of community unrest and political flux. It might be tempting to think that this growth has taken place *in spite* of the province's disturbed political and social context and depressed economy. But it is more likely that this is one of a resilient people's responses to adversity. Certainly the period has seen a remarkable emergence of voluntarism, self-help, and community leadership. The 1970s and 1980s have seen major innovations in government and administration. A succession

Note: I wish to thank the following for their insights in connection with this chapter: Nick Acheson, Tim Blackman, Ralph Kramer, Paul Sweeney, and Roberta Woods.

of new structures have been invented (and as often discarded) as part of the continuing attempt to govern without consensus, to find more effective ways to deliver public and social services, and to provide for citizen rights while combating terrorism. Northern Ireland is a social laboratory in which late twentieth-century democratic assumptions about the relations of government and the governed are being thoroughly tested (Birrell and Murie, 1980; Darby and Williamson, 1978).

In a population of one and a half million people, there are at least one thousand active voluntary organizations and community groups, a ratio of more than one group for every two hundred people. Assuming a level of voluntary activity similar to that of adults in Great Britain (five hours ten minutes per month), it is estimated that voluntary activity in Northern Ireland is equivalent to more than thirty-five thousand person years of full-time work (Saxon-Harrold, 1989). The sector receives more than £100 million each year from government (Acheson, 1986; "Scrutiny of Government Funding . . . ," 1990).[1] Most of this is used to finance the work of the voluntary housing movement and a temporary employment scheme, Action for Community Employment. More than £40 million is channeled to voluntary housing associations to subsidize dwellings for groups such as the elderly and the handicapped and to encourage the growth of home ownership through equity sharing. The remainder supports the work of the Northern Ireland Council for Voluntary Action, the major umbrella organization in its field, which provides central advisory and training services for the voluntary sector, the Arts Council, the Sports Council, and many regional and intermediary voluntary organizations working in the social welfare and educational and recreational fields.

Public money is allocated by a multiplicity of funding agencies ranging from central government departments and local government to semi-independent boards composed of government nominees and to the Northern Ireland Voluntary Trust. Additionally, in the late 1980s the International Fund for Ireland (IFI) began to distribute large amounts of money contributed mainly by the United States and the European Community.

IFI is a supranational funding body that aims to engender stability and to develop the economic and social infrastructure, particularly in areas of social turbulence in the cities and along the frontier with the Irish Republic.

The primary focus of this chapter is the interface between government and the voluntary sector in the field of community relations and community development. Many issues are raised, including the function of the voluntary and community sector in a setting where formal political activity is moribund; how government uses the voluntary sector where statutory services are unacceptable to the local population; administrative structures developed by government in a situation where it rules without consensus; the tension between government's desire to encourage the voluntary sector and its need to prevent public financial support "leaking" into the paramilitary sector; the internationalization of concern about community instability and of funding for community development and community relations; how "new public management" (Hood, 1990) and the British government's new approach to the voluntary sector may be implemented in this quasicolonial setting. Underlying the whole discussion are questions about the interaction of the public bureaucracy state with a divided community that it administers without effective accountability.

The study of voluntary organizations in Northern Ireland is handicapped by the lack of an agreed classification system, very little academic research in the field, and lack of a central source of information on the extent of statutory support. This contrasts with a long-established tradition of academic research in statutory social policy, public administration, and political processes. Northern Ireland exemplifies Lester Salamon's statement that "the phenomenon of government-nonprofit interaction has been largely ignored in public debate and scholarly enquiry has focused instead on the evolution of government policy" (1987, p. 30). The development of government policy has been treated in a number of extensive studies, of which the most comprehensive is Birrell and Murie (1980).

British administrations in nineteenth-century Ireland relied heavily on paragovernmental boards for the delivery of pub-

The Voluntary Sector's Role in Northern Ireland 123

lic services (McDowell, 1964; MacDonagh, 1968). Local government has never rooted itself effectively in Irish soil. After experimenting with local government for about seventy years (from its establishment in 1898), the governments of both parts of Ireland passed legislation in the early 1970s that once again made the major public and social services the responsibility of nominated boards.[2] From 1974 the main responsibility for community relations remained with reorganized (and attenuated) local authorities (district councils). Given the current (and historic) propensity in Ireland for using paragovernmental organizations (PGOs), their role as intermediary organizations between government and the voluntary sector is of central importance.

The Northern Ireland Setting

What is the origin of Northern Ireland's divisions and why do its people find it so difficult to live at peace together? In other parts of the United Kingdom, people with more obvious cultural and social differences normally live alongside one another without resorting to violence.

Northern Ireland shares the island of Ireland with the Republic of Ireland. The two are separated by an international frontier extending over some two hundred miles of mountain and bogland. Northern Ireland has a population of about one and a half million, of whom about 1 million are of English and Scottish origin. Their ancestors immigrated to the northern part of Ireland in the seventeenth century as one of the great migrations of that time (another contemporary westward surge colonized the Atlantic seaboard of North America). They were granted, or seized, land in fertile valleys running northward and westward from Belfast on the east coast. These English and Scottish settlers were mainly of the Protestant faith. Their descendants today regard themselves as British and consider their linkage to England very important. In political terms they call themselves Unionists or Loyalists, signifying their commitment to the British connection (Darby, 1976, 1983).

About half a million people are of Irish descent and have close cultural and religious affinities with the rest of Ireland.

Most have ancestors who were displaced by the new settlers from England and Scotland. Most aspire to political union with the rest of Ireland and are, in political terms, called Nationalists. Moderate Nationalists usually support the Social Democratic and Labor Party (SDLP). Some Nationalists are Republicans who believe that violence is an appropriate way to achieve political objectives. They support Sinn Fein, the political arm of the IRA (Irish Republican Army), or one of a number of similar organizations such as the Irish National Liberation Army, which is a Marxist organization. It has been shown [Market Opinion Research International (MORI), 1984] that two-thirds of Sinn Fein's support comes from those in the eighteen to thirty-four age group. In some working-class areas of the cities and in rural settings along the frontier with the Irish Republic, a large part of the population exhibits virtually total alienation from the state. Republican Nationalists and their leaders are committed to an armed struggle to overthrow the British administration.[3]

In the mid 1960s, after four decades of political stagnation, a new generation of middle-class Nationalists led a civil rights campaign that echoed the civil rights movement in the United States. This succeeded in eliminating most of the more important grievances experienced by the Roman Catholic population, with the important exception of disadvantage in employment (and corresponding experience of unemployment). The early 1970s saw the reemergence of the IRA and the beginnings of a sustained terrorist campaign that has cost twenty-seven hundred lives. Following a bitter hunger strike in the early 1980s, the IRA (which had until that time not been involved in party politics) committed itself to a political agenda and reestablished a political party, Sinn Fein, which has emerged as a major political force.

The British government viewed that emergence with grave concern, particularly the close integration of political and military objectives between Sinn Fein and the IRA, with their twin weapons of Armalite (an explosive) and the ballot box. The competence and eagerness of Sinn Fein to deal with welfare and social security problems and to give leadership in the community have done much to enhance the credibility of the organization and its support, at the expense of the more moderate but less socially aware SDLP. A major thrust of recent government policy, and an area with many implications for the voluntary sector, is stronger cooperation with the Roman Catholic church, to support moderate nationalism (through the SDLP) and to try to reduce the strong appeal that Sinn Fein and the IRA have gained.

A political vacuum at provincial level (since 1974 there has been no provincial parliament) leads to relations between governed and government that resemble many features of a classic colonial setting. An indigenous civil service is responsible for public and social services. Government is in the hands of English members of the Westminster parliament who, in addition to their normal parliamentary duties, have ministerial portfolios in Northern Ireland and who work there on a part-time basis. Government perceives itself to be under continual pressure to demonstrate its evenhandedness and impartiality on sectarian matters and to sustain an image of credibility, effectiveness, and even benevolence. Meantime, in a situation of endemic terrorist violence, security policy has the highest priority. The police and the British army work, under political direction, to isolate and curb elements that threaten an uneasy status quo and that are responsible for daily terrorist activities and frequent deaths.

A further pressure on government, and one that drives the recent decision to give the highest political priority to improving community relations, is the economic inviability of Northern Ireland. No less than the Irish Republic (which has an intolerable burden of foreign debt), Northern Ireland suffers from grave economic disadvantage. Two decades of economic recession and a narrow industrial base have led to endemic unemployment reaching, in some areas, levels of more than 60 percent. Top priority for all administrations has been the imperative of attracting inward investment. However, poor community relations, chronic political instability, and a vociferous Irish-American propaganda machine and political lobby in Washington have done much to discourage multinational companies from investing in Northern Ireland. In the late 1980s these realities compelled government to acknowledge the importance of a propaganda counteroffensive in North America. If that is to be successful, community relations must be a central aspect of its broad strategy for economic development.

Voluntary Organizations and Their Context

Every voluntary agency or community organization in Northern Ireland is exposed to the pressures that are features of everyday life. How may its leaders and constituency relate to the part of the community on "the other side"? What kind of partnership with government is possible when an organization's staff, clients, and management reject the very basis of the state? These and similar questions are constant preoccupations for all involved in management.

For government the questions are no less difficult. How may civil servants treat organizations and groups led by local leaders whose political loyalties are to organizations committed to the overthrow of the British administration? How should government relate to the churches and to their leaders? Senior clergy (on both the Catholic and Protestant sides), reflecting as they do the intractable divisions in the society, are among government's most persistent, and credible, critics. In this setting government accords a heightened importance to voluntary agencies, seeing them as a means of dispersing social power, providing opportunities for citizen participation, and increasing a sense of civic efficiency—provided they are not controlled by leaders who are committed to the overthrow of the state.

Several further factors are essential for understanding the backdrop for voluntary and community activity. The first stresses continuity with the rest of the United Kingdom. In most respects Northern Ireland is administered much like the other countries of the mainland United Kingdom. Levels of taxation and social security are the same. The National Health Service operates in much the same way and medical care is free at point of need. Both the agencies of government that provide services, and the professionals who manage and administer those services, share the values of their counterparts elsewhere in the United

Kingdom. However, overshadowing the theme of administrative and professional continuity are important contrasts which, though often unrecognized by the superficial observer, mark the fact that public and social administration in Northern Ireland is like no other part of the United Kingdom. A significant part of the population withholds its consent from government (Rose, 1971). Violent political upheaval in the last twenty years has led to the invention of many administrative devices in the field of public administration and the voluntary sector.

The ideological climate in which voluntary agencies operate has changed greatly since the early 1980s. Until that time, for nearly forty years they had struggled to survive on the margins of the British welfare state. By contrast, by the end of the decade the actual and promised retrenchment of the welfare state led to a new and potentially much enlarged role but one in which they depend more than ever on government as the source of their funds. Now accountability, coordination, cost effectiveness, and the discipline of contracts for service promise to lead to a new kind of partnership and indeed to a fear of colonization (Kramer, 1989).[4] The recent and continuing emphasis on contracts for service and on practical outcomes to specific individuals will restrict the vital contribution made by the voluntary sector to public policy debate. Given the absence of normal political discourse in Northern Ireland, this is particularly important. Furthermore, it is likely to reduce the capacity of voluntary organizations to innovate, the very objective that government has declared it wishes the sector to pursue (Acheson, 1989b).

As an integral part of the United Kingdom, Northern Ireland experiences the full effects of changes in government's policy toward the voluntary sector. Driven by conservative ideology and by concern about welfare state paternalism, inefficiency, and alleged resistance to innovation on the part of the civil service bureaucracy, the Thatcher governments of the 1980s eschewed the statist assumptions of the 1960s and 1970s. Not since World War II has policy so favored the voluntary sector. But there is strong evidence that the new policies are based on assumption rather than on empirical evidence (see Kramer, 1981).

Government and the Voluntary Sector: Community Relations

The community relations experience provides an interesting case study of two decades of innovation in public administration as successive governments have attempted to respond to the region's deep community divisions. Further, it illustrates changing patterns of central-local relations and shows how, when central government became disenchanted with the waywardness of local authorities, it invented new structures through which to channel money to voluntary and community groups.

The history may conveniently be divided into two periods. The first began with the onset of political violence in 1968, and in 1972 saw the abolition by London of Northern Ireland's Unionist government (which had ruled without a break since 1922). It also saw the introduction (1972–1974) of direct rule from London (known sometimes as "Helicopter Rule"), followed by a short-lived initiative, the power-sharing Northern Ireland Assembly, which existed for a few months and ended abruptly in May 1974 after a Unionist and Loyalist general strike. The second, and longer, period (also of direct rule) lasted from mid 1975 until the late 1980s. During that phase, community relations were given relatively low priority by government.

In 1968, faced with unprecedented disorder and civilian protest, the Unionist government created a new government department, the Ministry of Community Relations, and a new paragovernmental agency, the Community Relations Commission. The main function of the commission was to make financial grants to voluntary agencies and community groups. The commission engaged in a community development policy that was carried forward by a field staff working with community groups and voluntary agencies. It articulated a two-stage approach. In the first stage it would help deprived communities combat anomie and develop morale, self-confidence, and leadership by supporting and encouraging voluntary organizations, community groups, and initiatives in the field of community services (Rush and Althoff, 1971). It was thought that, as communities developed confidence through protopolitical participation, leaders would emerge. This process would take place simultaneously in communities on both sides of the political divide. At an appropriate stage leaders from both sides would be brought together to discuss common problems and approaches. Umbrella associations would be formed to provide a forum to discuss and formulate policy. Community development would metamorphose into community relations.

Although the commission's development and freedom were severely curtailed by the ministry's tight financial controls over expenditure, for a while much good community development work was done. Then in 1974, both the commission and the ministry were abolished by politicians in the power-sharing assembly who were jealous of the commission's independence and its support for unelected community leaders who often rivaled their influence (Griffiths, 1974). Such are the political and sectarian realities of urban life in Belfast, and the constant backdrop of violence, that communities were preoccupied with survival and security. Attempts to form linkages with "the other side" were regarded with deep suspicion; leaders simply could not afford to become involved in such activities. Little was seen of the intended metamorphosis of community development into community relations.

The second period in the history of government's initiatives in the community relations field began in 1975, when there was a division of responsibility between the role of central government and that of local government. The functions of the Community Relations Commission were transferred to twenty-six local authorities (district councils); those of the Ministry of Community Relations became the responsibility of the Department of Education (DENI). Government stipulated that the Department of Education should have responsibility for formulating and sponsoring policies for the improvement of community relations in Northern Ireland. DENI inherited from its predecessor a funding relationship with a number of voluntary agencies and community organizations, and it continued to fund these and similar groups. However, it did not acquire a settled policy toward the voluntary sector, and it brought to its new responsibilities no evident enthusiasm or commitment.

During the rest of the 1970s, DENI was preoccupied with other policy issues. Community development and community relations became low-priority matters.[5] The main emphasis of the direct-rule administration was on improving Northern Ireland's infrastructure and on trying to attract inward investment projects. The most spectacular of these was John DeLorean's ill-fated car assembly plant in Catholic West Belfast.

In the late 1970s the community development and community relations work of local authorities was increasingly interpreted in "community services" terms. Most existing recreational facilities had been provided and continued to be controlled by churches. District councils, with the assistance of DENI, embarked on an ambitious capital program of building community centers and other leisure and recreational facilities. Well-appointed and well-equipped facilities were provided in most urban centers. DENI continues to reimburse district councils 75 percent of their approved expenditures for the staff employed on community services work, the operating costs of resource and community centers, and grants to voluntary groups. Groups assisted by district councils are typically local citizens' advice bureaus, which give consumer advice and advice about welfare rights, tenants' groups, and community and neighborhood groups.

Debate in council chambers was totally overshadowed by security issues in 1981–82 following the Sinn Fein hunger strike (when Bobby Sands and more than a dozen other activists died) and again in 1986 after the signing of the Anglo-Irish Agreement. This international treaty between the governments of the United Kingdom and the Republic of Ireland gave the Dublin government the right to comment on and to some degree to influence the administration of government in Northern Ireland. From 1986 to 1988 many councils with Unionist majorities ceased to function, in protest against the agreement. In 1986 the Belfast City Council withheld funding of about £500,000 from seventy-one voluntary and community groups because the council suspended itself and refused to allow council business to be carried on. Funding was released only when, in exercise of its statutory reserve powers, the government appointed an anonymous commissioner to conduct the financial business of the council.

The Voluntary Sector's Role in Northern Ireland 131

By the early 1980s it was clear that the strategy of making local authorities the primary funding agencies for local voluntary and community groups was a failure. A full discussion of the gradual paralysis of local government in Northern Ireland lies outside the scope of this chapter, but it is now accepted that the twenty-six local authorities (most of which are themselves bitterly divided along Unionist/Nationalist lines) are unsuited to conduct community relations initatives. Despite the enthusiasm and professionalism of some of their community relations staff, most local authorities, with the notable exception of Belfast City Council, restricted their efforts to promoting leisure and recreational opportunities, to the detriment of community development and community relations work. During the 1980s in some local authorities, relations between local politicians and their professional community staff also underwent serious deterioration, largely because some councilors believed that their staff were fostering the development of community groups on "the other side," some of which they suspected of being front organizations for paramilitary groups.

Established patterns of funding community services, community development, and community relations are in flux. In 1988, reflecting the antipathy of its councilors to community development, Belfast City Council cut the budget of its community services division by £24,000. Unionist members have been bitterly accused of disparaging leisure services in disadvantaged Nationalist areas. In light of this experience it is little surprise that government has for some years gradually reduced funding to Belfast City Council for community work.

In early 1987 government was ready to begin a new approach to promoting community relations. Its new enthusiasm for the subject was undoubtedly influenced by the priority of attracting inward investment and was in part a response to the effective campaign waged in the United States to deter corporations from investing in Northern Ireland. From the mid 1980s onward, a growing number of states introduced stringent criteria for investment in Northern Ireland that draw attention to the region's poor community relations and in particular to the degree of economic and employment disadvantage suffered by the Catholic community. Now, after twenty years of tentative initiatives, government appears ready to tackle the community relations agenda with substantial resources and strong determination coupled with a new approach. This new approach has as its guiding principle the view that each of the two traditions has equal validity and that members of majority and minority communities should be educated about the cultural heritage and values of the other (Foster, 1989).

There is also a fresh determination to eliminate Catholic economic disadvantage. The Fair Employment Commission was established, effective January 1, 1990, with tough powers to pursue affirmative action policies in employment. School curricula have been reshaped to include Education for Mutual Understanding. Government spending on community relations will be increased from £3 million to £4 million in the 1991-92 financial year.

Two other new agencies, announced by government in January 1990, are central to this strategy: the Central Community Relations Unit (CCRU) and the Community Relations Council. The CCRU is located in the office of the secretary of state. Two of its main functions are to monitor and influence all government policy from the standpoint of community relations and to support voluntary bodies working in this field. Its annual budget of £2 million is used to support organizations such as Women Together, the Peace People, and the Corrymeela Community. A total of £50,000 has been allocated to support local history projects, and a similar sum has been given to the Northern Ireland Voluntary Trust to fund community groups promoting contact across the traditions. The CCRU also supports publishing activity and has made available £70,000 to sponsor books and television and radio programs dealing with the diverse cultural heritage of Northern Ireland's people. A major initiative of the CCRU has been to establish the Community Relations Council, and it is likely that up to £2 million will be available to that body for distribution to the voluntary and community sector to encourage community relations activity. The establishment of the council was foreseen and recommended in an influential discussion paper titled "Improving Community Relations," written in 1986 by two practitioners in the field of community relations (Fitzduff and Frazer, 1986).

The Community Relations Council (CRC) will act as a central facilitating and research body in the field of community relations and community development and will serve as a focal point and catalyst for the many voluntary organizations working in this field. The existence of a powerful independent community resource agency could do much to enhance the potential of voluntary bodies and community groups working for community regeneration and paralleling the more modest work of the Community Relations Commission in the early 1970s. There is likely to be concern in some quarters in government that the new body could become a potent source of criticism of government policies and activities. It will be interesting to see if it can maintain its independence and integrity and indeed whether it can survive for longer than its predecessor. Remembering the conflict between the Ministry of Community Relations and the first Community Relations Commission in the early 1970s, it will be interesting to see how the new CRC will relate to its funder, the CCRU, and to the civil servants and ministers who formulate government policy.

Government and Voluntary Organizations: Community Development

In addition to new agencies with a direct involvement with community relations, the 1980s have seen the development by government of a range of other intermediaries to channel support to the voluntary sector, each of them distinct in origins, purposes, and methods of operation. The Northern Ireland Voluntary Trust, although established by government, is a wholly independent charitable foundation. Funded by the Department of Economic Development, Action for Community Employment exists primarily to provide work experience for the long-term unemployed; it contributes more than eight thousand person years of support to the voluntary sector. Belfast Area Teams is a project of the Department of the Environment and operates only in Belfast. Consisting of eight interdisciplinary teams of civil servants, it acts as a channel of statutory funding across the range of local initiatives in the social and environmental field. Finally, and most recently, the International Fund for Ireland represents a cooperative response by the international community to the social and economic problems of Northern Ireland and has become a major source of funding of voluntary and community activity.

The concept of Belfast Action Teams (BAT) was first developed in 1986, out of concern about the social and physical infrastructure of Belfast, where many areas had been decimated by a decade and a half of civil disturbances and urban distress.[6] Years of high levels of public and private investment had succeeded in improving the physical conditions in many parts but large areas continued to experience severe social deprivation. The BAT initiative was announced on February 17, 1987, as part of a £28 million package of measures. Teams of civil servants drawn from a number of government departments distribute £500,000 a year according to their own criteria. In the first eighteen months four teams supported 150 local initiatives. In July 1988 four more teams were established, making a total of eight teams with a total annual budget of £4,000,000.

No information on the BAT teams' allocation policies has been made public. It is extraordinary, and illustrative of the unusual situation in Northern Ireland, that such large sums of public money are spent without any published policy, review machinery, or indeed public discussion of their objectives. The development of this initiative in Northern Ireland is an example of a "direct drive" approach by government (bypassing local government), which contrasts significantly with policy and practice on the United Kingdom mainland, where local government is a much more significant force and possesses deeper roots. The size of this program, the lack of professional expertise and training of most of its teams, and the lack of public accountability or monitoring of its spending should be matters of considerable public concern.

The Northern Ireland Voluntary Trust (NIVT) is an unusual and highly significant vehicle for funding voluntary and community activity; it will be of particular interest to those concerned with developing new structures for facilitating voluntary and community activity. Founded by government in 1979, the trust was established to channel small-scale financial support to local groups. Its creation was an acknowledgment of the fact that Northern Ireland had very few indigenous sources of independent charitable funding (Northern Ireland Voluntary Trust, 1980-1989). Only a handful of major corporate donors existed locally, and it was recognized that a new source of funding was necessary. Notwithstanding the deadlock in local politics, there was vigorous voluntary activity in communities across Northern Ireland. Many exciting initiatives were being developed in adult education, conservation, culture, community care, and the relief of poverty. How might government support these initiatives, so vital to the well-being of deprived communities experiencing severe unemployment and recovering from violence and urban redevelopment? A responsive and effective channel of funding was necessary to bring support and hope to people living in beleaguered communities who felt that they had been betrayed by politicians and deserted by government.

The intention was to set up a form of community chest for Northern Ireland. Initially a board of seven independent trustees was established and to this board the government made a capital grant of £500,000. A further £250,000 was promised on a pound-for-pound matching basis. This was later extended, with the result that, by 1989, the trust had a capital base of £2,283,655.

Since its inception, NIVT has given a lifeline to many groups in disadvantaged areas of cities, towns, and villages. Some of the neediest areas have informal community organizations, which have the capacity to restore social, cultural, and environmental vitality to their neighborhoods. Between 1979 and 1988 the trust made grants of £1,370,000 to many hundreds of community-based projects. In the financial year 1988-89, 521 groups received grant aid of £741,735. The particular emphasis of the trust has been on projects that help people in areas of need to acquire the skills, knowledge, and self-confidence to tackle serious social problems and that improve understanding and communication within and between communities. More than half of its grants are for sums less than £500 and only 8 percent are for more than £3,000. Its annual grant-making program is now more than £400,000 (which, though considerable for a grant-making foundation, is only 10 percent of the annual expenditure of the BAT teams). Grants are made under eleven headings: community development, community care and poverty, community education and arts, unattached young people, rural projects, intercommunity grants, unemployment and community enterprise, community health, women's groups, networking and mutual understanding, and crime prevention.

The trust has been responsible for or has collaborated with other bodies to facilitate a range of highly innovative projects: the Rural Action Project, the Rural Awards Scheme, the Community Support Scheme, and the Inter-Community Contact Grants Scheme, for example. The Rural Action Project involves a partnership between a number of voluntary organizations with funding from the department of Health and Social Services and the Anti-Poverty Program of the European Community. The project is a "bottom-up" community development process in four pilot areas of Northern Ireland with scattered populations marked by poverty and high levels of social need. The Rural Awards Scheme was launched in 1983 with support from Shell UK and the Calouste Gulbenkian Foundation. Some 315 projects have been assisted, ranging from local history and community newspapers to women's groups and from village improvement schemes to community centers and enterprise projects. The Community Support Scheme represents a major initiative in the field of community care and involves expenditure of £450,000 over three years. Under this program the trust will fund a small number of pilot projects demonstrating a community development and mutual aid approach to tackling the problems of those in need. Groups will be given £20,000 a year to help them define their own needs and take part in responding to them.[7] Under the Inter-Community Contact Grants Scheme, established in 1986, forty grants totaling £39,415 were made in the year 1988–89. Although some of these grants were for short-term projects, others were continuation grants to organizations that require longer-term financial support, such as the Northern Ireland Council for Integrated Education and the Northern Ireland Conflict and Mediation Association.

The role played by the NIVT since its establishment in

The Voluntary Sector's Role in Northern Ireland   137

1979 is of great importance. Since that time the trust has been virtually alone in Northern Ireland in addressing the community development agenda. The trust accepts that problems between communities must be mitigated by well-resourced and sensitive strategies, but believes that the problems *within* communities are of no less importance. NIVT has demonstrated the enormous value of assisting communities to develop greater strength and resilience. The standing of the organization and the quality of its work assure its continuance and growth.

Established in 1981 by the Department of Economic Development, Action for Community Employment (ACE) is, in volume terms, the most important source of government support for the voluntary and community sector. Financed in large part by the European Community under its Social Fund's training budget, in the financial year 1989–90 ACE spent over £40 million to give employment to nearly ten thousand people, of whom the large majority worked in more than six hundred bodies in the nonprofit sector. A condition of eligibility for grants under the ACE scheme is that workers have been unemployed for one year. Furthermore, they may participate in the scheme for only one year. Most communities across Northern Ireland have a spectrum of ACE schemes, some of which give employment to up to two hundred workers engaged in nonprofit social and community activity. This work ranges from environmental projects to social research in universities and from community care (which employs about three thousand workers) to church visitation, secretarial work, adult literacy, and Irish-language projects. Virtually every voluntary organization uses ACE workers, and the availability of ACE staff has enabled many bodies to develop their programs in a way that would otherwise have been impossible.

Security or "political" vetting by the police or army is an aspect of the ACE scheme that has become the subject of vehement political controversy. Decisions by government about whether or not to fund ACE projects relate not only to their purposes but to the associations of their leaders. Since 1985 funding has been made available on the basis of an unequivocal statement by the secretary of state that no body receiving funding may have links with a paramilitary association. Funding has been withdrawn from a number of voluntary bodies on the grounds that they had "sufficiently close links with paramilitary organizations as to give rise to a grave risk that to give support to those groups would have the effect of improving the standing and furthering the aims of a paramilitary organization" (Hurd, 1985; see also Stanley, 1987, and Lyell, 1988).[8]

Accordingly, policy toward the voluntary sector is influenced by the necessity and desire to foster its work of filling the gaps in public services, by the wish to sustain what Lipset calls the "social requisites of democracy" (1959, p. 69), and by the dictates of security policy and the pressing need to insulate and isolate the paramilitaries. It is hardly surprising that the leaders of community groups with social welfare objectives sometimes occupy positions of leadership in locally based paramilitary "active service units" whose very purpose is often seen as community protection. Sinn Fein has run a vigorous campaign against what it calls "political vetting" ("Political Vetting," 1988). The centerpiece of this protest was a public inquiry in the summer of 1988 that received considerable publicity. Acheson (1989a) has criticized vetting on the grounds that it has the effect of inhibiting the fundamental freedom of the right of association. In the special conditions of Northern Ireland, government believes that it must place limits on that right by reference not to the legitimacy of the purposes of the agencies but on grounds of security to the affiliation of their members.

International Concern for Community Stability: Support for Community Development and Community Relations

The conflict in Northern Ireland is a source of concern not only to the governments of the United Kingdom and Ireland but also to countries with strategic interests in the North Atlantic area anxious about increasing political instability in Ireland and the rise of Sinn Fein. The salience of the Northern Ireland problem led in 1986 to the establishment of the International Fund for Ireland (IFI), a kind of Marshall Plan for Ireland, which followed the signing of the Anglo-Irish Agreement. By the end of 1989 the fund had received the equivalent of £104 million from the United States under the AID program, as well as donations from Canada and New Zealand and a substantial grant from the European Community.

IFI's purpose is to channel economic aid to disadvantaged areas of Northern Ireland and to parts of the Irish Republic close to their frontier. It works to support moderate interests and to enhance community development, particularly in interface areas or areas where alienation from government is greatest and community morale is lowest — that is, areas where Republican advocates of political violence have their strongest following. The fund appears to be guided by a wish to raise community morale by filtering money into projects that might not otherwise be funded and generally to increase levels of economic and community activity. Many of the projects it has funded have nominees of the Catholic church on their boards, ensuring that moderate Nationalist projects are supported and contribute toward the marginalization of terrorist interests (Rolston and Tomlinson, 1988).

During its first two years the fund tended to pursue priorities that were more economic than social. Its third annual report indicates that it had provided assistance of £57 million to 1,261 projects. In September 1988, in response to criticism, the board decided to adopt a new definition of "disadvantaged," and to allocate an increasing proportion of its resources to social programs under a Disadvantaged Areas Initiative. A total of £12 million has now been allocated to this program and a further £2 million to community relations. The fund has also given £250,000 to the Northern Ireland Voluntary Trust to enable it to encourage the development of neighborhood infrastructures and to help leaders of neighborhoods establish relations with bodies outside their immediate areas (International Fund for Ireland, 1988, 1989).

The fund was described by Sir Charles Brett, its first chairman, as independent and nonpolitical, but it is difficult to see how that statement can be defended. It is highly political in the sense that it is under political direction from Dublin, Belfast,

London, and Washington. Its main board is assisted by an advisory committee appointed by the two governments, and it is required to take account of the wishes of the donor countries, who have the right to be represented at its meetings.

The work of the fund is an example of the influence of supranational interests in combating political instability in their sphere of influence by means of a broad program of community development. On one level it represents a large and novel source of funding to the voluntary and community sector. On another it represents international concern with the North Atlantic strategic implications of the Northern Ireland conflict. It might, however, be observed that for many years the Republican paramilitaries have derived much of their finance and inspiration from North American sources. The internationalization of the conflict is not a new phenomenon. With regard to its aegis and to its management the fund is a unique (and very substantial) body dedicated ultimately to political change and to the reduction of radicalism and dissent in Northern Ireland. There is some evidence that previous levels of support for Sinn Fein are waning, but it is unlikely that financial interventions such as are being made by the fund will significantly reduce commitment to Sinn Fein and the IRA in areas where, for several centuries, opposition to British rule in Ireland has expressed itself with political violence.[9]

Conclusion

Lester Salamon (1987) has drawn attention to important weaknesses in contemporary theories of the welfare state and the voluntary sector. He advances the concept of "third-party government" as an amendment to prevailing theories of the welfare state; he posits a new theory of the voluntary sector around the idea of "voluntary failure," replacing the common notion of government or market failure (where gaps left by the incapacity of government or the market are plugged by a subsidiary voluntary sector). His theoretical analysis suggests that government involvement is less a substitute for, than a supplement to, private, non-profit, action.

This chapter has described and illustrated some aspects of the relationship between government and the voluntary sector in Northern Ireland in regard to community relations and community development. In some important respects Northern Ireland illustrates the phenomenon of "societal failure": few of the conditions for stable democracy exist (Lipset, 1959); and the potential for political violence and insurrection is always present. The dominance of the constitutional question over normal politics and the consequent failure to develop conventional political parties in the manner of Western democracies have resulted in the failure of the province's political apparatus. State failure has led the direct-rule government to acknowledge, in this realm at least, government failure. Far from treating voluntary organizations as derivative or subsidiary institutions, governments have been increasingly glad to acknowledge their central role in Northern Ireland society. Such is the perceived importance of strengthening the voluntary and community sector that central government has found it necessary to develop PGOs to mediate with it, recognize the failure of local government (because its competence to make local policy is vitiated by sectarian politics), and set up Belfast government's own structures (the Belfast Action Teams) to provide generous resources to the voluntary and community sector.

The resulting partnership between government and the voluntary sector (often with Nationalist bodies, which are deeply opposed to the political ideology of the British government) illustrates both the operation of third-party government and what Salamon calls nonprofit federalism. Research into the mechanisms and procedures by which this unusual partnership in one of the countries of the United Kingdom is sustained would no doubt provide fascinating insights into the *realpolitik* of government without consensus.

Notes

1. Finance for education is not included in this total. Many schools retain a considerable measure of independence in their management. Most schools in this "maintained" sector

are managed by the Roman Catholic church, which is responsible for a school system that parallels the state system. "Maintained" schools receive 85 percent of their capital costs from government.
2. There are numerous examples from Northern Ireland of paragovernmental organizations (PGOs) managed by boards composed of government appointees. Public housing, primary and secondary education, health, and personal social services are all administered in this way. Hood (1987) has shown that PGOs are an effective way of coming to terms with ethnicity as well as religion; they give institutional form to national or religious minorities and allow the cooption of elites.
3. The IRA obtains support from Irish groups in North America. In the late 1980s it also received an estimated 250 tons of sophisticated East European guns, rockets, and explosives from Libya.
4. The recent White Paper on charity law (*Charities: A Framework for the Future,* 1989), speaking about the future of relationships between the voluntary sector and government, draws attention to government's desire to seek a "free, vigorous and creative partnership . . . in which each partner is able to make its distinctive contribution." It applauds the sector's ability to respond flexibly and swiftly to changing needs and circumstances and perhaps above all its ability to innovate. But new policies seem to be based on conventional Conservative Party wisdom rather than on empirical realities and appear to ignore the evidence that voluntary associations may only rarely live up to expectations concerning their vanguard role. Kramer (1979) examines both the need for conceptual clarification of the vanguard role and the common assumption that voluntary agencies are more innovative than local authorities.
5. In the financial year 1988–89, DENI's total expenditure (including the 25 percent contribution from the local authorities) on staff, resource centers, community centers, and on voluntary groups was £2,386,000. Total grant aid by local authorities for the support of voluntary organizations

was £487,460, of which 75 percent was refunded by DENI (see McGinley, 1989).

6. Belfast Action Teams (BAT) is part of a government-sponsored campaign called "Making Belfast Work" and is similar in many respects to the interdepartmental team pioneered in Liverpool in 1981 by Michael Heseltine after the Toxteth riots in the summer of that year. BAT is only one of the policies introduced in Northern Ireland that are similar to initiatives previously used in England. Another example is the Community Development Projects of the 1970s.

   Antipathy to local government is not confined to the direct-rule administration in Northern Ireland. The Thatcher government in Britain was inimical to local political power. Its most controversial move in this direction was the abolition of the Greater London Council. I am grateful to Tim Blackman for pointing out this parallel with the experience of central-local relations in Northern Ireland.

7. The Community Support Scheme has recently been evaluated by staff working at the Center for the Study of Conflict at the University of Ulster at Coleraine.

8. Groups that had their funding withdrawn have included a tenants' and community group in West Belfast, which lost support for five staff, a community group in Derry, and an Irish-language group in Belfast. In Sinn Fein's battles with SDLP, vetting has become a major issue; Sinn Fein has made its objection to vetting a touchstone of fidelity to Nationalist and Republican principles, with voters being urged to challenge SDLP candidates on their stand on vetting. It is interesting to note that, despite this, some Loyalists have participated in a campaign against vetting which parallels that being conducted by Sinn Fein.

9. Conor Cruise O'Brien, an eminent international political commentator, has observed that "the idea that economic advances can promote inter-ethnic and other religious harmony is an illusion." Writing in *The London Times* (Jan. 20, 1990, p. 10), he drew attention to the fact that the most prosperous of India's communities — the Sikhs of the Punjab — are also the most given to religious and political violence.

References

Acheson, N. "Large Charities Taking Lion's Share of Cash." *Scope,* Feb. 1986, pp. 16, 17.

Acheson, N. "Looking Towards the Nineties: Emerging Roles and Relationships Between the Voluntary and Community Sector and Government." Paper delivered at a "Towards an Uncertain Future: Voluntary Organizations and the State in Northern Ireland" conference held at the University of Ulster, Coleraine, Nov. 24, 1989a.

Acheson, N. *Voluntary Action and the State in Northern Ireland.* Belfast: Northern Ireland Council for Voluntary Action, 1989b.

Birrell, D., and Murie, A. *Policy and Government in Northern Ireland: Lessons of Devolution.* Dublin: Gill and Macmillan, 1980.

Charities: A Framework for the Future. London: Her Majesty's Stationery Office, 1989.

Darby, J. *Conflict in Northern Ireland: The Development of a Polarized Community.* Dublin: Gill and Macmillan, 1976.

Darby, J. (ed.). *Northern Ireland: The Background to the Conflict.* Belfast: Appletree Press, 1983.

Darby, J. and Williamson, A. *Violence and the Social Services in Northern Ireland.* Portsmouth, N.H.: Heinemann Educational Books, 1978.

Fitzduff, M., and Frazer, H. "Improving Community Relations." Unpublished paper for the Northern Ireland Standing Advisory Commission on Human Rights, 1986.

Foster, R. "Varieties of Irishness." In M. Crozier (ed.), *Cultural Traditions in Northern Ireland.* Belfast: Institute of Irish Studies, The Queen's University of Belfast, 1989.

Griffiths, H. *A Case Study in Agency Conflict.* Coleraine: New University of Ulster, 1974.

Hood, C. "Public Administration" and "Policy Analysis." In V. Bogdanor (ed.), *The Blackwell Encyclopedia of Political Institutions.* Oxford: Blackwell, 1987.

Hood, C. *Beyond the Public Bureaucracy State? Public Administration in the 1990s.* Extended text of an inaugural lecture at the London School of Economics, Jan. 16, 1990.

Hurd, D. House of Commons, written parliamentary answer to Mr. John Taylor concerning the intention to withdraw

government funding from community groups with connections with paramilitary organizations. *Hansard,* June 27, 1985.
International Fund for Ireland, *Annual Reports,* 1988-1989.
Kramer, R. "Voluntary Agencies in the Welfare State: An Analysis of the Vanguard Role." *Journal of Social Policy,* 1979, *8* (4), 473-478.
Kramer, R. *Voluntary Agencies in the Welfare State.* Berkeley: University of California Press, 1981.
Kramer, R. "Voluntary Organizations in the Welfare State: A Look into the 90s." Paper presented at the Scottish Council for Voluntary Organizations, Edinburgh, Oct. 12, 1989.
Lipset, S. M. "Some Social Requisites of Democracy: Economic Development and Political Legitimacy." *American Political Science Review,* Mar. 1959, *53*(1), 69-105.
Lyell, L. House of Lords, written answer to Lord Blease concerning grants to voluntary bodies. *Hansard,* July 1, 1988, col. 1879.
MacDonagh, O. *Ireland.* Englewood Cliffs, N.J.: Prentice-Hall, 1968.
McDowell, R. B. *The Irish Administration.* New York: Routledge & Kegan Paul, 1964.
McGinley, A. "District Councils and Community Services: Who Really Cares?" In E. Deane (ed.), *Lost Horizons, New Horizons.* Belfast: Workers Educational Association/Community Development Review Group, 1989.
Market Opinion Research International (MORI). Poll for London Weekend Television, May 1984.
Northern Ireland Voluntary Trust, *Annual Reports,* 1980-1989.
"Political Vetting." *Women's News,* June 1988.
Rolston, W., and Tomlinson, W. *Unemployment in West Belfast: The Obair Report.* Belfast: Beyond the Pale Publications, 1988.
Rose, R. *Governing Without Consensus: An Irish Perspective.* London: Faber and Faber, 1971.
Rush, M., and Althoff, P. *An Introduction to Political Sociology.* London: Nelson, 1971.
Salamon, L. M. "Of Market Failure, Voluntary Failure and Third-Party Government: Toward a Theory of Government-Nonprofit Relations in the Modern Welfare State." *Journal of Voluntary Action Research,* 1987, *16*(1), 24-49.

Saxon-Harrold, S. "Volunteering: Statistics from North America and Europe." *Charity Trends* (12th ed.). Kent, England: Charities Aid Foundation, 1989.

"Scrutiny of Government Funding of the Voluntary Sector." London: Cabinet Office, 1990.

Stanley, J. House of Commons, oral answer to Mr. Bowis concerning the disbursement of funds by the International Fund for Ireland. *Hansard,* Nov. 12, 1987, col. 548.

7

The Changing Role of the Nonprofit Sector in Britain: Moving Toward the Market

Marilyn Taylor

Governments across the globe are looking for new ways of meeting human need. Demographic trends, technological advance, economic restructuring, environmental stress, and organizational change are all making new demands on finite resources. Many governments wish to put limits on their responsibility for welfare and encourage a more pluralistic system with a greater input from the nonstatutory (that is, nongovernmental) sectors, whether in the desire to release more resources or the belief that such a system is both more efficient and more responsive to individual need.

In principle, this policy trend presents considerable advantages to the voluntary or nonprofit sectors, with new opportunities for service provision and the prospect of new resources. But experience suggests that there are risks as well as opportunities. To assess the likely implications of such a change of direction, this chapter looks at the British experience (exclusive of Northern Ireland), where welfare policies have been moving, over the past ten years, from a system based on government provision and financing of welfare toward one modeled on market principles. The first section examines the changing relationship between government and the voluntary sector through the 1980s and the different ideologies of welfare that have applied to the United Kingdom.[1] The second section assesses the impact of current policies on the voluntary sector and its activities, first in relation to service delivery, then in relation to service finance. The chapter concludes that new welfare policies pay too little attention to the role that government should continue to play in a more plural system, particularly at the local level. It argues for a partnership between government and the voluntary sector that recognizes the strengths of the latter not only in service provision but also in the democratic control of welfare—an element of the voluntary sector role that is neglected by policy makers and voluntary sector theoreticians alike.

Changing Welfare Strategies

Developments to 1979

The voluntary sector has long had a role in British welfare. Charity law was introduced in 1601 to encourage private citizens to share the burdens of welfare in a period of economic upheaval (Ware, 1989, p. 16). The nineteenth century saw a renewed emphasis on philanthropy, with the birth of some of today's best-known charities. Other elements of the voluntary sector tradition also grew in importance during the Victorian era: mutual aid, especially among working-class communities; and public education or campaigning, for example, on poverty, prisons, and public health.

During the first half of this century, government came to recognize the inequities and patchiness of a system of provision that depended so much on voluntary philanthropy. During the 1940s legislation on income support, health, and education was the climax to the development of a comprehensive

The Changing Role of the Nonprofit Sector in Britain 149

welfare state, with the public sector taking primary responsibility for the delivery, financing, and regulation of welfare. Under this system, the voluntary sector was for many years seen as marginal, although it is important to recognize that there was never a complete state monopoly. Aspects of welfare remained with voluntary organizations, including residential care, provision for special needs, the lifeboat service, and independent counseling and advice.

The 1970s saw growing dissatisfaction with state welfare. To some extent the system bred the seeds of its own destruction. The improved standards of living to which it contributed, coupled with rising incomes, meant that initial satisfaction gradually gave way to rising expectations and frustration with the lack of choice offered. But there was more to the criticism than that. Provision of services was felt to be standardized and insensitive. Critics argued that public welfare was overloaded with bureaucracy and had been taken over by the professionals and the public service unions. "Public services continued often to treat people as a potentially recalcitrant mass, while the private supplier of goods and services wooed them as individuals of taste, discrimination and independence" (Corrigan, Jones, Lloyd, and Young, 1988, p. 3).

Whether these shortcomings were an inevitable consequence of public-sector provision of services is open to debate. Efforts were made during this period to introduce more participation into the decision-making process, particularly in housing, planning, and community development (Loney, 1983). By the end of the 1970s alternative models of welfare, involving a reduced role for the state, were being canvassed. Prominent among these was the concept of "welfare pluralism" (Wolfenden Committee, 1978; Gladstone, 1979), which allowed voluntary organizations a much greater role. Gladstone argued for a "preference-guided society" where government, in the interests of equity and social justice, would retain a major responsibility for financing welfare but the voluntary sector would take over much of the delivery. This bears considerable similarities to the pragmatic partnership model of Kramer (1981) or the third-party government model of welfare suggested by Salamon (1981,

1987a). Welfare pluralists also introduced the concept of political pluralism, where voluntary organizations are viewed as a medium not only for delivering services but also for giving different interests a voice in the political process (Hatch and Mocroft, 1983).

Critics from the right of the political spectrum saw no major role for government in welfare. Public-sector provision was accused of "stifling innovation, denying choice, and voraciously and insatiably consuming people's money" (Anderson, Lair, and Marsland, 1981, p. 14). Known as the New Right, this school of thought advocated using the market as the principal mechanism for welfare, claiming that its neutrality made it the only mechanism that could both respect individual liberty and, through competition, guarantee the efficient use of resources. Thinkers on the political right also preached the values of self-reliance and individual enterprise. They believed that state welfare had encouraged a "culture of dependency" (Lawson, 1987). Too much emphasis on entitlements and rights to benefits, in their eyes, undermined people's ability and will to help themselves, weakened the traditional role of the family, and "privatized" compassion, leaving nothing to the individual but the pursuit of self-interest. Where the market failed to meet need, by implication, philanthropy and the family should provide a safety net. These different approaches are summarized in Table 7.1.

Table 7.1. Alternative Approaches to Welfare.

Approach	Function		
	Provision	Finance	Regulation
Welfare state	Government	Government	Government
Welfare pluralism	Voluntary sector	Government	Government and voluntary sector "mediating structures"
New Right	For-profit sector (with a voluntary sector safety net)	Private sources	The market (through individual purchase)

The Changing Role of the Nonprofit Sector in Britain   151

By 1979, public-sector services were facing growing pressure from their consumers. During the 1970s a new wave of voluntary activity had arisen in direct response to the weakness of state welfare. Criticism of the growing power of professionals in public services led to the formation of self-help groups. Concern about red tape, bureaucracy, and inefficiency was reflected in the growth of advice, information, and advocacy services. Disabled people developed their own advocacy services to counteract the loss of dignity involved in state services; black and ethnic minority groups joined forces to bring into their communities the jobs, training, and services that neither the state nor the private sector was delivering. These new organizations took issue not only with the insensitivity of state bureaucracies, but also with the more traditional voluntary-sector service providers, who were seen as paternalistic and disabling. These, too, were under pressure to develop more community-based approaches to their work.

Significant new advocacy bodies came into existence during this time; for example, Shelter (an organization concerned with homelessness) and the Child Poverty Action Group started in the mid 1970s. Old and new, voluntary organizations drew on their experience as providers and as consumers to provide feedback to policy makers and draw public attention to new or neglected needs. For example, MIND (a national mental health agency) played a major part in drawing up the legislation enshrined in the Mental Health Act of 1983, and a coalition of voluntary organizations worked on drafting the Disabled Persons' Act of 1986.

The Thatcher Era

Economic recession, rising unemployment, and a series of crippling public-sector strikes combined in 1979 with more general criticisms of state welfare to pave the way for the election of a Conservative government committed to rolling back the frontiers of the welfare state. During its three terms in office, this government introduced a range of policies reflecting the influence of the New Right approach: priority for economic regeneration, in the belief that social regeneration will inevitably follow on from economic buoyancy and that the benefits accruing to the wealthy will "trickle down" to the disadvantaged; a more open market in social welfare with the withdrawal of the public sector from service delivery; and the generation of new resources for welfare with a corresponding limitation of the state's financial responsibility.

This transition took place in two phases. The first, which spanned the first two terms of the Thatcher administration (1979-1987), featured tax cuts and the relaxation of controls over industry as well as the introduction of the more politically attractive reforms in welfare (such as the sale of public housing). This period also saw the opening moves in the dismantling of local government powers, with increasing financial controls over local government spending, the abolition of a tier of local government in the metropolitan areas, and the introduction of nonelected public bodies at the local level for specific programs, particularly in the field of economic development (for example, urban development corporations).

During this phase also, however, many local bodies, which remained in Labour Party control, sought to fashion their own response to the dissatisfactions of the 1970s by introducing decentralization and participation policies designed to bring services closer to the consumer and the community. They drew on the experience of other countries, notably in Scandinavia, in introducing a "public-service orientation" (Clarke and Stewart, 1986). They also increased considerably their levels of funding to voluntary organizations. Local-authority financial support for voluntary bodies grew by 19 percent in real terms between 1983-84 (when figures were first collected) and 1987-88 (Charities Aid Foundation, 1989, p. 40), although it experienced a dip toward the end of this period as financial restraint began to bite. The role of voluntary organizations in extending economic development and training to disadvantaged communities and people with special needs was recognized, and joint ventures were developed. Environmental groups worked with local authorities and the private sector to reclaim wasteland or develop cooperative housing. In community care, recognition of

The Changing Role of the Nonprofit Sector in Britain   153

the unique strengths of the voluntary sector led to joint packages in, for example, special-needs housing.

The pace of this change was slow and very patchy, dictated as much by the survival instincts of a beleaguered local government as by belief in the merits of voluntary activity. And efforts at sharing power left much to be desired (Taylor, 1986). Nonetheless, the tension between the old and new orders was productive for the voluntary sector and began to foster many of the principles promoted by the welfare pluralists, including greater pluralism in provision and greater empowerment of the consumer. Voluntary organizations were not, however, looking to substitute for public-sector provision but rather to supplement it. A continued major government role in finance and delivery was essential if good practice was to be guaranteed, especially to minority groups. A symbiotic relationship began to develop between the two sectors, which sought to extend the opportunities for choice within the welfare state, with government still providing the major finance but with a mixed delivery system and a voluntary-sector role in regulation (broadly defined). Voluntary organizations were needed to supplement and complement public-sector provision, by reaching isolated or special needs that large-scale services could not meet and by catering to the diversity of need where state services were too uniform (service pluralism), and to promote good practice in the public sector (and elsewhere) through advocacy and campaigning and through developing and demonstrating innovative alternative models for provision (democratic pluralism).

Before these local reforms could really take hold, however, the Thatcher government moved during its third term to accelerate the legislative program and introduce more far-reaching changes in relation both to local government and to the central welfare state services of health, community care, and education. These changes included legislation that allows schools, housing, and hospitals to be taken out of local government control, as well as the introduction of compulsory competitive tendering in some public services and the encouragement of contracting out in many others.

Measures were also introduced to further restrict the autonomy and role of local government, changing its system of raising finance to one based on the community charge or poll tax, which government sees as being more accountable to ratepayers; and effectively reducing local-authority influence on a range of new bodies and joint ventures through legislation that, with some exceptions, places similar restrictions on companies with a local-authority interest as those placed on local authorities themselves. New legislation on community care provided the exception to the general trend, by giving primary responsibility for the planning and management of care to local authorities while encouraging them to contract out the delivery of services. However, the announcement of delays in the implementation of significant parts of this legislation until after the next election raises considerable doubts as to both the resources that will be made available to support the new arrangements and the continued political commitment to the local authority's lead role. A major review of the structure and finance of local government is currently underway (Department of the Environment, 1991). Meanwhile, the implementation of new legislation on the health service is going ahead, and could affect the balance of power between local and health authorities in this field.

The third Thatcher term also saw new efforts to contain public spending on welfare and to generate private and charitable funding. At the individual level, social security legislation reduced income support for young people on the assumption that they can still turn to their family. In 1988 entitlements to special-needs grants were changed in most instances to discretionary loans through the introduction of the Social Fund. Under this system, claimants are expected to exhaust all other sources of help before coming to the state, and applicants are frequently referred to voluntary organizations in the first instance. As a result, voluntary bodies report greatly increased demand.

Beyond this, individuals are being urged to recognize their responsibilities not only toward themselves and their families but also toward others. Government is promoting the idea of "active citizenship," where those who have gained from increased affluence are expected to recognize parallel social responsibilities. "We are moving from the 'I care, therefore the state must provide' attitude of the 1960s to the much more practical and

The Changing Role of the Nonprofit Sector in Britain   155

effective 'I produce and consume, therefore I have a moral duty to care and provide' imperative" (Patten, 1988, p. 23). Parallel to this is the promotion of corporate responsibility, harking back to the benevolent paternalism of the Victorian city fathers. Where government funding is provided, there is more of an emphasis on stewardship and value for money, with an Efficiency Scrutiny of government funding to the voluntary sector (Home Office, 1990) and with a growing emphasis on performance indicators and financial monitoring.

These policies may be influenced by the New Right ideology described earlier but they are not in complete harmony with it. Public spending on welfare has proved difficult to reduce, for both practical and political reasons. Opinion polls still show considerable public support for public spending (Bosanquet, 1988), and government has acknowledged a continued financial responsibility for health and education, while seeking to introduce outside funds where possible. Government agencies are being encouraged into the fundraising business, one of the most successful appeals of the past two years is the Wishing Well Appeal organized by a National Health Service children's hospital in central London. Private health insurance has been given a boost through tax advantages, and the delays in the implementation of new community care legislation are encouraging private insurance companies to look at this field. Market principles are also being introduced wherever possible through contracting out and the introduction of internal markets.

The primary role for the voluntary sector in this scenario is that of an instrument of government (Salamon, 1989), competing with the private sector in the contractual marketplace. As the channel for "active citizenship," it also has a role as a safety net for needs that cannot be met through the use of market principles. Government finance is increasingly likely to be tied to specific government policy objectives rather than providing general support (Home Office, 1990, p. 9).

The Impact on the Voluntary Sector

In assessing the impact of these changes on the voluntary sector and its activities, the second part of this chapter will address two questions: Will the new policies allow voluntary organizations to play their part in a more pluralist and diverse delivery system? Will they release new, nongovernmental resources into the welfare field?

Pluralism in Delivery

British welfare is moving from a position where the voluntary sector complements state delivery toward one where the voluntary and for-profit sectors are expected to substitute for state delivery. The introduction of compulsory competitive tendering in a range of service fields, the promotion of purchase-of-service contracting in others, and the introduction of "opting-out" legislation that allows agencies to become private all offer new opportunities to voluntary organizations and will bring more services into the sector. Voluntary organizations will have new partners to work with, and the introduction of wide-ranging new legislation could encourage a valuable overhaul of service provision, which would recognize the different contributions that each sector can make. The emphasis on the consumer in the market could provide opportunities to consumer- and community-based organizations, both to provide advice and information to service users faced with a more fragmented system and to develop their own forms of provision. Many voluntary organizations feel, too, that contracts imply a more equal partnership than the paternalistic relationships that were so often a feature of grant aid.

Nonetheless, there are anxieties that a more open market in service delivery may discourage the innovation, diversity, flexibility, and responsiveness to consumer need that voluntary organizations are supposed to bring, and indeed that the progress made in this direction during the first two terms of the Thatcher government may be reversed. There are fears that replacing grant aid with purchase of specific services as the main form of government support may compromise organizational independence or even distort the aims of an organization, that services will become increasingly bureaucratized, and that voluntary organizations will lose their distinctiveness in relation to the statutory services they were meant to replace. Many in the voluntary sector are concerned that the marketplace will favor the larger service-providing organizations at the expense of smaller, community-based organizations. Finally, there are questions about the survival of consumer and citizen empowerment functions in a system that sees voluntary organizations as primary service providers. It is too early to say whether these fears will be realized, but evidence from other countries suggests that while anxieties over independence may be exaggerated, those who are concerned about the diversity of the sector and its empowerment functions may well have grounds for their concern.

Will a move toward purchase-of-service contracts mean that government funders will increasingly dictate the content of a voluntary agency's work? U.S. researchers suggest that multiple funding, political influence, and government's own failure to put adequate resources into monitoring all mean that contractor organizations still have considerable room for maneuver. The work of Kramer and Grossman (1987) and de Hoog (1985) suggests that voluntary organizations with an expertise that government wants are able to exert considerable influence on the shape of the final contract and that once a contract is made it is likely to be renewed.

However, commentators in the United Kingdom feel that a "contract culture" will inevitably favor certain kinds of activities. Contracts tend to reflect the status quo and are unlikely to allow for innovation, risk taking, or uncertainty. "The whole notion of contracted services reflects a culture that has little time for values and principles . . . a culture of management in which goals are not worth setting unless they are achievable" (Dowson, 1989, p. 10). The fear is that agencies will find themselves compromised not through direct pressure from a funder, but through a gradual process of diversion into the areas that are amenable to contract funding—those that are quantifiable and easily specifiable and those that carry out government objectives. A successful bid for a contract covering part of the agency's work could absorb its energies to the extent that other work suffers. Or the agency may seek to follow the money into new areas, with the result that existing work is squeezed out. Those who voice these fears point to voluntary organizations' use of Community Program funding (a government program to promote job creation); they believe the opportunity to get money for providing jobs of community benefit pulled a number of agencies away from their initial aims into becoming employment and training agencies (Addy and Scott, 1988).

If government contracts do not dictate the content of voluntary agency work, will they dictate its style? There is a danger that voluntary organizations that take on mainstream services will become more and more like the statutory service providers they were meant to replace. Maria Brenton, in her study of nonprofits in the United States and the Netherlands, suggests: "The process of development of the voluntary sector to the role of monopoly or major provider with the aid of state funds seems inevitably to follow a path similar to that taken by our statutory services—the path toward professionalization and bureaucracy" (1985, p. 206).

Contracts are likely to be framed in the tried and tested operating culture of the contracting authority rather than that of the contractor, and may undervalue the different ways of working used by voluntary organizations. De Hoog's suggestion (1985) that familiar professional systems may serve as a substitute for assessing the actual outcomes of suppliers' services would reinforce this point. Kramer and Grossman (1987, pp. 47-48) see the skills that are needed in order to bid for contracts as being quite "different from the traditional competencies associated with the administration of voluntary agencies dependent on community contributions." They note a tendency for successful, small agencies to become larger and more bureaucratic through engaging in the contracting process and comment that "while government agencies prefer contracting because it avoids inflexible civil service requirements, it is the voluntary agencies that inherit the rigidity of line budgeting" (p. 45). It is even possible to suggest that local authorities will put out to contract the services that can be easily specified (mainstream provision) and keep the more innovative, less easy to specify work in house. This would be a complete reversal of former patterns.

The Changing Role of the Nonprofit Sector in Britain 159

The introduction of competition may, however, pull voluntary organizations into the culture of the for-profit sector rather than that of government and lead to a shift toward income-generating, as opposed to mission-based, objectives (Perlmutter and Adams, 1990). One commentator suggests, "In a market economy non-profit organizations share the same dynamic for expansion as profit-making organizations. Indeed the dynamic may be the stronger because of limits to the ways in which non-profit-making organizations can financially reward those who direct and manage them. Expansion provides a justification for regrading senior staff and increasing their salaries" (Maxwell, 1989, p. 9). British voluntary organizations may yet find themselves in a situation similar to that faced in the United States, where for-profit organizations have challenged the tax breaks received by not-for-profits in their field.

Some of the more pessimistic commentators are suggesting that voluntary organizations will become a stepping stone on the path to true privatization: once the for-profit sector has entered the market, they will find themselves taking a back seat. But there are other competitors too. Recent years have seen the appearance of a number of "hybrids" in the margins between the voluntary, statutory, and for-profit sectors. Opting-out policies are creating new voluntary or nonprofit organizations; for example, the new National Health Service (NHS) trusts—opted-out hospitals—may well be looking to expand their field of enterprise. There are a growing number of management or employee buyouts, where local-authority workers set up an independent organization, which then contracts with the authority to provide previously in-house services. In the years to come, such trends may force a complete rethink of current distinctions between the public, private, and voluntary sectors (Rein, 1989).

Critics of the market point to its tendency to concentrate production and distribution in the hands of corporate giants, who are then able to exercise considerable control over the market and over patterns of consumer choice (for example Corrigan, Jones, Lloyd, and Young, 1988, pp. 8-9). In theory, the voluntary sector should be in a strong position to counteract this. By its nature it spawns many local, small-scale, close-to-the-consumer initiatives that offer an alternative to large institutional welfare and promote democratic pluralism by involving the consumer or community. But there is no reason to believe that, left to itself, the services market will behave any differently from the private-goods market. British researchers point out that "from the point of view of the local authority, a single large contract has the advantages that there is only one contractor to deal with and that there should be economies of scale" (Kunz, Jones, and Spencer, 1989, p. 11). Kramer and Grossman (1987, p. 44) found that in the United States "larger agencies with 'track records' tended to receive contracts . . . more frequently." They suggest further that the larger organizations are most likely to be able to negotiate flexibility into their contracts and thus maintain their independence, and that they are also the most able to bear the uncertainty and costs involved in preparing and negotiating contracts.

If contract funding becomes the preferred form of government support to the voluntary sector, the diversity of the sector may be threatened. Many of the smaller, community-based voluntary organizations are not in the market for large-scale service contracts and rely on more general "arm's length" funding in support of their general objectives (National Council for Voluntary Organizations, 1984). Especially in a period of financial restraint, this kind of funding is likely to be at risk. They also depend on a well-developed network of intermediary and development agencies, which provide the information, training, and support that allows the small organizations to survive on very limited funding. This voluntary-sector infrastructure is no longer likely to be at a premium in a market oriented to front-line services.

The advocates of the market see individual consumers as the regulators of provision, selecting the commodity that meets their needs most effectively. But there is no guarantee that all consumers will be able to exercise this power. Nor is it a foregone conclusion that voluntary organizations will improve on public accountability through the democratic system. "The history of voluntarism is not one simply of benevolence and altruism . . . but also of self-interest, self-protectionism and class interest"

(Davies, 1986, p. 24). The introduction of a market style of operation may even reverse the efforts that have been made in this sector toward involving more members of the consumer community in running local projects and services. "To the market, democratic structures of accountability and management will appear an unnecessary cost . . . the model for a 'market-fit' organization will be a non-profit-making trust or company with a self-perpetuating leadership and a management structure organized around profit centers. These will be ill-equipped to combine the provision of services with a 'community development' role" (Maxwell, 1989, pp. 8–9).

Consumers will need advice and advocacy if they are to make informed choices, especially when they are, as so often in the case of social welfare, under considerable stress. This advice will become even more critical in a fragmented market. However, the emphasis in new policies has been on the voluntary organizations' role as service providers. Advocacy is supported in principle but not in the detail of new legislative requirements and, although a new funding power for advice has been put into recent local government legislation, there are no parallel resources. Indeed the pressures of poll tax are reducing the amount of money available for discretionary services, which puts existing advice services at risk and makes it difficult for new services and groups to get established.

Meanwhile, a number of major service providers in the voluntary sector are concerned that their advocacy work could suffer as they move into mainstream provision (Billis and Harris, 1986; Etherington, 1987). The larger organizations may be able to exert considerable influence as major providers and could use this influence to ensure better services and policies across the board as well as in their own service agreements. But there are questions as to how far independent advice and advocacy for service users can be provided by organizations with a central position as service providers.

The market deals with consumers as individuals. But many voluntary organizations are concerned with the impact of individual choices on the public good (they have a long tradition in combating the environmental consequences of production and promoting public health) and thus consider the individual not only as a consumer but as a citizen. Through collective action and community development, they have helped people to realize their common experience and common strengths as consumers and to tackle the wider interests of the community at large. At best, they have regard to patterns and styles of overall provision as well as individual choices, and their perspective is about changing provision by transforming its nature, not just by finding another—what Hirschman (1970) describes as the Voice as well as the Exit option. These kinds of empowerment are likely to have low priority in a welfare system designed around individual choice. While there is nothing in market theory that prevents groups of consumers from acting together in their own or the public interest, right-of-center thinking is suspicious of allocating government or charitable money for such purposes, and it is on such income that community development and the empowerment of the disadvantaged consumer has often relied.

Pluralism in Finance

The argument so far is that, although government finance has been maintained in many services, as the welfare pluralists decreed, the change in its nature, with priority for purchase of service, means that it may not yield genuine pluralism in welfare. But voluntary organizations have access to alternative resources, philanthropy, and volunteering; indeed, many would see these as essential features of the sector. It could be argued that greater use of these alternative resources will overcome some of the difficulties. This brings us to the second question raised at the beginning of this section: will the new policies release new nongovernmental resources into the welfare field?

Government's promotion of "active citizenship" has led to tax concessions, first on payroll giving and most recently on single donations by individuals that are above £600 (Gift Aid). It has also been a factor in a new initiative to promote volunteering, launched by the Prince of Wales, and a Speaker's Commission on Citizenship, which has proposed several initiatives concerned with the promotion and recognition of volunteering. Corporate giving, too, has been encouraged and is gaining pace. Some financial institutions have introduced credit cards that generate income for charity; one of them claims to have raised £1 million in 1989. The media have put their considerable resources behind major fundraising appeals such as BandAid, Children in Need, Comic Relief, and the Telethon, and the latter three raised some £80 million from corporate and individual donors in 1988. The relaxation of previous controls on charity advertising on television and radio opens up still more potential avenues.

However, these new developments are taking place against a background of a standstill in government funding. During the first two terms of the Thatcher government, total government funding for the voluntary sector rose by about 221 percent (in real terms 92.4 percent) to an estimated £4,147 million. But central government funding (direct or through central government agencies) has been standing still in real terms since 1986, while local government funding actually fell in real terms during 1985–87, although it has since recovered to its 1985 level (Charities Aid Foundation, 1988, pp. 32–33).

The restriction of local government finance intensified with the introduction of poll tax, or capitation tax, and the efforts in some jurisdictions to place caps on this tax; there are growing reports of large cuts to voluntary-sector budgets imposed by authorities that have in the past had a good track record in funding voluntary organizations. Initial evidence suggests that advocacy and infrastructural services are particularly hard hit. Meanwhile, major central government funding programs in the Department of Health and the Department of Education and Science have shifted their emphasis away from long-term core funding toward short-term project funding, and although the Efficiency Scrutiny supported investing central government funding in core and infrastructural work, this was not reflected in the minister's response, which emphasized short-term funding.

Meanwhile, the shift of funding criteria from social to economic programs, as has happened in inner-cities initiatives, and the transformation of the Community Program into employment training geared more specifically to the needs of industry, have made it far harder for social programs to find government funds. In the financial year ending March 1988, the Training Agency (which ran these programs) provided some £700 million to the voluntary sector, but in 1988-89, although the change took place halfway through the financial year, the level of support was already down by 26 percent and several organizations, whose work was dependent on this funding source, reported serious difficulties. Cuts in the program during 1989-90, as government sought to transfer responsibility to the private sector, caused further retrenchment and closures.

Government wishes to see other sources taking more responsibility for such programs and welfare in general, but there are question marks over their ability to do so, their willingness to do so, and the pattern of welfare that would result. Salamon (1987a, p. 39) has referred to the "insufficiency," "particularism" and "paternalism" of U.S. philanthropy. What has the British experience been so far?

Total private charitable support for the British voluntary sector was estimated to be £3,442 million as of 1987-88, mostly from individuals (Charities Aid Foundation, 1989). The sources of this support are noted in Table 7.2.

Table 7.2. Private Charitable Support for U.K. Voluntary Organizations, 1987-88.

Source	Amount (£ million)
Households	£2,260[a]
Grant-making trusts	572[b]
Legacies	325
Company giving (1988)	285[b]
Payroll giving	4
Total	£3,442

Sources: [a]Based on an average between estimates by Charities Aid Foundation (1989) and Department of Employment, *Family Expenditure Survey*, 1987.
[b]Charities Aid Foundation, *Directory of Grant-making Trusts*, 1989, p. xi.

What is the capacity for increased giving? Donations from the private and corporate purse are on the increase. Both have more than doubled since 1979, and corporate giving is estimated to have grown by nearly 20 percent during 1988. However, corporate giving has not increased in line with profits and there are signs that it may be reaching a plateau, especially among the larger donors (Directory of Social Change, 1989). Recession in the economy and industrial restructuring as a consequence of the introduction of the single European market could affect these levels. Moreover, while business has shown that it is willing to engage more generously with community and voluntary organizations, there is little evidence that it is prepared to take over where it feels that government should take financial responsibility. Plans to set up twenty technical colleges in association with industry have failed to raise sufficient private-sector finance, and leaders in business have criticized government for withdrawing subsidy for the arts as business sponsors are attracted. Moreover, government has an important role in promoting private investment and drawing it into new fields. Leat, Smolka, and Unell (1986) found that financial support from government increases the capacity of voluntary organizations both to raise funds from elsewhere and to recruit volunteers.

Charitable trusts are estimated to have given £572 million to the voluntary sector in 1987–88. They, too, see their role as funding innovation and experiment and do not wish to take on responsibility for mainstream service provision (Burkeman, 1988). Charity Commission guidance in relation to benefit changes reinforces this stand. "Trustees are in breach of trust if by making a grant they bring about a reduction in statutory benefit to which a person otherwise has a right. . . . Funds for the relief of need, hardship or distress cannot properly be used to pay for relief or assistance which might otherwise be given by the State" (Charity Commission, 1988, p. 1).

What about individual giving? Central government's hope that individuals would give more does not seem to be bearing fruit. The introduction of payroll giving has had disappointing results so far, while recent evidence indicates that slightly fewer people than in previous years are giving to charity and that the typical (median) amount given is also going down (Halfpenny, 1990, p. 32). Economic recession and rising unemployment suggest that a reversal of this trend is unlikely in the immediate future.

Meanwhile, some of the major agencies concerned with volunteering are reporting a drop in numbers of new volunteers. Demographic changes may well make recruitment even more difficult at a time when the increasing numbers of frail elderly will increase demand. Rather than a surplus, which could be drawn into volunteering, there is likely to be a shortage of young people going into the labor market. Married women are therefore being encouraged back into employment, a trend that further reduces the pool from which volunteers can be recruited and puts pressure on informal care. There seems little sign as yet that early and new retirees are taking up volunteering (Rankin, 1989). However, there is a growing interest in company volunteering programs.

The one area where there is an increase in commitment and voluntary activity is environmental concern, where membership and subscriptions are increasing by leaps and bounds (Taylor, 1990). But whether this interest will spill over into social welfare remains doubtful. And increased subscriptions are not an option for voluntary organizations whose members have low incomes, which includes many self-help and community groups.

Whatever the capacity for increasing resources, the surplus is unlikely to be sufficient to make serious inroads even into the £3.68 billion given by government to the voluntary sector in 1987–88 (Charities Aid Foundation, 1989, p. 33), let alone into public expenditure on welfare as a whole. A charitable trust administrator reported in 1989 that the £42 million raised for a major children's hospital appeal over four years would "only keep the nation's health services going for one day" (Best, 1989, p. 3).

Fees and charges are another potential source of income. Posnett (1988) found that such fees accounted for 61 percent of voluntary-sector support in 1985 out of an estimated income of £12.65 billion. But in Posnett's study, 96 percent of this fee income was raised in the fields of housing, arts, and education, and only one in three voluntary organizations received any fee income at all (Peterson, 1988, p. 30). Social welfare organizations at that time raised less than 1 percent of total fee income. It is likely that these proportions have risen since that study, which found that newer charities were more likely to receive fee income. But raising more money from fees may well be at the risk of serving those most in need. Voluntary organizations in the fields of residential care and housing are experiencing increasing difficulties as they are forced to increase their charges, and many community-based organizations operate "in areas where paying for any other than the most essential services, such as housing, is not an option and where dealing with the results of lack of money is more urgent" (Berry, 1988, p. 270).

"Charity, though the noblest of virtues," argues Edwards (1988, p. 136), "is a quixotic one, subject to the vagaries of happenstance, fads, fashions, sex appeal and media hype. . . . Whatever else the market and charity may achieve, they will not, severally or in combination, *guarantee* welfare provision." There is plenty of evidence to suggest that giving is unevenly spread. It would appear that public generosity is more appropriate for relieving disaster, stimulating innovation, and filling gaps than for providing dependable basic services. It is not so readily tapped for drug addicts, ex-prisoners, or people with mental health problems. Its geographical coverage is patchy, too. Leat (1985, p. 30) concludes that "the voluntary sector tends to be least strong where statutory provision is least adequate, where need is greatest."

British philanthropy is most likely to go to children, animals, hospices, and medical research. Donors want to give to something they can see and are notoriously suspicious of administration. They are not likely to give to the voluntary-sector infrastructure, even if it does make the difference between survival and extinction for many small and new groups. Evidence from the United States suggests that corporate foundations tend to shy away from controversy (Salamon, 1987b). Neither advocacy nor the assertive self-help and ethnic minority organizations that have given a voice to so many disadvantaged consumers are likely to be a saleable commodity compared with the image of a helpless child. But these are the very activities that are finding it more difficult to raise government funds.

Government ministers have argued that it is state welfare that creates dependency. Hence the current appeal to "active citizenship," which is framed in terms of individual responsibilities rather than rights to state help. But charity can, to quote Salamon (1987a, p. 41), "create a self-defeating sense of dependency on the part of the poor since it gives them no say over the resources that are spent on their behalf." In Great Britain, Hall (1989, p. 26) recalls "the indignities—what I would call the offensive social contempt—which have always gone along with a system of welfare which depended only on private patronage."

The financial climate for agencies that speak out for the disadvantaged consumer has deteriorated considerably with the collapse of consensus politics. Legislation to curb the use of local authority funds for political publicity also constrains those voluntary organizations whom local authorities fund from making political statements. The White Paper on Charity Law (Home Office, 1989, p. 12) did endorse the current guidelines on the political activities of charities so long as efforts to influence policy remained "ancillary to a charity's primary purposes, which must be clearly charitable and non-political." This judgment was reinforced by the Efficiency Scrutiny (Home Office, 1990, p. 26), but Scrutiny did allow the right of departments to define the areas of activity they wished to exclude from a particular funding agreement. In addition, there have been several attacks on campaigning activity from the political right, along with media reports of government concern about left-wing influences in charities. The minister's response to Scrutiny—that projects and bodies receiving government money must uphold "accepted ethical standards, for example, to support family life" (Home Office, 1990)—has caused concern among voluntary organizations working outside traditional family structures and more generally among those working with people who are not always seen as the deserving poor.

Conclusions

This chapter has described a range of policies that seek to transfer responsibility for welfare away from the state and toward other providers and funders. The voluntary sector has a crucial role in such a transfer. But it suggests that, although moves toward the market in the United Kingdom aim to promote choice and diversity and to release new resources through the increased use of voluntary organizations in welfare provision, they will not do so unless they recognize a continued government role, not only in financing welfare but also in guaranteeing that choice is available to all.

A number of writers have argued that government and the voluntary sector should not be seen as alternatives, but that systems of welfare should draw on the different strengths of both (Brenton, 1985; Kramer, 1981; Salamon, 1987a). The welfare pluralists saw a central role for government in providing the finance of welfare in the interests of equity and social justice (see, for example, Gladstone, 1979, pp. 103-4). The link between government finance and social justice is reinforced by Dahrendorf (1982, pp. 167-68): "Less government is a very pertinent political demand though it must not be misunderstood as a free pass to cut services which are needed to back up the citizenship rights of all. . . . Governments. . . . have the job of ironing out the injustices brought about by the market. . . . Unless full participation in the life of society is regarded as a right for all, liberty remains an empty phrase, even a smokescreen behind which privilege thrives."

Certainly without continued government finance, choice is likely to extend only to those with money, while philanthropic provision will be weighted toward the more socially acceptable in society (the deserving poor). But earlier discussion suggests that real choices across the board depend not only on whether government finances welfare, but how it does so.

Merely to transfer service delivery from a monolithic state to large independent providers will not of itself transform the nature of service provision or bring it closer to the consumer.

If real pluralism is to be encouraged, government has a role in promoting diversity within a framework of guaranteed universal provision. In such a role, government would fund specific services but would also take some financial responsibility for sustaining the health and vitality of the sector on which it depends for service delivery. This means providing development and support to allow smaller, community-based groups to get to the point where they can take on services if they so wish. It involves supporting the core costs of some organizations as a basis for innovation and project development, and investing in the voluntary sector infrastructure, which is so necessary in a time of change and new demands. It also involves recognizing advice and advocacy as key services if consumers are to make their choices effective.

But government's role is not confined to finance. If the range and pattern of provision are to be appropriate to the diversity of need, and if fragmentation and confusion are to be avoided, some form of planning and oversight are necessary. This is a role that government, especially at the local level, is uniquely equipped to perform. But if government is to resume this role, then ways have to be found of resisting the centralism that overwhelmed the welfare state. To do this, government must learn to promote democratic pluralism as well as pluralism in provision. The devolution of service delivery is a first step toward this, but it is not sufficient. It requires democratic mechanisms through which people, as consumers and citizens, can influence patterns of service provision. In this respect, the erosion of local government and the poverty of current political thinking in relation to local democracy are a cause for considerable concern. But democratic mechanisms, too, are insufficient without parallel investment in the community development and public education that gives people, especially those with least power, the ability to use these mechanisms. These are not activities that find favor with the private donor, except perhaps in the environmental field.

To expect government to support this range of activities may seem utopian. But the recent Efficiency Scrutiny supported the case for core and infrastructure funding. And the growth of both the voluntary-sector infrastructure and its empowerment work owes a lot to government funding during the 1970s and 1980s, especially at the local level. To suggest that government has a role in these areas is not to ask for a blank check. Nor does it negate the need to mobilize new resources from nongovernmental sources. Indeed, these will be all the more necessary if genuine welfare pluralism is to be supported. What is required is a recognition that government has a different role from that of the private donor. What is worrying many voluntary organizations now is the trend in government funding toward the very activities the private donor prefers to support: those which are short-term and visible, which are new, and which make for good public relations.

In such a scenario, government funding would still need to be subject to the definition of priorities and objectives and to the test of cost effectiveness. Difficult decisions would still need to be made and worthwhile work would continue to go unsupported. But a model of welfare that gives government a vital role in planning and supporting the delivery of welfare in the interests of social justice seems a more appropriate aspiration for welfare than one that leaves the fortunes of the most disadvantaged in society to the rough justice of the market.

Note

1. Voluntary organizations in Britain are defined as self-governing associations of people who have joined together to take action for public benefit. They are not created by statute, or established for financial gain. They are founded on voluntary effort, but may employ paid staff and may have income from statutory sources. Some, but by no means all, are charities. They address a wide range of issues through direct service, advocacy, self-help and mutual aid, and campaigning. Because it is the most commonly used term in Britain, "voluntary sector" is used throughout this chapter to refer to what in other countries may be more familiarly known as the nonprofit or nongovernmental sector.

References

Addy, T., and Scott, D. *Fatal Impacts? The MSC and Voluntary Action.* Manchester: William Temple Foundation, 1988.

Anderson, D., Lair, J., and Marsland, D. *Breaking the Spell of the Welfare State.* Agenda for Debate No. 1. London: The Social Affairs Unit, 1981.

Berry, L. "The Rhetoric of Consumerism and the Exclusion of Community." *Community Development Journal,* 1988, *23*(4), 266-272.

Best, R. "Future Directions for Charitable Trusts." *Search.* York: Joseph Rowntree Foundation, 1989, p. 3.

Billis, D., and Harris, M. *An Extended Role for the Voluntary Sector.* Uxbridge: PORTVAC (The Brunel Program of Research and Training into Voluntary Action), 1986.

Bosanquet, N. "An Ailing State of National Health." In R. Jowell, S. Witherspoon, and L. Brook (eds.), *British Social Attitudes: The Fifth Report.* Social and Community Planning Research. London: Gower, 1988.

Brenton, M. *The Voluntary Sector in British Social Services.* London: Longman, 1985.

Burkeman, S. "Plugging the Gap." *Poverty, 71,* pp. 20-21. London: Child Poverty Action Group, 1988.

Charities: A Framework for the Future. London: Her Majesty's Stationery Office, 1989.

Charities Aid Foundation. *Charity Trends.* (11th ed.) Kent, England: Charities Aid Foundation, 1988.

Charities Aid Foundation. *Charity Trends.* (12th ed.) Kent, England: Charities Aid Foundation, 1989.

Charities Aid Foundation. *Directory of Grant-making Trusts.* Kent, England: Charities Aid Foundation, 1989.

Charity Commission. Charities for the Relief of the Poor: The Social Fund: Guidance Notes. London: Charity Commission, 1988.

Clarke, M., and Stewart, J. *The Public Service Orientation—Developing the Approach.* Working Paper No. 3. Luton: Local Government Training Board, 1986.

Corrigan, P., Jones, T., Lloyd, J., and Young, J. *Socialism,*

Merit and Efficiency. Pamphlet No. 530. London: Fabian Society, 1988.
Dahrendorf, R. *On Britain.* London: British Broadcasting Corporation, 1982.
Davies, B. "The Future for Voluntary Organizations in Manchester." In D. Sott and P. Wilding (eds.), *Beyond Welfare Pluralism?* Manchester: Manchester Council for Voluntary Service, 1986.
de Hoog, R. "Human Services Contracting: Environmental, Behavioral and Organizational Conditions." *Administration and Society,* 1985, *16*(4), 427-454.
Department of Employment. *Family Expenditure Survey.* London: Her Majesty's Stationery Office, 1987.
Department of the Environment. *The Structure of Local Government* and *New Tax for Local Government.* London: Her Majesty's Stationery Office, 1991.
Directory of Social Change. *Company Giving News.* London: Directory of Social Change, 1989.
Dowson, S. "Innovation and Advocacy." In Community Care Project, *Should Voluntary Organizations Provide More Services?* London: National Council for Voluntary Organizations, 1989.
Edwards, J. "Justice and Social Welfare." *Journal of Social Policy,* 1988, *17*(2), 127-152.
Etherington, S. "Heading for the Big Time." *Social Services Insight,* Nov. 1987, 27.
Gladstone, F. *Voluntary Action in a Changing World.* London: Bedford Square Press, 1979.
Halfpenny, P. "The 1989-90 Charity Household Survey." *Charity Trends.* (13th ed.) Kent, England: Charities Aid Foundation, 1990.
Hall, S. *The Voluntary Sector Under Attack?* London: Islington Voluntary Action Council, 1989.
Hatch, S., and Mocroft, I. *Components of Welfare.* London: Bedford Square Press, 1983.
Hirschman, A. O. *Exit, Voice and Loyalty: Responses to Decline in Firms, Organizations and States.* Cambridge, Mass.: Harvard University Press, 1970.
Home Office. "Efficiency Scrutiny of Government Funding of

Voluntary Sector Published" (news release). Apr. 4, 1990.

Kramer, R. *Voluntary Agencies in the Welfare State.* Berkeley: University of California Press, 1981.

Kramer, R., and Grossman, B. "Contracting for Social Services: Contract Management and Resource Dependencies." *Social Services Review,* Mar. 1987, 32–55.

Kunz, C., Jones, R., and Spencer, K. *Bidding for Change.* London: Community Projects Foundation and Birmingham Settlement, 1989.

Lawson, N. "All Mankind's Concern . . . " The Arnold Goodman Charity Lecture. *Charity,* July 1987, 13–16.

Leat, D. *Privatization and Voluntarization.* Paper presented to research seminar on "The Future of Welfare." London: Economic and Social Research Council, 1985.

Leat, D., Smolka, G., and Unell, J. *A Price Worth Paying?* London: Policy Studies Institute, 1986.

Loney, M. *Communities Against Government: The British Community Development Project.* Portsmouth, N.H.: Heinemann Educational Books, 1983.

Maxwell, S. *Riding the Tiger.* Edinburgh: Scottish Council for Voluntary Organizations, 1989.

National Council for Voluntary Organizations. *Relations Between the Voluntary Sector and Government: A Code for Voluntary Organizations.* London: National Council for Voluntary Organizations, 1984.

Patten, J. "Launching the Active Citizen." *The Guardian,* Sept. 28, 1988.

Perlmutter, F., and Adams, C. "The Voluntary Sector and For-profit Ventures: The Transformation of American Social Welfare." *Administration in Social Work,* 1990, *14*(1), 1–13.

Peterson, J. "Fees and Charges Paid to the Voluntary Sector." *Charity Trends 1986–7.* Kent, England: Charities Aid Foundation, 1988.

Posnett, J. "Trends in the Income of Registered Charities, 1980–1985." *Charity Trends 1986–7.* Kent, England: Charities Aid Foundation, 1988, pp. 6–8.

Rankin, M. *Active Citizenship: Myth or Reality.* Berkhamsted: Volunteer Center UK, 1989.

Rein, M. "The Social Structure of Institutions: Neither Public nor Private." In S. B. Kamerman and A. J. Kahn, *Privatization and the Welfare State*. Princeton, N.J.: Princeton University Press, 1989.

Salamon, L. M. "Rethinking Public Management: Third-Party Government and the Changing Forms of Public Action." *Public Policy*, 1981, *29*, 255–275.

Salamon, L. M. "Of Market Failure, Voluntary Failure and Third-Party Government: Toward a Theory of Government-Nonprofit Relations in the Modern Welfare State." *Journal of Voluntary Action Research*, 1987a, *16*, 29–49.

Salamon, L. M. "Partners in Public Service: The Scope and Theory of Government–Nonprofit Relations." In W. W. Powell, (ed.), *The Nonprofit Sector: A Research Handbook*. New Haven, Conn.: Yale University Press, 1987b.

Salamon, L. M. *Beyond Privatization: The Tools of Government Action*. Washington: The Urban Institute Press, 1989.

Singleton, R. Letter to *The Guardian*, Oct. 1988.

Taylor, M. *New Times, New Challenges: Voluntary Organizations Facing 1990*. London: National Council for Voluntary Organizations, 1990.

Taylor, M., with the Newcastle and Sheffield Tenants' Associations. "For Whose Benefit? Decentralizing Housing Services in Two Cities." *Community Development Journal*, 1986, *21*, 126–132.

Ware, A. "The Changing Relations Between Charities and the State." In A. Ware (ed.), *Charities and Government*. Manchester: Manchester University Press, 1989.

Wolfenden Committee. *The Future of Voluntary Organizations*. London: Croom Helm, 1978.

8

A Resurgent Third Sector and Its Relationship to Government in Israel

Benjamin Gidron

When analyzing the relationships between the government and the nonprofit sector in Israel, with its unique history and social structure, we need an approach that focuses on the primacy of government as the source of public policy and the provider of services.

In her comparison of the nonprofit sector in different countries, Estelle James suggests that existing "theoretical paradigms of nonprofit organizations . . . [have] developed with the American context in mind . . . [and] concentrate on the comparative advantage of NPOs versus profit maximizing organizations (PMOs) rather than NPOs versus government" (1987, p. 397).

Note: I would like to thank Professor Yeheskel Hasenfeld, from UCLA School of Social Welfare, for his very important comments on an earlier draft of this chapter, and Francis Wood, for his help in collecting some of the data.

The Third Sector in Israel

Thus, she adds, these paradigms fail to relate to four aspects that are crucial in understanding the nonprofit sector worldwide: (1) they do not explain why the size of the nonprofit sector varies from one country to another; (2) they do not relate to the division of responsibility between government and nonprofits; (3) they do not address the issue of government contributions to nonprofits; and (4) they ignore the fact that nonprofits are founded by organized religious (or other ideological) groups. She goes on to suggest that the relative size of the nonprofit sector in a society is determined by the "excess demand and differentiated demand for quasi-public goods and by the supply of religious entrepreneurship in . . . society; the sources of venture capital and operating funds for NPOs"; and the relative costs of public versus private provision of services (p. 398).

These basically economic categories are helpful in a comparative analysis of the size and the nature of the nonprofit sector. Yet when the analysis focuses on the processes that lead a society to change the balance of relationships between the nonprofit sector and the government, a trend that we witnessed in the 1980s in practically all industrial societies, we will also need to relate to historical, political, and sociological forces shaping this relationship, and our framework should reflect this broader perspective. Furthermore, in analyzing the relationship between government and the nonprofit sector, the common approach is to use the entire society as a frame of reference. Yet, if the society has specific characteristics or features, such as being an immigrant society, we would also need to analyze the relationship between government and the nonprofit sector within the specific area of immigration absorption, which would shed additional light on the overall picture.

Conceptual Framework

A five-point framework is suggested to analyze the changing relationships between the nonprofit sector and government. It partially draws on James's conceptual framework, but it uses additional perspectives. It will be used in this chapter to analyze the government-nonprofit relationship in Israel.

1. Is the provision of human services in society organized within a basically centralized (highly controlled from one center) system? A centralized system would curtail the existence of both autonomous nonprofit and for-profit (human service) organizations, by regulating them and by effectively controlling their potential funding sources.

2. Historically, in the transition into the era of the welfare state, when government took upon itself the responsibility for the welfare of its citizenry, in what areas did it actually substitute the nonprofit sector in delivering services, and in what areas did it leave the nonprofit service systems intact but incorporate them in the overall system? Such an arrangement would usually entail governmental financial support to nonprofits in return for service provided to a specific population under guidelines set by the government. As it is easier to change agreements with nonprofits than to dismantle government bureaucracies, a change in the relationship between the nonprofit sector and government will evolve at first around those nonprofits with which the government had such arrangements.

3. To what extent are religious and other ideological nonprofit organizations providing comprehensive human services to their followers? A change in the relationships between government and these organizations on a political level will determine the size and the nature of their human service endeavors.

4. Have the different groups composing a heterogeneous society developed a differentiated demand awareness? Such an awareness will lead to a formation of nonprofit organizations to cater for this demand.

5. In countries with a large immigrant population, is immigration a part of the national ethos, and is there a national policy to encourage it? If so, the government is likely to directly engage in immigration absorption (or use quangos), and thus limit the need for immigrants' nonprofit associations.

A note of caution is needed for the term "nonprofit sector." The term assumes an entity, recognized and related to as such. In Israel this is far from the case. A wide variety of voluntary organizations, associations, nonprofit organizations, and quasigovernmental organizations, has always existed in Israel.

The Third Sector in Israel

Yet they would not consider themselves a part of a "sector," and neither would outsiders. Actually, for a variety of reasons, demarcation lines dividing the sectors are particularly hard to trace in Israel. Three obvious reasons for this are the political significance of all collective action, the personal nature of the society, and the close and often informal contacts among officials of different sectors.

I use the term "nonprofit sector" because no better one was found, but readers should recognize it as imposed. It is used here to include organized and institutional activity that is neither public nor for-profit.

Major Characteristics of the Israeli Society

In 1988 Israel's population was 4,406,000, of which 3,613,000 are Jewish and the rest are mostly Arabs (Moslems, Christians, and Druze). Its Jewish population grew from 84,000 in 1922, to 650,000 in mid 1948, when the state was established, to 2,855,000 in 1968, and to its present size—all primarily because of immigration (*Statistical Abstracts of Israel,* 1969; *Monthly Bulletin of Statistics,* 1988). Immigrants to Israel came from more than a hundred countries, the vast majority from societies without a democratic tradition.

In addition to its heterogeneity along religious, national, and ethnic lines, Israeli society, at least the Jewish part, is further divided between the religious, those whose vision for the Israeli society means following, in varying degrees, a way of life based on Jewish law (about 25 percent of the population), and the secular, whose vision is for Israel to follow, again in varying degrees, a way of life similar to other Western democracies.

Another important characteristic of Israeli society has to be taken into consideration: the long tradition of support (financial and other) by Diaspora Jews of the Jewish community living in the Holy Land. This practice, which dates back to the era following the destruction of the First Temple and continues ever since, has to do with the special role the land of Israel plays in the Jewish religion and tradition.

A historical analysis of modern Israeli society usually starts at the end of World War I (the Balfour Declaration) and divides the past seventy years into three distinct periods:

1. The prestate (Yishuv) era (1920–1948), when the infrastructure was laid for most political and social institutions for the future state (the political parties, health and education institutions, labor unions, and so on).
2. The formative era (1949 to mid 1970s), the period during which, out of a mass of new immigrants and against the background of three wars and economic hardships, the foundations for an Israeli society were laid, within an institutional framework set forth in the previous period.
3. The pluralistic era (mid 1970s to present), the period during which the heterogenous character of Israeli society is gradually finding expression in its institutional framework.

This division of Israel's social history more or less parallels major changes in the relationships between the government and the nonprofit sector during the same periods. The transition from the Yishuv to the formative era marks the move from a social and political system based on voluntary nonprofit organizations into a system based on national public administration vested in a formal legal framework. The transition from the formative to the pluralistic era marks the trend (similar to other Western welfare states) of government retrenchment and the renewed importance attributed to nonprofit organizations.

The Yishuv (Prestate) Period

Zionist ideology, developed during the second half of the nineteenth century, was the major force in starting a trend of secular Jewish immigration into Palestine. Yet Zionism was a broad umbrella under which different movements with specific ideological orientations operated. In the early part of the twentieth century the immigration was not of individuals but of groups representing such ideological (often socialist) movements. Under their auspices the cooperative settlements (kibbutzim and moshavim) were formed. But in addition to settlements, each of these movements was also building an infrastructure to absorb more immigrants under its auspices. That infrastructure included comprehensive services in education (the "workers' movement's" schools), health (the various sick funds), welfare, housing, and employment. The concept of a Histadrut (labor union), which deals not only with labor issues but also provides a variety of social, cultural, educational and health services for its members, was developed during that period. This approach — providing comprehensive services to their members — developed by what would amount to nonprofit voluntary organizations was the Jewish community's response to living under a foreign power (British mandate) that was not interested in providing human services. At the same time, the approach could also be seen as both a community preparing itself for independence by building an infrastructure for national services, and as a form of competition among the various ideological movements for actual and potential immigrants; a power struggle for influence in the future state (Eisenstadt, 1967, 1972).

In addition to the Zionist, basically secular, ideological movements and their independent service organizations, there existed for many centuries a religious, non-Zionist Jewish community living mostly in the holy cities of Jerusalem, Safed, Tiberias, and Hebron. This community had its own independent infrastructure of human service organizations, such as Torah-learning institutions (Yeshivot) and health and welfare organizations, financed largely by funds raised abroad. Members of this community took no part in the actions of the Zionist movements, which it opposed on ideological and religious grounds. They believed that working for the establishment of an independent Jewish state before the coming of the Messiah was a form of sinful behavior.

The governing and representative body of the Jewish community in Palestine during the British mandate was the Va'ad Le'umi (National Council), which included representatives of the various Zionist movements and served as the "government on the way." It acted as a coordinating body and as an initiator of policy around all public issues, from external and defense issues to health and education. Representatives of the religious, non-Zionist groups were not a part of that council.

Thus, the institutional life of the Jewish community in Palestine during the British mandate was a coalition of independent movements, each with a strong ideological base, with roots in Jewish communities in the Diaspora, and with service components related to it. This process of institution building by independent entities was the Jewish community's way of preparing itself for independence from the British, and such endeavors were a part of the overall national effort. The service components of the various movements (which would be characterized today as nonprofits) were the actual infrastructure of the public social and human services of the state of Israel when it was established in 1948. Thus, we can say that the workers and volunteers in these organizations did not see themselves as serving only a sectoral interest but a national one as well. This is important in understanding the continuity and the relative stability in many of the human services in the period following the establishment of the state, and their acceptance of the state's authority (Eisenstadt, 1972, p. 3).

In summary, in the prestate era, systems for providing human services cannot be linked to economic considerations. The origins of what would today be called nonprofit organizations had to do primarily with political considerations — establishing an infrastructure for a future independent society — and with a struggle for dominance within that society among the various movements. Because of a lack of an accepted Jewish government, the Yishuv era is characterized by a loosely coupled system of multiple independent ideological movements with organizational branches, each providing a variety of human services to their members, forming a coalition because of their common goal. Such services were not provided by the existing governing power.

The Formative Era

In direct contradiction to the Yishuv era, when social institutions were organized around a loose coalition of ideological movements, observers of the Israeli society during the 1950s and 1960s characterize it as centralistic and dominated by a large public sector, with a bureaucratic-hierarchical form of decision making (Eisenstadt, 1967; Fine, 1967). The locus of power was the central government, and it worked through an intricate system of direct and indirect controls by its ministries and other quasigovernmental organizations. The rationale for such a structure had to do with the national character of the main issues during that period: security, building an economy, and absorption of mass immigration (Weingrod, 1964). It also fit the need to develop a national solidarity, to recrystallize a national tradition, to form the immigrants into one "Israeli" identity (Eisenstadt, 1985; p. 425). Furthermore, it also fit the welfare state ideology, adopted by the coalition of Labor parties that held power during that period, of central government's responsibility for certain aspects of the welfare of its citizenry.

The idea of an autonomous nonprofit sector could under no circumstances fit into such a social and political structure; indeed, as Galnoor claims, the Israeli political establishment showed "hostility towards autonomic participation of citizens and towards independent, non-established groups" (1982b, p. 75). This point is further emphasized by Eisenstadt (1967), who writes about the "tendency to see in the citizen an 'object' of governmental and administrative regulations, which knew better than any citizen—or group of citizens—what the ultimate good of the country and the citizens may be" (p. 322).

This government attitude was not exactly opposed by Israelis. Kramer notes, for example, that in contrast to the Anglo-Saxon tradition, in Israel "there is no Lockean dichotomy of the individual versus the state, nor is there an anti-state philosophy which views with apprehension the expanding scope of central government. Instead, state intervention is generally welcomed, and the prevailing expectation is the somewhat paternalistic one that 'the government will take care of it', since the state is perceived as the central source of benefits to which everyone is entitled" (1976, p. 12).

During the 1950s and 1960s the overall political climate and the official rhetoric were built on "nationhood": the national interest (as reflected by government policy) is superior to any sectoral interest (such as social class, for example). Yet, because the government consisted of a coalition of primarily Labor parties, those in power were in a position to advance their own political goals under the auspices of the state. It is within this context that we must analyze the relationships between the government and the nonprofit sector.

Defining the nonprofit sector in Israel is problematic. For many years there were no clear demarcation lines between sectors, the result being a social system that Kramer terms "holistic" (1976, p. 12). Within the so-called nonprofit sector, he distinguishes between public and voluntary organizations. The public ones would include quasigovernmental organizations such as the very powerful labor unions (Histadrut), Hadassah, the Jewish Agency, and the Joint Distribution Committee. The voluntary organizations would include the traditional religious organizations and charities, women's organizations, immigrants' associations, and the like (Kramer, 1981, p. 90). While such an approach highlights the differences between the "established" organizations, very close to government, and the smaller philanthropic ones, from a legal point of view both types would be nonprofits; indeed, later literature on the subject includes both types in its definition of the nonprofit sector (see for example Rotter, Shamay, and Wood, 1985).

In this period one of the first questions the government had to ask itself regarding human services was, which services should be provided directly by government agencies, and which could be provided by existing sectoral nonprofits?[1] The process of answering that question lasted several years, required negotiations, legislation, and building an administrative infrastructure. After several years, the following results emerged.

In the field of education, the government provides primary and secondary education. This is done through a national education system controlled by the Ministry of Education. The nonprofit sector provides higher education, adult education, informal education, and vocational education. The private sector provides nursery school education. This division of labor was not the outcome of a planned process, but rather of political negotiations. It covered the vast majority of the population, including a large section of the religious population (for which a special "national religious system" was created). However, one part of the religious population, the Haredi or ultraorthodox, do not use the national educational system; they have their own independent systems, for all age groups, which are run as nonprofit organizations and draw on private as well as governmental financial sources (see Jaffe, 1992).

In the field of health, the nonprofit sector, through its sick funds (health insurance schemes), is providing most of the hospital and other direct medical care, emergency ambulatory services, and some psychiatric services. The largest sick fund (Kupat Cholim of the Histadrut) would almost resemble a national health scheme in terms of its coverage. Its clinics can be found in practically all communities, and fees are lower than in other sick funds. The Labor parties in power chose this method to provide almost universal services under auspices they controlled. The government is providing public health services, including well-baby clinics and psychiatric services; these services were practically nonexistent before the state was established. The private sector is providing dental care. While the Haredi community does not have an independent health system, it does have special arrangements with certain hospitals and clinics to treat its population.

In the field of welfare, government is providing basically all income-maintenance services; some through the National Insurance (social security) scheme, some through welfare bureaus on the local level. Government, the nonprofit sector, and the private sector all provide a variety of welfare services for the aged, the handicapped, and the chronically ill. The Haredi community is making use of the national income-maintenance services, but has hundreds of small welfare funds to help the needy, and very often its own homes for the aged, the chronically ill, and the like.

In the field of immigrant absorption, government and the Jewish Agency (a quango) are providing all the crucial services for the first three years: housing (subsidized rent, mortgages), employment including retraining, welfare services, language instruction, and so on. The nonprofit sector provides primarily cultural services. As with welfare services, the Haredi community is using government services and in addition has its own system of helping immigrants, such as providing them with housing in specific neighborhoods, providing educational services for children, and so on.

If we look at the general picture that emerged, it seems that government took upon itself the provision of services in areas of national importance (education, absorption), as well as in areas where no appropriate infrastructure existed (psychiatry, public health). In other areas, it left nonprofits and the private sector to provide services they had provided before. This is reflected in the figures of the national expenditures in health and education, where most of the large nonprofits exist. According to the National Bureau of Statistics, whose records on these issues begin in the early 1960s, government, the nonprofit sector, and the private sector all provide certain services and are responsible for a certain share of the overall expenditure in health or education. This picture is rather stable throughout the 1960s and 1970s, suggesting in effect a certain division of labor among the three sectors.[2] But given the centralistic nature of the system, the government developed a variety of mechanisms to control the nonprofits. The first and most obvious one was the rate of government financial support (in various forms). Both in health and in education, government's support of institutions often amounted to between 30 and 50 percent of their budgets. Furthermore, if an institution, such as the Histadrut sick fund, encountered financial difficulties because of the cost of new programs, a common practice was to turn to government to bail it out.

In addition to financial support, there were also other formal and informal means to control the nonprofits. The formal ones included regulations on salary levels of employees, membership fees (in the sick funds), and tuition (in the preschools and universities). The informal ones included a system where careers of officials were interchanged between government, Histadrut, and the Jewish Agency (Kramer, 1981, p. 90). Another means of control was the centrally managed distribution system of contributions coming from Diaspora Jews in support of health, education, or welfare programs in Israel. By providing a small number of centrally controlled channels through which funds were raised (United Jewish Appeal, Israeli bonds) and later funneled to Israel (the Jewish Agency), the government was able to direct these funds into programs and institutions it was interested in.

In sum, the system that emerged ideologically supported the notion of government's responsibility for providing many human services, yet the actual implementation of that responsibility was sometimes exercised by nonprofits, over which government maintained a high level of control. In other words, the nonprofits were acting as substitutes or extensions of government in prescribed areas, and were perceived as such, not as autonomous entities.

This picture was not limited to the relationship between the government and the large "public" nonprofits; that pattern of relationship was maintained with the smaller, voluntary ones as well. Kramer (1981) observed this in his study of voluntary service agencies; the organizations he studied in the areas of blindness, deafness, mental and physical handicap, and so on were engaged first and foremost in service provision on a fee basis to a certain category of people, which was what the government expected them to do. They seldom filled the roles of improver, value guardian, and vanguard.

The formative era was characterized by building a centralistic system of governance, in most aspects of life. To build one society of the very heterogeneous population that constituted the state, the common denominators were stressed rather than the divisive ones. In such a system there was very little room for differentiated demand in the population, and there was no need (and no political advantage) for the institutional arrangements to reflect it. One exception was the Haredi community, with whom no agreements could be reached to participate in the process of nation building. This community maintained its own, independent system of human services, either as a substitute for national services (especially in education), or, when it suited, in complementing them.

The Pluralistic Era

Since the mid 1970s, Israel has witnessed a gradual process by which its central government is no longer able, perhaps no longer willing, to maintain the same central, omnipotent role it played in the previous era. Several political events—the Yom Kippur War (1973) and its aftermath, ethnic tensions highlighted in the Black Panthers' demonstrations[3] (1970–71), the Labor party's loss of power (1977)—seriously challenged the centralistic-hierarchical form of relationships that had characterized Israeli society. As a matter of fact, collective action by independent, nonestablished groups spurred the resignation of the Golda Meir government following the 1973 war and was the prime mover for change in the government's attitudes and policies toward ethnic problems and youth in distress after the demonstrations of 1970–71. These political events, together with the fruition of demographic, economic, and psychological processes on the one hand (see Gidron and Bargal, 1986) and a policy of government retrenchment on the other, set the stage for the society to move toward a less monolithic system, with additional centers of power.

These changes at the societal level also touched the relationship between the government and the nonprofit sector. The relationship was affected on two levels: there was a dramatic growth in the number of new nonprofits during the 1980s; and the rate of government financial support of nonprofits is gradually decreasing, whereas the rate of other sources (fees, donations) is increasing.

Growth in Nonprofits. In 1980, a new law required nonprofits to be registered with the Ministry of Interior.[4] By December 1989, 12,320 nonprofits were registered (personal communication, the ministry registrar, Jan. 1990). For technical reasons, no breakdown according to purpose, size, year of establishment, or other categories was possible at the time. Yet, from personal observation I can say that the vast majority of these organizations are new; they are small, often local, and tend to be financed by independent funding sources rather than by government.

They operate in a vast variety of areas. Some of them came into existence to provide services formerly provided by government, such as the organizations that provide informal educational services within schools, services that were discontinued because of budget cuts in education. Others engage in activities that were not necessarily considered a part of government responsibility, such as advocacy or public education; examples are the numerous self-help groups dealing with a variety of social or health issues, from AIDS to alcoholism, or with religious freedom, environmental protection, and so on.

Interestingly, this growth includes another category of organizations: funding organizations. Independent foundations, collecting funds both in Israel and in the Diaspora, always existed in the Haredi community, but they were rare among the rest of the population. Since the late 1970s, numerous foundations have been established in Israel, many with independent funding sources in the Jewish Diaspora. Recently, an umbrella organization, the Foundations Association in Israel, was established, with a membership of over twenty.

This change in funding can also be seen in the weakening of the centralized funding mechanisms (the Jewish Agency), and the building of additional, sometimes alternative, mechanisms for Jews in the Diaspora to support Israel. A good example is the New Israel Fund, a partnership between Israelis and North Americans, set up to fund nonprofits engaged in advocacy around issues of civil rights, women's rights, Arab-Jewish cooperation, religious pluralism, and community development. Between 1979 and 1989 the fund grew from $350,000 to $7,000,000.

Even in immigration absorption, a domain where little nonprofit activity was present in the 1960s and 1970s, a change occurred in the 1980s. The government's policy of aiding newcomers with housing and employment has not changed. However, immigrants of the 1980s did not feel that the governmental programs met their specific needs, and established their own nonprofit organizations for advocacy and self-help. One example is the Association of Americans and Canadians in Israel (AACI), which raises some of its funds in North America and, since the early 1980s, helps its members with counseling, loans, and social activities. Another example is the Association of Ethiopian Immigrants, which engaged its members in a dramatic battle against the Rabbinate, when it demanded that Ethiopian Jews undergo a form of conversion.

This overall development demonstrates that Israelis are getting acquainted with a new tool for independent collective action and are beginning to use it. Yet, philanthropic contributions on a regular basis to sustain those organizations are not very prevalent in Israel. There are no federated fundraising mechanisms; corporate giving (or laws to encourage it) does not exist. Fundraising campaigns are usually characterized by mass solicitations, and the result is a large number of small gifts.

These developments are too recent to enable us to understand their impact on society, but it is apparent that many of the controversial issues have moved away from the traditional, established arenas, to the public arena, involving new actors in the process. There is no doubt that immigrants from North America, with their concepts of participatory democracy and citizen involvement, have contributed a great deal in shaping these trends.

Decrease in Governmental Financial Support. Nonprofits have seen a major decrease in government support of their budgets and a parallel increase in fees for service and contributions. A case in point is the major sick funds (membership health care schemes): Histadrut and Maccabi.[5] Membership fees, together with the parallel tax (employers' share in health insurance) amounted to between 60 and 70 percent of their budgets throughout the 1960s and 1970s; in 1986-87, the percentage had grown to 80.8. Direct government transfers, which fluctuated between 15 and 30 percent in the 1960s and 1970s, were only 3.2 percent in 1986-87. The balance comes from sales of services, which grew slightly (3 to 4 percent) from the 1970s (see also Yanay, 1990).

This development — increased fees charged by nonprofits — also increased the nonprofits' input in human services, and their presence is beginning to be felt more in this domain. This was especially marked in the health field. Throughout the 1960s and

The Third Sector in Israel

1970s, government's share of the national expenditure for health was between 28 and 30 percent, the nonprofits' share was 53 to 55 percent, and "other" (primarily for-profit organizations, or FPOs) accounted for 18 to 20 percent. Since 1980, the FPOs' share has gradually increased; in 1986 it reached 24 percent, the nonprofit share remained at 53 percent, and government's share dropped to 23 percent (*Monthly Bulletin of Statistics*, 1988, May supplement).

This reduction in government support to nonprofits had already affected their policies. To make up for the loss of government funding, many nonprofits have raised membership fees (sick funds) or tuition (universities) and also engaged in profit-making activities. For example, the sick funds are building and running homes for the aged, and also sell special medical insurance policies (for additional coverage); universities are enlarging their extension programs.

Household budgets for health care also changed. In the total household expenditure, health rose from 4.2 percent in 1979-80 to 5.2 percent in 1986-87 (Rosen, 1989, p. 29). That trend also affected the decision-making processes within the nonprofits. Yanay (1989) reports on the change in the composition of boards of directors of the community centers affiliated with the Israeli Association of Community Centers. Each center has an independent board that is basically in charge of managing the local center. In 1976 the central government (in most cases the Ministry of Education) was represented on the boards of 93.5 percent of the centers, the local population on only 32.4 percent. In 1988 the government was represented on only 56.1 percent of the boards, local population on 93.9 percent (pp. 9-10). A government representative on the board usually means at least some governmental financial support for that particular center. Representation of the local population means a high degree of involvement (financial and other) in the life of the center.

When the centralistic model of relationship between the government and its citizenry loosened up, the pluralistic nature of Israeli society could be better expressed. One result of this trend was a growth in the number of new nonprofits. Many of them, such as the vast variety of self-help groups and organizations, the various community and civic organizations, the various women's, ethnic, and immigrant associations, the advocacy groups, reflect an awareness for a "differentiated demand." This demand could no longer be satisfied by the basically uniform and standardized services provided by governmental agencies, or for that matter by traditional nonprofits closely controlled by government.

Paradoxically, while government curtailed its spending in practically all human service programs during this era, the Haredi community was able to *increase* governmental support for its independent institutions, especially the educational ones. This had to do with both its numerical increase and its pivotal role in the coalition-building process under the present electoral system. Thus, the government deviated from its own policy when it had to encounter an ideological group that could not be ignored politically.

Finally, government retrenchment policies have expressed themselves thus far primarily by cuts in financial support to nonprofits, not in major shifts of responsibilities between the sectors. Even when government-run programs were cut, such as the cuts in certain programs in schools, they involved relatively peripheral elements (in the music and art curriculum) in which the nonprofit and the for-profit sectors were also involved in providing services.

Conclusions

The conceptual framework used to analyze the process of the changing relationships between government and the nonprofit sector in Israel is based mostly on a political-sociological-historical approach. Such an approach is needed in countries where political and sociological considerations (rather than economic ones) are often used to steer public policy, and they can better explain the relationships between government and the nonprofit sector.

We have seen that in Israel, the relationship to the nonprofit sector is a facet of the *overall* relationship between the government and the population, and it reflects the government's attitudes toward autonomous collective and private action. A shift in this attitude in the 1970s resulted in shaping a different form of relationship with the nonprofit sector. This shift is, no doubt, related to the shift of attitudes of the population on the government's role in society. Here there has been a dramatic change in the Israeli population, from welcoming almost unconditionally government as the major actor in the public policy in the 1950s and 1960s, to a more critical and sophisticated view of government's involvement. This process became possible when the population developed an awareness to specific needs that could no longer be met by government, and the educational, and financial capabilities to act on this awareness.

Another important aspect of the analysis has to do with the composition of society, especially the existence of relatively autonomous ideological groups. Such groups, which will not use government-provided services, will establish their own nonprofits, both to satisfy their specific needs and to maintain their separate group existence. Their political clout will determine how much this will be tolerated.

The idea that services in some areas, considered nationally important, are carried out directly by government determines to a large extent the need for and the functions of nonprofits in those areas. For instance, practically all welfare states have school systems run by the public sector, because of the national importance of education and socialization of the young generation; however, not all immigration countries provide direct services to immigrants via the public sector, for immigration is not necessarily considered a vital aspect of society. Government involvement or noninvolvement in immigration absorption is the major variable explaining the difference in the functions of immigrant associations in different countries (see Jenkins, 1988).

The framework used, focusing on the primacy of government in steering social processes, was found helpful in analyzing the changing relationship between government and the nonprofit sector in the Israel. Other cases would be needed to test it and to perfect it.

Notes

1. It is important to note that with the establishment of the state in 1948, most of the ideological movements became political parties and continued their ideological feuds in the political arena. Later, some of the religious groups also formed their own political parties.
2. In health, government's share ranged from 28 to 30 percent, the nonprofit sector 53 to 55 percent, and the private sector 18 to 20 percent. In education, government's share varied between 50 and 55 percent, the nonprofit sector 40 and 45 percent, and the private sector 5 and 9 percent (*Monthly Bulletin of Statistics,* 1988).
3. The Black Panthers was a militant group of second-generation immigrants, mostly from North Africa, that borrowed its name from the original Black Panthers in the United States and engaged in social action activities in a demand for more power.
4. The 1980 legislation replaced a law dating back to the Ottoman Empire.
5. I thank Francis Wood for providing these data.

References

Eisenstadt, S. N. *Israeli Society.* London: Weidenfeld and Nicolson, 1967.

Eisenstadt, S. N. "The Social Conditions of the Development of Voluntary Association—A Case Study of Israel." *The Journal of Voluntary Action Research,* July 1972, *1*(3), 2–13.

Eisenstadt, S. N. "The Israeli Political System and the Transformation of the Israeli Society." In E. Krausz (ed.), *Politics and Society in Israel.* New Brunswick, N.J.: Transaction Books, 1985.

Fine, L. *Politics in Israel.* Boston: Little, Brown, 1967.

Galnoor, I. *Steering the Polity.* Newbury Park, Calif.: Sage, 1982a.

Galnoor, I. "Israeli Democracy and Citizen Participation." *Molad* 1982b, *41,* Spring, 71–87 (in Hebrew).

Gidron, B., and Bargal, D. "Self-Help Awareness in Israel: An Expression of Structural Changes and Expanding Citizen Participation." *Journal of Voluntary Action Research,* Apr.-June 1986, *15*(2), 47-56.

Jaffe, E. D. "The Role of Nonprofit Organizations Among the Ultra-Orthodox Jewish Community in Israel." In K. D. McCarthy, V. A. Hodgkinson, R. D. Sumariwalla, and Associates, *The Nonprofit Sector in the Global Community: Voices from Many Nations.* San Francisco: Jossey-Bass, 1992.

James, E. "The Nonprofit Sector in Comparative Perspective." In W. W. Powell (ed.), *The Nonprofit Sector: A Research Handbook.* New Haven, Conn.: Yale University Press, 1987.

Jenkins, S. (ed.). *Ethnic Associations and the Welfare State.* New York: Columbia University Press, 1988.

Kramer, R. M. *The Voluntary Service Agency in Israel.* Berkeley: University of California, Institute of International Studies, Research Series no. 26, 1976.

Kramer, R. M. *Voluntary Agencies in the Welfare State.* Berkeley: University of California Press, 1981.

Kramer, R. M. "Voluntary Agencies and Social Change in Israel 1972-1982." *Israel Social Science Research,* 1984, *2*(2), 55-72.

Monthly Bulletin of Statistics. Jerusalem: Central Bureau of Statistics, 1988.

Rosen, B. *The Public-Private Mix in Israeli Health Care.* Jerusalem: Brookdale Institute, 1989.

Rotter, R., Shamay, N., and Wood, F. "The Nonprofit Sector and Volunteering." In Y. Kop (ed.), *Israel's Outlays for Human Services, 1984.* Jerusalem: The Center for Jon'ai Policy Studies in Israel, 1985.

Statistical Abstracts of Israel. Jerusalem: Central Bureau of Statistics, 1969.

Weingrod, A. "Immigrants, Localism and Political Power." *Amot,* Feb.-Mar. 1964, *4,* 15-22 (in Hebrew).

Yanay, U. "Organization in Transition: From Government to Non-government Service Centers." Paper presented at the International Conference on Voluntarism, Non-governmental Organizations and Public Policy, Jerusalem, May 1989.

Yanay, U. "Service Delivery by a Trade Union—Does It Pay?" *Journal of Social Policy,* 1990, *19*(2), 221-234.

9

Voluntary and Public Social Services in Italy

Sergio Pasquinelli

In a traditionally Catholic-dominated welfare system, Italy has in the last fifteen years discovered the emergence of a large third sector in the personal social services; that sector figures increasingly in discussion about remedies for the long-standing crisis of the Italian welfare system.

This chapter presents information on the principal characteristics that voluntary action has assumed in Italy, with particular reference to the relationship established with public agencies, and considers some conceptual problems deriving from the current debate. To begin, it is important to clarify some terminology. "Voluntary action," "voluntarism," and "third sector" are

Note: I would like to thank Ugo Ascoli for his helpful comments on an earlier version of this chapter, which appeared in *Nonprofit and Voluntary Sector Quarterly*, 1989, *18*(4).

Voluntary and Public Social Services in Italy

actually misleading terms, since they embrace a plurality of meanings, orientations, and forms of action that are often confused. To clarify the phenomena described in this chapter, it is necessary to introduce at least two distinctions.

The first clarification involves the concept of absence of profit. This absence can refer either to an organization or to single individuals who act within the organization. On the organizational level, we can find collective actions that have no profit objectives, where the "nonprofit constraint" is in force (Powell, 1987) but where staff are paid; for example, in schools or hospitals. On the other hand, absence of profit at the individual level means considering the area of voluntary action in its literal sense — individuals contribute their efforts as nonpaid volunteers. The second focus is the topic of this chapter. So, I will not treat the whole Italian nonprofit sector but rather only a more circumscribed area within it — what is called *volontariato,* that is, collective forms of action whose actors (at least the majority) participate on a nonpaid basis. It is this type of participation on which current Italian debate and research are concentrated.

The second clarification involves those who directly benefit from voluntary action. A specific characteristic of voluntary action is the responsiveness to a need that is not directly related to the volunteers themselves, while the area known as self-help is composed of people who organize around their own interests and needs of others. In responding to the needs of others, volunteers may also be responding to their own needs (friendship, personal growth, or self-gratification).

No doubt there is continuous overlap between these two dimensions of profit versus nonprofit and self-needs versus others' needs. Nevertheless, most of the Italian voluntary action, as defined here, is committed to the delivery of personal social services in the welfare arena. It is useful to examine the social and political context within which this action occurs.

The Italian Scenario

In the last thirty years the Italian welfare state has gone through remarkable transformations.[1] For example, the monetary expenditure from 1960 to 1984 alone almost doubled, reaching 30.3 percent of the gross national product in 1984 (among the Organization for Economic Cooperation and Development countries, it is the highest percentage after France and Germany (Ascoli, 1989). Certainly, these transformations were not easily achieved.

From the time Italy became a unified state in 1861 to the beginning of the 1900s, social intervention by government was of very modest proportions. Until then, social policy was the practically exclusive domain of the Catholic church, whose charitable structure was based on a dense network of national and local institutions of a philanthropic nature. At the turn of the century, Italian social policy began to develop. A slow process of conversion to democracy (for example, the universal right to vote for men, introduced in 1912) was initiated under the leadership of Giolitti, who inaugurated state intervention into the economy and into the society. In particular, the evolution of the social security system was given a decisive boost. In 1910 the first public appropriation for the unemployed was approved.

The fascist period saw a further expansion of national policy by a strong centralization process, a feature that would deeply influence successive development. The major innovations in this period concerned protection from illness, state-subsidized maternity care, and the social security system. While a number of institutions under direct state control were founded, most were to be progressively eliminated with the fall of the regime.

Immediately after World War II, social policies were subordinated to the party government. Since then, increasing government instability, owing to the precarious system of party alliances, has heavily influenced the development or nondevelopment of welfare policies. From the 1950s to the mid 1960s, the Italian economy went through changes that have been called an "economic miracle." The transformational processes followed the lines of the urban-industrial model already established in other capitalist countries, but with some differences. For example, the discrepancy between northern and southern Italy was increased—the big industrial centers were all established in the north, and a rise in the internationalization of the economy

Voluntary and Public Social Services in Italy

brought about an increased dependence on the foreign market. In this situation, the main function of the political system was to repress imbalances created by the chaotic growth, instead of responding in a satisfactory way to the major social problems. In the 1950s some attempts at reform were made, but the results, even in the best of cases, essentially amounted to only a multiplication of bureaucratic structures, inserting the new in place of the old. More substantial efforts to change the institutional profile of the welfare state came only at the end of the 1960s, with the transformation of the hospital structure, and were intensified in the following years.

The 1970s in the United States are typically viewed as less dynamic than the 1960s. In contrast, the same period is remembered in Italy as a time of great social fervor. Beginning with the large-scale worker and student mobilizations in 1968-69, the 1970s were marked by great social conflicts through which groups such as youth and women saw their symbolic as well as substantive political power increase. As a result of the diffuse conflicts, the political system was obliged to abandon, at least partially, the inclination to control and contain the social demands. The laws on abortion and divorce were subjected to major revisions during those years. In terms of social policies, a reform in the psychiatric field of the public health service and a law pertaining to drug abusers were approved at the end of the decade.

In the 1980s the Italian version of the welfare state seemed to be quite close, at least in principle, to that of other advanced capitalist countries, especially when compared to the conditions of the preceding decades. In practice, however, there are difficulties. For example, the radical reform of the public health service, approved in the early 1980s, has encountered formidable application problems, owing in particular to the decentralization of services and the attempted integration of social and health services. Toward the end of the 1980s, there was a trend to reverse earlier changes in the health sector by introducing market elements in a highly bureaucratized, statist-dominated system. In addition, a more punitive law concerning drug addicts was adopted in June 1990 that contrasted with the 1978 version, and even the psychiatric reforms of 1978, considered one of the most advanced in the world, were also slated for change (Ascoli, 1989).

The last few years have seen, in addition, a proliferation of activities, promoted locally by public agencies, to benefit youth and other social groups with special needs. Great vitality at the local level, together with great inertia at the central or federal levels, is one of the characteristic features of the Italian political scene, and it affects the voluntary sector. Funds for volunteer groups are mostly of local origin (regions and municipalities), and partnerships among these groups and government agencies are found mostly at the local level as well.

The great current ambiguity of Italian policy making (Dente, 1990) concerns the conflict between centralization and decentralization. Local authorities have various delegated tasks, including the implementation of personal social services, but they are heavily dependent, financially and otherwise, on central government. The result is a fragmented situation dominated by the financial crisis of the state, public debt having now reached the record level of the total amount of the gross domestic product. Against this backdrop of financial crisis, further uncertainties appear because the necessity to reduce public expenditure goes against the major political parties' interests in maintaining consensus and avoiding unpopular decisions.

In terms of intellectual underpinnings, it was at the end of the 1970s that a debate on the crisis of the welfare state began to develop, centered on the failure of social policies, despite the enormous quantity of resources deployed, to create a just and equal society (Ascoli, 1987, 1989). In general, two remedies have been proposed. The first is called the neoliberal position, which, appealing to the concept of free exchange, seeks deregulation of the public apparatus in favor of a general and uncontrolled laissez-faire. The second position, on the other side, seeks to empower governmental institutions. What is recommended is a technocratic solution of a system planned by experts, according to regulations that preclude citizens' participation.

Between these two solutions, a third position has emerged that does not represent a simple compromise. According to this

Voluntary and Public Social Services in Italy

third viewpoint, the huge bureaucratic-administrative apparatus should be reorganized in favor of a more responsible and responsive administration. *Responsible* means that government should limit its functions with a well-defined scope, as opposed to a more broadly defined jurisdiction. *Responsive* means that government should be able to explain its day-to-day activities to the users of its services. The desired goal, then, is public services that are more independent of the political system, with more flexibility and greater capability of using the resources of other social service providers. The idea that the state must be the only social service provider—the last legacy of an orthodox reading of Marxism—is no longer commonly held. The diversity of groups who contribute to the welfare scene and the interdependence among them have to be recognized. It remains to be seen whether these diverse groups are destined to live together peacefully, exploring the possibilities of contact and communication. Clearly, among these groups are the voluntary associations.

Voluntary-Sector Associations and Their Characteristics

Voluntarism in Italy witnessed a rapid growth from the beginning of the late 1970s until the mid 1980s. I refer here not only to the birth and diffusion of new forms of commitment, often bringing with them innovative modes of response to social needs, but also to changes in established groups and associations.

The phenomenon of voluntarism stirred up research activity that has intensified since the early 1980s. To be sure, even with due consideration to differing proportions of social scientists, the level of research activity in Italy cannot be aptly compared to that, say, in the United States; yet there have been twelve recently published research studies in Italy on voluntary-sector groups.[2] Almost all of them have focused on specific geographical areas as well as, in some cases, organizational issues. The research by Rossi and Colozzi (1985) remains the only study conducted at the national level. Although the generalizability of their data is subject to dispute, there is no doubt that the survey findings have begun to fill a great void of knowledge. This study took into account more than 15,000 groups, of which 7,024 were analyzed by means of a questionnaire. It is worthwhile to examine some of these data to provide a characterization of the Italian case as a whole.

Of these 7,024 groups, 43.5 percent are legally recognized associations, while the remaining are informal groups without a bureaucratic structure; other research demonstrates that the informal associations are larger in number than Rossi and Colozzi indicated. Small groups tend to prevail: 49.8 percent have fewer than twenty members, 26.4 percent have between twenty and fifty.

In terms of function, charitable activities (home assistance, economic aid, and so on) are carried out by 34.4 percent of the groups; 20.3 percent provide services in the health sector (first aid, hospital assistance); 21.1 percent are involved in educational and free-time activities; and the remaining 24.2 percent engage in activities outside the field of personal social services, generically defined as "cultural," which often have an advocacy function.

The data reveal some interesting trends in age and sex of the volunteers. There is a strong presence of youth: 29 percent of the groups are composed only or predominantly of youth; 44.4 percent only or predominantly of adults (persons between thirty and sixty years of age); 5.9 percent only or predominantly of the elderly; and the remaining 20.7 percent are mixed. In contrast to other national contexts, Italian voluntarism is not carried out mainly by women, as the presence of the two sexes is equally distributed. The female presence was predominant in the past, but it is less evident today.

"New" Forms of Voluntarism

The "Italian case" is better understood by noting the growth that has occurred in recent years and the effects of this growth. Forty percent of the groups analyzed in the national survey were founded after 1977. Also, between 1981 and 1984, 54.5 percent saw growth in membership and 42.6 percent saw growth in the number of service users. Thus, many have talked of a "new" voluntarism, as opposed to more traditional forms of social service activity. Although ideological content is often obscured by the opposition between old and new forms of voluntarism, it is clear that a great many of the groups recently formed express new orientations and characteristics.[3]

First of all, we can observe a tendency, more marked than in the past, to carry out personal social services where public activities are most deficient, particularly in the area of "special needs" groups such as drug addicts, people with disabilities, minors at risk, and those who are called the "new" poor. In addition, the "new" voluntarism has quite precise organizational characteristics: groups are generally small in size; they tend to maintain an informal structure and to avoid rigid hierarchies; they generally have a local radius of action, restricted to a well-defined territorial context; their presence is strong, especially in the big metropolitan centers; and they have a great many youth as members. Referring to this last feature, many scholars have seen here a new kind of social commitment among the young, after the crisis of the social movements of the 1970s. Actually, these groups show both breaks and continuities with the past. The central continuity is seen in the role that many of these new associations attribute to themselves. To use the terminology proposed by Kramer (1981), their role is not just that of a service provider but also, and mainly, that of a vanguard and an improver.

Traditional voluntarism is rooted in the broad network of charitable parish groups. Before the late 1970s, voluntarism in Italy was mainly composed of such groups. Nowadays, this "old" structure remains effective and has kept pace with the expansion of voluntarism. Although it has partially assumed the new characteristics described above, new groups claim that the traditional voluntary associations remain imprisoned in the role of a substitute for governmental intervention, in which they are a remedy for social inequities, without focusing on the sources of these inequities and without trying to hold state organizations to their social responsibilities. In contrast, new voluntary-sector agencies want to work on the *causes* of social marginality.

Their aim is to create a network of solidarity and to build a different social standard, instead of just filling the social gaps. Regarding the political system, these "new" groups generally have a critical outlook. Many of them exert political pressure not only to improve public social policies, but also to assert their place as rightful participants in the welfare decision-making process. The purpose of these new groups is not to remain on the service-provision level of collaboration, where public organizations tend to keep voluntarism, but rather to promote cooperation based on their definition of social policy targets. Their attempt is to plan new programs together, rather than transfer them to the public organizations.

If this is the new philosophy, to what extent is it practiced? Although there does not exist in Italy any specific data on these new forms of voluntarism sufficient to give empirical substance to this vanguard role, it is evident that the major innovation of the new groups concerns their mode of intervention, or how they treat and respond to social needs. Faced with needs that are becoming increasingly complex, these agencies propose a broad approach to the social services. If the focus of the old voluntarism is on specific personal problems, such as physical disabilities, the new voluntarism focuses on developing quality services, not only at a technical and specialized level but also at a general level of human relations. In sum, the new voluntary sector has an activist social role, documenting new social problems in addition to trying to resolve them.

For both the old and new forms of voluntarism, there are apparently no processes through which programs are eventually transferred to government agencies. These voluntary agencies prefer to support and finance their activities because they know voluntary work has qualities that public agencies either could never have or could have only at a high cost. This issue of capability directly addresses the issue of professionalism in voluntary associations. In recent years the debate in Italy has focused on the problem of adequate training of volunteers. Although increased funding has produced greater professionalization of the groups, the overall degree of professionalization remains low, constituting one of the peculiarities of Italian voluntarism in comparison with other countries (Kramer, 1981). Studies have demonstrated that training sessions are seldom conducted, usually only by large national associations, and that, when they do occur, it is at a local level, mainly to reinforce and regenerate commitment rather than to help volunteers acquire specific technical abilities.

A Theoretical Problem and Its Implications for Research

In Italy, the majority of the scholars concerned with voluntarism are from the field of welfare studies. As a consequence, voluntarism is considered primarily in relation to the welfare state and its crisis. Thus, research is centered on the roles that nongovernmental organizations play on the macro-level. The major issue is where to place the important resource of volunteers in order to maximize their capacity to provide services, that is, to produce "social utility." Two major theoretical reductions follow from this approach.

First, there is the risk of again falling into old functionalist schemes, wherein collective actions are considered and valued mainly for their contributions to the cohesion and equilibrium of the social system. Therefore, greater emphasis is typically placed on the workings of government, but volunteers, especially those engaged in the provision of personal social services, struggle for something that goes beyond this functionalist approach. The message that this conveys to the rest of society may be comprehended only at a symbolic (or "cultural") level, similar to what happens in social movements.

Second, and directly related to the first problem, voluntarism is not viewed as an autonomous object of analysis. Reseachers always link the phenomenon to something else, such as the political environment in which the action occurs. No attention is given to the processes through which partnerships are constructed, which can be seen as "events," as unified empirical phenomena. Few attempts are made in Italy to carry out a sociological analysis, to explain how and why groups and agencies develop different types of intergroup relations.

To understand Italian voluntarism, analyses must be conducted at a micro-level, which allows the dynamics of intergroup relations to be seen. Eventually, new conceptual schemes must be formulated.[4]

Micro-Level Dynamics

Let us now turn to the relations between the voluntary sector and public agencies. The "public sphere" can be divided into two functions—political and service provision—and the relationships and logic underlying each of them are so different that it is necessary to study them separately. This functional distinction is very clear in the findings of Italian studies that have examined the connections between agency types (Ranci, De Ambrogio, and Pasquinelli, 1991). For instance, within a hospital there are either service-provider departments or political structures concerned with decision making, such as the board of directors. In an absolute sense, of course, we cannot separate political and service-provider agencies because we can find a political level in every organization considered as a whole.

Overall, between public and voluntary agencies, there do not seem to be homogeneous and unitary relationship strategies; rather, the situation is characterized by complex relations and attitudes. According to the national survey by Rossi and Colozzi (1985), 61.3 percent of voluntary groups have relationships with public (local or national) agencies, but only 7.4 percent of them receive grants of public funds, although this percentage has undoubtedly increased during the past few years. Disaggregating this data, the study demonstrates that the informal groups have fewer connections than the formal groups of volunteers.

These relationships become clearer when we move from these quantitative findings to more qualitative studies such as those conducted by the Istituto per la Ricerca Sociale (IRS).[5] The research done by the IRS in Milan, for example, specifies that it is not the *diffusion* of connections that varies among more or less formalized organizations (Ranci, 1985). It is, instead, the *type* of relations and public interventions that changes, if we consider informal local groups with respect to organizational dimensions.[6] Within informally structured groups, relations are generally more informal: these voluntary agencies do not want to compromise themselves with the political expression of the state, but when they do compromise, it is because they want to influence public decision making. In contrast, more formal groups tend to establish contacts with public service-provision agencies; these contacts are generally concentrated around single individuals such as the homeless or drug addicts who are users of one or the other type of agency. As we approach more formally structured organizations, we find more formal connections, also at the political level, and we find more formal conventions through which voluntary groups secure public support.

The IRS analysis proposed, then, a typology of relationships between public and voluntary agencies that ranges from no contact to full integration of voluntary and governmental interventions. In heterogeneous situations, the predominant orientation seems to be toward collaboration that respects the differences between agency types. Voluntary agencies accept and often consider their relationships with governmental agencies a necessity, but warn of relationships that are too close because they fear losing their autonomy. According to Ranci (1985), the principal task is that the relationships may become purely instrumental, that is, reduced to pure exchanges of resources, information, or even individuals who pass from one agency to another. Such instrumental relationships can prevent voluntary organizations from assuming active roles in public policy planning by confining them to marginal positions and thus reducing them to "tools" in the hands of the public agencies.

Interagency relationships can also vary with respect to geography. The study conducted by Cesareo and Rossi (1985), which analyzed the situation in southern Italy, clearly demonstrates this geographical variation. In southern Italy, where the welfare system has lost much of its credibility, contacts between public and voluntary-sector agencies are very sparse, and they are marked by a reciprocal diffidence. This is far different from the relationships in the north, where interagency communication seems to be relatively more widespread. Also, another important variable is the cultural inspiration of voluntary associations, which include both secular and Catholic groups. The secular groups, especially those engaged in health services, have developed consistent relationships with statutory bodies, whereas Catholic associations still seem to be highly mistrustful and receive very little public funding (Ranci, De Ambrogio, and Pasquinelli, 1991).

In summary, regarding the nature of the relationships between voluntary and public agencies in Italy, it is difficult to provide a definitive description. There is an openness and receptiveness of voluntary groups to the establishment of social service contracts with government agencies, though these contacts vary in degree of formalization, contextual features, and type of public agency involved. Contacts are increasingly with local public authorities rather than with national ones, but even with close ties to these public agencies, the major fear of voluntary agencies remains that of losing their independence.

More specifically, there is a cultural distance that is noticeable whenever a voluntary group contacts a public service-provider agency. They see themselves as "value guardians," conveying deep ethical meanings, and as capable of really listening to others' needs, of acting flexibly with altruism and solidarity. On the other side, they see the public institution as a prisoner of its aseptic procedures and its rigid bureaucratic administration.

Thus, in the experiences of collaboration between the two parties, volunteers view rigidity of intervention as the major limitation of governmental action, while governmental operators see a lack of competence and professionalism in voluntary action. Essentially, this is an impasse where all parties speak their own language: volunteers speak the language of creativity and personal sharing, and government staff members speak the language of techniques and professional preparation. What emerges is a "difficult agreement," a relationship based on some segment of a program that the two parties share.

To be fully comprehended, however, the situation must be put in a wider context. Altogether, this ensemble of initiatives is commonly assessed for what it does, or for what it appears to be. Its most important contribution, however, is found not on a factual level but instead on a symbolic one. This symbolism goes beyond Kramer's concept of the "value guardian" role (1981). According to this concept, voluntary action can serve to integrate individuals into the social system. But the Italian experience shows instead a break between the values that these forms of collective behavior propose and the socially dominant values. In fact, it could be argued that voluntary action has a potentially antagonistic role. Solidarity, quality of life, struggle in support of special-needs groups, and advocacy are indeed issues that cast doubt on the goals of society, that ask where we are going and why.

This symbolic dimension indicates the deep contradiction between what voluntary agencies actually propose — alternative definitions, different meanings — and what they are valued for. The consequences of this contradiction become evident in the relationships of these agencies at the political level. Today, public financial support of voluntary associations, especially by municipalities, is multiplying. Though the accountability problem does not seem to worry public administrators very much, these grants inevitably lead associations of volunteers to turn their energies and resources away from the provision of services and toward organization and professionalism. Thus, they see themselves as likely to be measured by productivity and efficiency, gradually uprooted from original attributes, and distracted from the goals on which they were founded.

Italian voluntary action is facing a serious dilemma: to play the game of a society in rapid tranformation and to undergo some major changes, or to stay aside and carve out room where it is possible to promote the values of solidarity. With the first choice, processes of organizational change often lead to greater professionalism, with groups losing their specific cultural features. With the second choice, there is the risk of marginality, the risk of becoming one of the many interest groups that enter the social system and have little influence.

There probably exists room for a third choice, but there are still many open questions. How will voluntary agencies strengthen their own collective identity and presence without undermining their original attributes? How will they seek governmental support without becoming new institutions? These are the crucial questions facing Italian voluntary groups at the current time.

Toward a Contract State

Some of the more recent changes in the emergence of a third sector in Italy relate to the growing use of voluntary agencies to provide social services to various handicapped groups as part of a governmental contract. Despite the growing importance of this practice, Italy still lacks any legislation regarding voluntary agencies or any other nonprofit organizations (Barbetta and Ranci, 1990).

In the absence of any national policy, a "contract state" may, however, be developing as the number of *convenzioni* (contracts or legal agreements) increase between local and regional governments and voluntary organizations. Public funding occurs mainly on the local level and is dependent on the willingness of individual politicians and either heads of local institutions or single departments within them. The pattern is quite fragmented and varies from community to community, sharing in the instability characteristic of local government.

While there is little data about governmental funding in the nonprofit sector, two recent studies begin to suggest some trends in Lombardy and Milan in the most heavily populated part of the country: nearly nine million people out of a total population of fifty-seven million. A survey of 598 voluntary organizations in Lombardy by De Ambrogio and Ranci (1989) found that 37 percent of them — mainly smaller organizations — received some governmental funds, which averaged about 10 percent of their income. On the whole, almost 60 percent of the income of all these organizations came from contributions. The funding pattern for voluntary associations contrasts, of course, with the income sources of nonprofit organizations that provide a social service to the community, such as the 126 surveyed in an unpublished study by the Istituto per la Ricerca Sociale in Milan. It was found that voluntary organizations serving the disabled received over 40 percent of their income from local government; those treating drug addicts averaged 60 percent, and hospitals obtained 82 percent of their revenue from government. These proportions are similar to those found by other research in progress (Pasquinelli, 1991; Bassanini and Ranci, 1990).

The most frequent form of funding voluntary agencies is by contracting (*conventioni*), which is regulated by regional laws covering eligibility criteria and rather loose accountability requirements. The major incentive for contracting by local government is the restriction on hiring new employees that has been in effect since the early 1980s: four employees must be released for every new one hired.

It seems likely that if these funding patterns continue there may well be increasing pressures to formalize these relationships between voluntary organizations and government and to require more accountability, as has occurred in other countries.

Notes

1. One of the best studies of the Italian welfare system is Ferrera (1984), a research project promoted by the Istituto Universitario Europeo of Florence, Italy, and directed by Peter Flora. A detailed comparative analysis of the American and European welfare states is in Flora and Heidenheimer (1981). On the Italian case, see also Ascoli (1987).
2. I have reviewed this research in Pasquinelli (1989).
3. What follows is not based on quantitative data, but rather is the partial result of research conducted at the Istituto per la Ricerca Sociale (IRS), in Milan, Italy; see note 5.
4. This situation is seemingly different from the American one, where a need for new theory is emerging (Ostrander, Langton, and Van Til, 1988).
5. The research work of the IRS consists mainly of two projects. The first was concluded in 1984 and was carried out in Milan. The second was completed in 1991 in the Reggio Emilia area. In each case a census was conducted of all the existing organizations and approximately eighty were subsequently interviewed. In addition, in the second project, a case study of seven agencies was made regarding two issues: the individual involvement in a collective identity and the relationship between the volunteers and users or those who benefited from voluntary-sector activities (see Ranci, De Ambrogio, and Pasquinelli, 1991).

6. Thus, the Italian case shows once again the importance of distinguishing between local and national levels. It would be very useful to have comparative analyses of voluntary-statutory relationships in other national contexts, such as the study conducted in Britain by Brenton (1985).

References

Ascoli, U. "The Italian Welfare State: Between Incrementalism and Rationalism." In R. R. Friedman and others (eds.), *Modern Welfare States*. New York: New York University Press, 1987.

Ascoli, U. "The Italian Welfare System in the 80's: Less State and More Market?" In R. Morris (ed.), *Testing the Limits: International Perspectives on Social Welfare Change in Nine Countries*. Hanover, N.H.: University Press of New England, 1989.

Barbetta, G. P., and Ranci, P. *The Nonprofit Sector in Italy*. Paper presented at the INDEPENDENT SECTOR Spring Research Forum, Boston, 1990.

Bassanini, M. C., and Ranci, P. (eds.) *Non per Profitto* (Not for Profit). Perugia, Italy: Quaderni della Fondazione Olivetti, 1990.

Brenton, M. *The Voluntary Sector in British Social Services*. London: Longman, 1985.

Cesareo, V., and Rossi, G. (eds.). *Volontariato e Mezzogiorno* (Voluntary Action in the South of Italy). Bologna, Italy: Dehoniane, 1985.

De Ambrogio, U., and Ranci, C. "Volontariato in Lombardia." *Prospective Sociali e Sanitarie*, 1989, *9*, 1–8.

de Hoog, R. H. *Contracting Out for Human Services*. Albany: State University of New York Press, 1984.

Demone, H. W., and Gibelman, M. (eds.). *Services for Sale*. New Brunswick, N.J.: Rutgers University Press, 1989.

Dente, B. "Partisan Politics and Bureaucracy in Italian Social Policies." In D. E. Ashford (ed.), *Discretionary Politics*. Greenwich, Conn.: Jai Press, 1990.

DiMaggio, P. J., and Anheier, H. K. "The Sociology of Nonprofit Organizations and Sectors." *Annual Review of Sociology,* 1990, *16,* 137–159.

Ferrera, M. *Il Welfare State in Italia* (The Welfare State in Italy). Bologna, Italy: Il Mulino, 1984.

Ferrera, M. "The Italian Welfare State." In P. Flora (ed.), *Growth to Limits?* Berlin: De Gruyter, 1988.

Flora, P., and Heidenheimer, A. J. (eds.) *The Development of Welfare States in Europe and America.* New Brunswick, N.J.: Transaction Books, 1981.

Gronbjerg, K. A. "Patterns of Institutional Relations in the Welfare State: Public Mandates and the Nonprofit Sector." *Journal of Voluntary Action Research,* 1987, *16,* 64–80.

James, E. "The Nonprofit Sector in Comparative Perspective." In W. W. Powell (ed.), *The Nonprofit Sector: A Research Handbook.* New Haven, Conn.: Yale University Press, 1987.

Kramer, R. M. *Voluntary Agencies in the Welfare State.* Berkeley: University of California Press, 1981.

Kramer, R. M. "Change and Continuity in British Voluntary Organizations, 1976 to 1988." *Voluntas,* 1990, *12,* 33–60.

Ostrander, S. A., Langton, S., and Van Til, J. (eds.). *Shifting the Debate: Public/Private Sector Relations in the Modern Welfare State.* New Brunswick, N.J.: Transaction Books, 1988.

Paci, M. "Il Sistema di Welfare Italiano tra Tradizione 'Clientelare' ed Esigenze di Cambiamento" (The Italian Welfare State Between Clientelism and Needs for Change). In U. Ascoli (ed.), *Welfare State All'italiana.* Roma-Bari, Italy: Laterza, 1984.

Pasquinelli, S. "Voluntry Action in the Welfare State: The Italian Case." *Nonprofit and Voluntary Sector Quarterly,* 1989, *18,* 349–367.

Pasquinelli, S. "La Privatizzazione dei Servizi Sociali a Milano" (Privatization of Social Services in Milan). *Politica ed Economia,* 1991, *2,* 70–72.

Powell, W. W. (ed.). *The Nonprofit Sector: A Research Handbook.* New Haven, Conn.: Yale University Press, 1987.

Ranci, C. (ed.). *Volontariato, Bisogni, Servizi* (Voluntary Action, Social Needs, and Services). Milan, Italy: F. Angeli, 1985.

Ranci, C., De Ambrogio, U., and Pasquinelli, S. *Identita e Servizio: Il Volontariato Nella Crise del Welfare* (Organizational Identity and Service Provision: Voluntary Action in the Welfare Crisis). Bologna, Italy: Il Mulino, 1991.

Rossi, G., and Colozzi, I. "I Gruppi di Volontariato in Italia: Elementi per una Classificazione" (Voluntarism in Italy: Elements for a Classification), In L. Tavazza (ed.), *Volontariato ed Enti Locali*. Bologna, Italy: Dehoniane, 1985.

Weisbrod, B. "Toward a Theory of the Voluntary Nonprofit Sector in a Three-Sector Economy." In E. S. Phelps (ed.), *Altruism, Morality and Economic Theory*. New York: Russell Sage Foundation, 1975.

10

Building Welfare Systems Through Local Associations in France

Viviane Mizrahi-Tchernonog

This chapter analyzes the relationships between local authorities and associations in the field of welfare policy. The French term *"association"* basically parallels, both legally and sociologically, the English term "nonprofit organization."

The World of Associations in France

In France the term *association* (the English and French spellings are identical) refers to a specific legal organizational structure. The Act of Associations of July 5, 1901, defines them as "organizational bodies in which two or more persons use jointly their knowledge, skill, or activities on a sustained basis to advance a certain cause which is entirely different from profit making." Clause 2 of that act states that associations do not need special authorization or declaration to function, but in such cases they are unregistered de facto associations. Only after they register with the regional police headquarters do associations have a formal legal status: they can open a bank account, receive donations or government grants, or engage in profit-making activities.

An *association* usually suggests a small organization, formed to provide mutual-aid frameworks or social services. Such entities are created by local initiatives and use local resources and energies. In most cases they rely on volunteer work of their members, and their financial resources come mainly from members' fees and donations. When the public authorities are involved, their contribution consists mostly of donations in kind and loaned equipment or premises.

While such traditional associations do exist, it would be safe to say that the core of the world of associations is more diversified and more complex. As the legal framework that defines French associations is not very restrictive, a great variety of associations can be found. In addition to the voluntary associations and those founded by local initiatives, there are quasipublic ones initiated by various public agencies, "figurehead" associations, which are actually a disguise of for-profit enterprises, religious or lay charities (local, independent, or branches of a national organization), advocacy groups, and associations to provide equipment or services for other associations.

The flexible legal framework that allows those associations to be formed also creates a situation that is complex and intertwined. On the superficial level, two distinct types of associations may be seen: (1) the so-called associations, sometimes also called "figurehead associations" or "relay associations" and (2) the real ones. The former use association structures, because this allows them to benefit from simple management regulations and possible discretion as to the origin and use of their funds or the identity of the persons who actually control spending. The latter group are the small independent associations mentioned earlier, also labeled "associative movements"; they rely on volunteer work, experiment with innovative ideas, and use a variety of communal resources. The actual situation is even more complex. Those two general types of associations are the

Welfare Systems Through Local Associations in France 217

extremes on a continuum, along which different types of associations have different degrees of involvement of public or private funding, local or national initiatives, voluntary and paid staff, and so on.

The Current French Associative Sphere

An important feature of the world of associations in France is the growth in their numbers, especially in the past decade. This can clearly be seen from the figures of new associations registered per year. Their number jumps from 12,630 in 1960, to 26,112 in 1980, to 39,437 in 1982, and to 54,130 in 1987 (Forse, 1984). Table 10.1 shows the breakdown of new associations created in a single year (1982), organized according to their primary mission. Reliable data on the numbers of associations that discontinued their operations are lacking, and thus statistics on the number of current associations are inaccurate. A study into the various available sources on this topic, undertaken by Archambault (1984), indicates that the number of associations in France is between 500,000 and 600,000. The National Institute of Statistics and Economic Surveys counted 166,365 associations at the end of 1986; 48.6 percent of them had no paid workers. Those which did, employed about 821,000 paid workers in 1987 (National Institute of Statistics and Economic Surveys, 1987).

The number of associations per inhabitants is larger in rural areas (particularly those with fewer than two thousand inhabitants) and small towns than in big cities. However, these associations are small and they have few paid positions, relying instead on volunteer work. In big cities and large metropolitan areas, a smaller number of associations employ a larger number of paid workers, mostly for skilled work.

The growth in the number of associations was accompanied by a change in their types. The field has for a long time been dominated by charitable or religious associations. Between 1960 and 1970, the number of leisure associations increased. Today, consumer groups or citizen organizations are common; they serve as links between citizens and public authorities and

Table 10.1. Number of New Associations Created in 1982.

Primary Goal	Number	Percentage of Total
Sports	7,237	18.4
Religion	676	1.7
Private schools	213	0.5
Political	1,163	2.9
Special boarding schools	1,076	2.7
National heritage protection	683	1.7
Research, training	2,599	6.6
Art	4,116	10.4
Alumni associations	379	1.0
Parents	1,104	2.8
Work, production	1,692	4.3
Friendly associations	2,072	5.3
Leisure	4,803	12.2
Social	3,558	9.0
The elderly	1,126	2.9
Environment	960	2.4
Landlords and tenants	1,362	3.5
Advocacy	1,541	3.9
Professional	1,792	4.5
Community radio stations	1,285	3.3
Total	39,437	100.0

Source: Forse, 1984.

introduce new forms of participatory democracy (Passaris and Raffi, 1983). The current association sector deals with issues that greatly overlap those dealt with in the public sector. Relations with public authorities can lead to conflicts, confrontations, or negotiations; associations can also serve as extensions of the government.

An analysis of associations by their economic sectors suggests that they are mainly concentrated in nonmarket services (see Table 10.2), particularly in the field of entertainment, culture, and sports (22.2% of associations and 8.4% of jobs), social welfare (10% of associations and 28% of jobs), and finally in teaching, research, and health. Another source (Ministry of Social Affairs, 1983–1984) analyzes the associations involved in health and welfare fields. It shows the important role played by associations in the French welfare field. The Ministry of Social Affairs claims that the number of associations involved in this

Table 10.2. Associations According to Economic Sectors (1986).

	Associations		Paid Employees	
	Number	Percentage	Number	Percentage
Agriculture, forestry, fishing and food industries	2,355	1.4	2,255	0.2
Manufacturing	1,568	0.9	9,830	1.2
Housing, civil engineering	310	0.2	705	0.1
Wholesale and retail trade	430	0.3	739	0.1
Hotels, bars, restaurants	13,469	8.1	53,214	6.5
Counseling, legal advice and assistance	6,973	4.2	35,968	4.4
Teaching and research	15,624	9.4	126,068	15.4
Health	4,245	2.6	118,146	14.4
Social welfare	16,685	10.0	237,565	28.9
Entertainment, cultural, and sports services	36,996	22.2	68,731	8.4
Insurance	601	0.4	5,561	0.7
Financial institutions	216	0.1	3,635	0.4
Prevention and social security	821	0.5	12,252	1.5
Others	68,107	40.9	144,754	17.6
Total	166,366	100.0	820,614	100.0

Source: National Institute of Statistics and Economic Surveys, 1987.

sector averaged 90,000 in 1982, with 7 to 8 million members. Of these, 7,000 managed residential homes with a total of 550,000 beds, employed 290,000 persons and ran a combined yearly budget of 46.5 billion francs. Associations seem to be important actors in the field of welfare as they constitute a major partner for public authorities. This is especially true for local authorities because associations function in a limited territorial area, which usually overlaps the administrative area.

The Organization of Local Welfare Policy in France

In France the term *welfare assistance* implies assistance guaranteed by law and provided by a national bureaucracy. This assistance is subject to strict regulations and applies only to a number of well-defined categories of the population (mainly the elderly, the disabled, children, and the sick). It is also subject to various tests, such as nationality and length of residence.

For a long time, local welfare programs were slow to develop in France, especially if compared with West Germany or Great Britain. Lately, however, France is seeing a fast growth in local welfare expenditures. This is coupled with the trend to decrease centralized welfare spending (National Institute of Statistics and Economic Surveys, 1987). Many expectations are raised in the process of development of a local welfare policy. Criticism of the welfare state and of public intervention in general is not directed at the local level. Local authorities are expected to intervene to supplement measures provided by the national level. Furthermore, the local government is expected to modify its policies so that they fit the specific characteristics of the population; to that end, local communities have a high degree of autonomy in their financial matters.

The 1982 Decentralization Act changed the traditional mode of territorial development in a highly centralized country, since it considerably strengthened the powers of local authorities. Three levels of local authorities were created and were expected to play new increased roles.

1. The regions, also called "territorial communities" by the act. There are twenty-two regions, and their main functions are local planning and regional development, building infrastructure for secondary schools, and vocational training.
2. The departments act as local, decentralized extensions of government services. There are ninety-five departments, and they oversee the provision of the national welfare services at the local level.
3. The boroughs are the smallest unit of local government.

The boroughs are an interesting feature of the French political system because of their number (over 36,000) and their potential impact. Their combined expenditure represents two-thirds of the total spending for local communities. They spend one-fourth of their budget on human services: health, welfare, education, and cultural services (Home Office). This in itself underscores the importance of this administrative level in the sphere of local welfare policy. Furthermore, boroughs are par-

Welfare Systems Through Local Associations in France 221

ticularly relevant in the field of welfare. The following points are noteworthy:

- Social problems are mostly found at the level of boroughs, where users, citizens, and public authorities interact.
- Except for fixed-income maintenance programs, boroughs have a high level of discretion as to the particular national programs they implement; this is called "optional assistance." They determine the relative importance of these programs or policies, choose the method of intervention (transfers in kind or cash, collective equipment or services), and decide on the persons or categories of people who will benefit from them.
- The political system at the borough level, the borough council, which is directly elected by the voters, and the proximity of the various actors to the issues create a situation where debates between concerned parties are continuous. This is particularly true for the relations between the local authorities and citizens. Naturally, citizens who are organized have an advantage; this gives associations an important role to play at that level.
- The funding sources of boroughs, based on tax collection both from individual households and business enterprises, create a situation of great inequalities between boroughs: smaller boroughs have less resources.

This last point is especially striking when we look at the distribution of boroughs by their population size (Table 10.3).

Historical Background

Both voluntary organizations and local authorities have always adapted smoothly to social and political changes in France. Charities, originally under religious auspices, are now called associations. They were able to develop new features and adapt to the present era and its particular needs. They have always been pioneers in detecting social needs and in defining policies and measures that needed to be implemented. With the evolution

Table 10.3. Number of Boroughs and Their Inhabitants.

Size of the Borough	Number of Boroughs	Percentage	Population (in thousands)	Percentage	Aggregate Percentage
Less than 500	31,208	85.8	11,448	21.1	21.1
From 500 to 2,000	1,205	3.3	3,120	5.8	26.9
From 2,000 to 5,000	2,456	6.7	6,500.6	11.9	38.8
From 5,000 to 10,000	800	2.2	5,645.7	10.4	49.2
From 10,000 to 30,000	553	1.5	9,543.7	17.6	66.8
From 30,000 to 100,000	194	0.5	9,552.9	17.6	84.4
More than 100,000	36	0.2	8,440	15.6	100.0
Total	36,452	100.0	54,250.9	100.0	

Source: National Institute of Statistics and Economic Surveys (1987), 1982 census data.

of the welfare state, the public sector took over the social services that were planned, tried out, and improved by associations. At a later stage of development, it was agreed that such services should be delivered at the community level by public authorities.

A few examples will illustrate this point. In the period before the welfare state, charities were seen as the proper organizational bodies to take care of the poor. Public authorities limited their role to maintaining law and order. This division of authority, however, was affected by the extent of poverty, and laws against vagrancy coexisted with institutions such as poorhouses, homes for the sick, and later general hospitals, all of which engaged in private fundraising to help the poor. This division of labor between government and associations already constituted the beginning of the complementary relationship that is still prevalent today.

In 1793, as a result of the French Revolution, the right to welfare assistance was recognized. Although the great assistance acts were not passed until the end of the nineteenth century, this new recognition implied that an actual involvement of government in welfare issues was beginning to emerge. At the same time, charities continued to help the numerous populations excluded from welfare assistance and developed several new programs, for example "reception centers" that housed, fed, cured, and took charge of the poor and abandoned children, soup kitchens, housing, assistance, and donations of food or clothes.

Since 1960, public welfare policy has focused more on building a proper community infrastructure so that other bodies can provide services. As a result, associations have oriented themselves toward providing services. For example, in the area of the care for the elderly, the government was building homes for the elderly and the associations were developing support services to help them remain in their homes (home helps, home care, meals on wheels). At a later stage, these services were taken over by local authorities. The actual services, organized by the boroughs, benefit from sizable public funds. The associations continue to detect new needs and to set up new programs. Recent examples are care for the social life of the elderly in the form of clubs, entertainment, and cultural services. These are created and developed by associations and are later transferred to become the local government's responsibility.

The development of the programs for the elderly highlights the process and the level of intervention by both government and associations. Yet the choice of the populations being cared for also illustrates the complementary aspect of both structures. For a long time, the elderly were a population that charities were most interested in, and indeed they were one of the major categories of poor people until 1977, when a "minimum living standard benefit for the elderly" was enacted. Today they are less likely to experience utter destitution but they are still the category most cared for by local authorities, both at the department and borough levels. They constitute a group that is very sensitive to neighborhood solidarity and their impact is becoming more and more important in the electorate. At election time they fastidiously take into account the achievements of the local candidates.

As care for the elderly is basically the responsibility of public authorities, associations are tending to shift their attention to other population categories that have inappropriate public schemes of social welfare. A case in point is the long-term unemployed, those who are no longer eligible for unemployment benefits and who, when single, cannot benefit from the family welfare benefits. With no public programs to resort to, they turn to charities for help, the charity groups provide meals, emergency assistance, and shelter, and sometimes exert pressure on the economic environment to try to create jobs. The introduction of the recent minimum income (1988) will mostly benefit the unemployed and will certainly affect the activities of associations in this domain. As a matter of fact, associations have already been involved in the investigation process of claims along this policy.

Characteristics of Public Institutions and Associations

When we analyze the specific characteristics of public institutions and associations, it is not surprising to find complementary functions between them; actually there are both complementary and interdependent aspects at many levels of decision, production, and planning. By focusing on those, we can get a good idea how associations and local authorities cooperate in a form of partnership to intervene in various areas. Here we are discussing the small associations that have kept their original spirit and function.

The differences between associations and public institutions can be seen as nine points:

1. *Self-organized versus publicly sanctioned.* Associations come into being as a result of self-organization of citizens; this in turn strengthens their participation and responsibility. The elected members of local authorities define and supply services to passive citizens, consumers, or users of social services.

2. *Selectivity versus universality.* Associations can be biased and can defend particular interests; they can be selective in their choice of services supplied or beneficiaries. Conversely, the principle of equality for all citizens before the law strengthens the universal nature of the services supplied by the public authorities in a given territory. An analysis of the current association movement in France shows that the self-organization of citizens takes place primarily among the middle class; lower-class populations, foreigners in particular, are excluded from services

Welfare Systems Through Local Associations in France 225

provided by associations and in general from participating in the social dialogue (Forse, 1984). Such populations have government services to count on.

3. *Volunteers versus professionals.* Associations are based on nonprofessional volunteers' work and initiatives. This limitation affects their activities and interventions; sometimes the situation requires the involvement of a skilled worker. The main advantages of using volunteer labor are lower costs, enthusiasm, and dynamism. But unpaid work often implies low skill and irregular service. Public authorities provide the competence of professionals and technicians, and the control of elected officials.

4. *Unstable financing versus regular budget.* Associations use funds from a variety of sources, which are often limited and unstable: public subsidies, private foundations, donations, members' fees, loaned equipment or premises, services of staff paid for by public authorities, and so on. This variety sometimes implies a lower level of costs in associations. Local authorities use regular budgets which are financed by compulsory taxes.

5. *Flexibility versus formal management.* Public administrations are subject to many constraining regulations, which put an additional burden on the agency's management, already burdened by the size and variety of the services supplied. Thus, for instance, the constraints of the wage scale and the skills scale of local civil servants can create a shortage of jobs for a number of skilled posts. Another example has to do with time lags in decision and production: public accounting systems cause delays and often prevent local authorities from intervening in emergency cases. On the other hand, associations are characterized by a flexible management structure, a result of their size and of the fact that the services they provide are few, well-targeted, and clearly identified, but also of the limited constraints of regulations governing associations.

6. *Flexible interventions versus standardized action.* Because of their management and their decision-making processes, associations can come up with quick, flexible, innovative solutions. Public authorities are associated with slow, standardized, yet proven and powerful solutions.

7. *Adaptability versus stability of structures.* Associations must

adapt to changing conditions and renew their structures or face extinction. Public structures are characterized by stability. Trying out a policy or program for a limited period raises considerable difficulties in public administration. An association seems more appropriate for short-time measures or for actions that require innovations.

8. *Private versus public origin of programs.* The identity of the founders of a movement or those who control its spending, as well as the origin of funds, are not always apparent in associations, for reasons that may be related to their diversity. On the other hand, public programs and their financing are clearly identifiable. Sometimes this determines which of the two auspices will be chosen for a specific program. For example, because public welfare assistance is frequently turned down by some people, such services are now provided by solidarity measures (associations) set up by the government. In areas that may be considered irrelevant in a period of recession, such as cultural programs, an association may be a more suitable provider than the local authority. Conversely, the private origin of associations may cause suspicion among some people, who might prefer the neutral aspects of public intervention.

9. *Local initiatives versus legitimacy.* Associations need not only public economic support, which represents the largest proportion of their resources, but also official recognition by the government, which gives them legitimacy. Local elected officials try to use associations as a means to get closer to the population, as a form of dialogue with the citizens. This represents an involvement in the assessment of their needs, and in the definition and implementation of the services offered. This helps them get the citizens' approval of their actions; it also helps them get reelected.

Types of Associations and Forms of Relationship with Local Authorities

This section of the chapter is based on the situation observed in a number of French towns; data from a survey conducted in a large number of French boroughs will enable us in a later

Welfare Systems Through Local Associations in France

section to complete these observations and to add quantitative dimensions on the type, position, and role of associations at the local level.

The present diversity of the French urban landscape, the different sizes of administrative buroughs, and the relative importance of metropolitan areas explain the unequal roles various boroughs play in the field of welfare policy. Furthermore, the economic, social, political, and demographic differences between urban and rural areas lead to major differences in local measures of welfare policy. The roles and scope of activities that associations may have in different localities can therefore be quite variable. Two criteria seem to play a key role: the size of the borough and its relative rural or urban nature.

The level of local welfare programs depends on the size of the borough. Small ones are unlikely to get programs that entail economic activities, which might bring employment and add funds to their budget; businesses are seldom set up in a borough that has no sufficient infrastructure and housing. In addition, tax revenues in small boroughs are low, and any change in the tax structure is not easily accepted. Bigger boroughs are able to welcome various economic activities that are a source of wealth, both from taxes levied on firms and individual income taxes.

Besides the question of financing, boroughs are confronted with the problem of the minimum number of participants in certain activities. In small boroughs, it is difficult to set up viable social services; it is generally agreed that below a population of ten thousand, no local social service can be reasonably provided.

Interborough cooperation is one way to compensate for the negative consequence of a very limited population. This is why the borough's location — urban or rural — is important. As the situation stands now, cooperation can take place only among neighboring boroughs, and therefore such arrangements are more readily found among boroughs within the same metropolitan area. Towns, as opposed to the rural areas, can supply various urban services, such as markets, that might compensate for a shortage in public services in some areas. For example, the issues pertaining to the care of the elderly in their homes do not raise the same questions in towns as they do in the country, and it is not surprising that these services were created in rural areas. Finally, the condition of the welfare program often depends on the location of boroughs within the metropolitan area; satellite boroughs, boroughs in the center city, and bedroom boroughs do not define their welfare needs in the same way.

The diversity of the local situations and the inequality of the welfare systems imply that the roles played by associations would greatly vary. The next section will discuss the characteristics of association features in rural and urban boroughs respectively.

The Association Life in Small Rural Boroughs

In small boroughs with fewer than two thousand inhabitants, there are few public welfare programs, because of a shortage of resources. A local, often part-time employee fills the main functions, particularly those related to a claimant's civil status. As far as welfare assistance is concerned, the only aspects the local authorities deal with are investigations for welfare assistance claims. However, in such small locales, solidarity plays an important part. Elected officials, confronted by a problem that concerns one of their constituencies, will try to solve it through neighborly solidarity or through their own network of supporters. In such situations, associations play a decisive role.

Two types of associations are likely to be found in rural areas: small local and intervillage voluntary associations, and local branches of large national associations.

Small Local Voluntary Associations. A substantial number of small local associations, created and maintained by volunteers, are operating. They generally have extremely limited resources, which mostly come from the members' fees, although they sometimes receive a very limited subsidy from the local authority and they often use loaned premises from the local authority. The most common local associations in rural boroughs are associations of war veterans and sports associations.

Welfare Systems Through Local Associations in France 229

Associations providing social services (such as for elderly or parents) are somewhat different. They involve larger budgets and entail certain costs for the participants (or a third party). Thus, social services associations are seldom confined to one village, for reasons of economies of scale. Rather, intervillage associations are created to provide a variety of services to the populations of several neighboring boroughs. These associations, when they provide services deemed to be very important, are subsidized by the boroughs on the basis of the number of users from each borough.

This situation creates a balanced relationship between local authorities and associations. As local financing of associations is minimal, the result is an independent operation of these associations. Thus, they are able to fill essential functions that would have otherwise had to be filled by the local authorities. This structure in turn leads to close collaboration between associations and local authorities in these boroughs.

Local Branches of National Associations. At another level, rural areas often host local branches of large national associations. They form federations at department level and they act both at the village and intervillage levels. Two major types of associations can be found in this category: charity associations and service associations.

Large charity associations such as Emmaus, the Catholic Assistance, the People's Help, and ATD Fourth World are present in rural areas. Here their major goals are similar to those in urban areas: to intervene in situations of total deprivation. They provide emergency cash, pay the rent or heating bills, and sometimes even provide groceries.

Large service associations, initially formed by several families, are connected to federations of rural families; they play a prominent role in rural association life. Most of these associations were founded around 1945, to fulfill the numerous collective needs resulting from the war. They have developed mutual help services in response to the changing needs in rural areas. The federation usually encourages the establishment of associations, most of which are intervillage associations. They are based on volunteer work and they provide a variety of social services. Often they provide mandated social services that local authorities cannot provide.

They are also involved in the process of establishing new associations by helping them locate volunteers or providing advice in managing them. They negotiate with local authorities for permission to use the premises. They train association leaders in obtaining public financing and provide consultation on organizational issues. The federation can also provide funds to encourage the establishment of an association.

Their services are financed by users' payments, which complement the private or public funds collected in other ways. Sponsorship by a local bank can be substantial. Other funds are raised by fairs, raffles, sales of donated products, and so on.

The relationship between these associations and local authorities is one of close collaboration. In fact, local authorities frequently ask these associations to provide a certain service at the village level, usually in premises loaned by the local authority. Associations and local authorities frequently discuss whether to initiate a new program and how to share the responsibilities for it. However, tensions or conflicts between the federation or its representatives and the local authority do occur, mostly because of personal reasons, and can sometimes lead to a situation where the parties refuse to collaborate. Ideological or political conflicts can sometimes neutralize collaborative relationships between local representatives and association leaders. Associations can be stereotyped as being left wing, Christian, or right wing, and therefore be turned down by biased local authorities.

Services provided by these associations are often intended for the elderly, who constitute a prominent and increasingly larger proportion of the rural population. Typical services include:

- Home help and domiciliary care services. These services, although part of the welfare assistance system, cannot always be provided by local authorities. Associations played an important role in creating them and continue to provide them, with the help of institutional funds, when local au-

thorities cannot afford to. In the past, before these services were included in welfare assistance, they were provided by voluntary home helpers. Today home help services in rural areas are important providers of part-time jobs.
- Home visits.
- Social clubs, with weekly meetings, outings, and holiday celebrations.
- Child care services, mostly during school holidays.
- Advocacy on behalf of an individual elderly person.
- Temporary shelter for the elderly. Some elderly people have problems living alone only during the winter. The associations have first resorted to neighbors, asking some families to provide temporary shelter for the elderly. Later they broadened their program by remunerating host families. Today, this service is provided on a large scale in rural areas. This is another example of the innovative, creative, and experimental abilities of the associations and how they can become a driving force for public welfare policy.

Associations and Urban Authorities in Urban Areas

The size of boroughs is directly related to the potential funding of welfare associations: larger budgets enable local authorities to develop extensive welfare programs that can be sufficiently diversified to account for the various needs and different claims at a given local level. Also, large urban boroughs can play a compensatory role in case of government shortcomings, by granting their social services additional means to act. Their intervention in the field of welfare policy has increased, diversified, and became more technical and sophisticated. For example, for a borough of four hundred thousand inhabitants, there are, on the average, nine hundred municipal staff employed by the various social services, whose salaries are exclusively drawn from the municipal budget. The basic services, which deal with situations of distress, are in most cases provided with the collaboration of large charity associations. In addition, these boroughs manage the main welfare assistance services, intended for the elderly and disabled people, which draw from various institutional funds. They have diversified not only their interventions but the beneficiaries as well: while local help in rural areas is primarily directed toward the elderly, a sizable part of municipal welfare action in large towns is geared toward families. Municipal administrations have sometimes introduced, as an option, various sophisticated services such as telephone safety services for the elderly.

While welfare policy in large boroughs is mostly managed by the municipal administration, numerous associations can be found there too, playing new roles and serving new populations. Despite their advantages in the field of welfare policy, larger boroughs face a number of problems related to their size, which have implications for the way they provide services and the way they use the traditional municipal structures and the associations. Three of these problems are noteworthy.

First, as a result of the distance between local authorities and the citizens, it is more difficult to evaluate citizens' needs, demands, and ideas and to incorporate them into programs administered by local authorities.

Second, local life can be a focus of debates on priorities in public spending, which can lead to change local authorities' certain choices. For example, the traditional debates between taxpayers and social service users can induce local authorities to hide their role in the development of some activities. This is often the case with leisure activities for the elderly. If the borough's tax rate is perceived as too high or if other needs, considered more important, are not fulfilled, local authorities will use an association to cover the cost of these activities.

Third, a fragile municipal political coalition or a possible conflict between the political and the administrative bodies, as in the case of a change in the political leadership after elections, can create difficulties in the decision-making or management processes and move local debates into the realm of service provision.

These conditions have clear implications for the local welfare policy structure and its recourse to associations.

In urban boroughs, five types of associations coexist along with the large charity associations mentioned earlier, dealing

Welfare Systems Through Local Associations in France 233

primarily, as in rural areas, with situations of distress and great emergency, and with the confederation of urban families, which are the urban equivalent of the federation of rural families. We will briefly consider each type.

Small Voluntary Associations. The small voluntary associations of unpaid and active members are numerous in larger boroughs; there are, on average, 150 associations of this type for a borough of one hundred thousand inhabitants. They provide important services, because they operate in areas that are hard to reach, such as detection of distress situations in households, psychological support, assistance in job seeking, advice on social rights and formulation of claims and demands for welfare assistance, and planning and implementing innovative schemes or programs. They also provide cultural and social services, stressing concepts of mutual help and empowerment; this gives them a prevention orientation. Although they receive a limited budget from local authorities, these associations heavily depend on those authorities for in-kind supports.

Boroughs of a certain size (from about fifty thousand inhabitants) usually have a "house of associations," which is overseen by an elected member, in charge of the association life in town. The house of associations is the meeting place for the town's associations, where they use its facilities: mail service, telephone, photocopier, meeting rooms, and so on. The local authorities take great pride in the existence of the local associations; their activities and dynamism provide testimony on the quality of the local debate between public authorities and its citizenry. In addition to the services they provide, they foster a local dialogue; through them, the authorities can get an initial idea of public opinion.

Free Expression and Claim Associations. Free expression and claim associations, which are basically citizens groups and consumer associations, have seen a tremendous growth in large boroughs. They play a significant role in bringing local authorities and citizens together. Some of them, for example the district committees, have been encouraged by local authorities, who see them as partners in debates on municipal projects. These associations have an important role as mediators between local authorities and citizens. They help in the formulation of community collective needs, enabling local authorities to act with more precision and better control their opposition. The famous Committees for the Protection of Environment are an example of this structure. Very often, local authorities work hard to get the approval of the "noisy" associations. In most cases, there is a cordial relationship between these associations and local authorities, but sometimes conflicts do appear.

Management Associations: Contractual Relations with Associations. Local authorities can sign contracts with associations, to allow them to use equipment or to provide health or social services, usually under the jurisdiction of the local administration. In such cases, associations receive public funding from the various bodies concerned and they are then called "management associations." A management association may decide to focus on a mission that will benefit the entire community and whose scope is broader than the interests of its members. Its domain of activity and its methods of intervention will be specified and regulated in the agreement. These associations usually have a large staff. The frequency of these contractual relationships increases with the size of the boroughs, as Table 10.4 illustrates. In the large towns where municipal management is possible, these associations are more dependent on the local authorities.

Associations in Which Local Authorities Are Partners in Management and Finance. The larger the town, the more associations develop where local authorities share in their management and finance. Usually these associations are large, both in budget and number of employees. They function because of the considerable municipal funds, which dominate other sources. The involvement of local authorities is sometimes so overwhelming that the term "associative management of municipal affairs" is used.

The form and the levels of involvement of local authorities in the management of these associations can be very different:

Table 10.4. Agreements Between the Social Service Offices of Boroughs and Associations, by Size of Boroughs.

Size of Boroughs	Inhabitants		
	Less than 2,000	From 2,000 to 25,000	More than 25,000
Frequency of agreements made with associations	6.7%	21.4%	31.4%
Object of the agreement			
Equipment management	2.9	20.6	37.2
Social service management	58.9	56.8	25.7
Other service management	2.9	7.1	16.2
Other	35.3	15.5	20.9
Total	100.0%	100.0%	100.0%

Source: Mizrahi-Tchernonog, 1983.

the mayor can be the president of the board of directors; elected members or executives from the city council can be members of the board; the city council representatives can even have the majority on the board. In other cases, the board of directors can be composed of representatives who are not connected with local authorities; however, their decisions are not supposed to contradict programs developed by the local authorities. The city council's support is predicated on the continued compliance with the guidelines defined by the local authorities.

Local authorities choose an association type of management principally because they need a partner and want to benefit from the favorable elements of associations: diversified resources, lower costs, flexible management and actions, volunteer work—assets that local authorities can readily use. This integrative structure provides the means for collaboration between political management, administrative services, and citizens. The partners bring their own legitimacy and competence, but this partnership cannot take place without a certain loss of identity for the associations.

Paramunicipal Associations. Some local authorities adopt the legal structures of associations to free themselves from the constraints of public management and employment regulations in the public sector, or to change the municipal origin of programs or their financing. Such associations, which operate only with municipal subsidies and whose general assembly and board of directors are exclusively composed of locally elected members, city councilors, or their representatives, are the mere extensions of the municipal social services. They have no other reason to exist but to avoid the managerial or financial regulations that apply in the public sector.

Summary

This survey of the French association at the local level has highlighted the incredible adaptability of association structures and the ways public authorities make use of these forms. Associations are sometimes partners of local authorities, sometimes mediators, and sometimes mere instruments in the hands of authorities. In using all the possible aspects of associations, local authorities have succeeded in considerably extending their activities, in differentiating their actions, and at the same time in benefiting from funds provided by associations. At the same time their interventions have provided a political advantage.

A new function of local authorities in the field of welfare policy, related to the intervention of the association sector, is taking shape. Historically, local authorities initially performed police functions, then moved into performing administrative and technical functions. Currently, it seems that municipal authorities are performing a function of animation, of organizing and steering the association life in the field of welfare policy.

References

Archambault, E. "The Total Number of Associations." *Cooperatives' Studies Review,* 1984, *12*(4), 11–41.

Delorme, C., and Andre, C. *The State and the Economy: An Attempt to Explain Public Spending in France.* Paris: Le Seuil, 1983.

Forse, M. "The Creation of Associations as an Indicator of Social Changes." *Economic Observations and Diagnoses,* Jan. 1984, 6, 125–145.

Ministry of Social Affairs. *Welfare Policy and Associations.* Inspector-General of Social Affairs, 1983–1984.

Mizrahi-Tchernonog, V. "Local Social Policy and the Management of Bureaus of Social Assistance." Paris: National Center for Scientific Research, Social Economy Laboratory, 1983.

National Institute of Statistics and Economic Surveys. SIRENE file of July 10, 1987. (List of all enterprises employing at least one person. Compiled from 1982 census data.)

Passaris, S., and Raffi, G. *The Associations.* Paris: La Decouverte, 1983.

Index

A

Abramson, A. J., 2, 5, 9, 14
Accountability, 209
Acheson, N., 121, 127, 138
Action for Community Employment (ACE; Northern Ireland), 133, 137–138
Active citizenship, 154–155, 163, 168
Adams, C., 159
Adaptability, 225–226
Addy, T., 158
Advocacy function, 4, 11, 161
Advocacy groups, 151
Alcoholism, care for, 80–82
Althoff, P., 128
Analysis, level of, 4, 9–11
Anderson, D., 150

Anglo-Irish Agreement, 130, 139
Anheier, H. K., 15, 17, 20, 21, 53, 54
Aquina, H. J., 10, 21, 22, 59
Arbeiterwohlfahrt (Germany), 43, 44
Archambault, E., 217
Ascoli, U., 198, 200, 211
Associations (France), 215–219
Associative movements, 216

B

Barbetta, G. P., 210
Bargal, D., 188
Bassanini, M. C., 210
Bauer, R., 33, 43
Belfast Area Teams (BAT; Northern Ireland), 133, 134, 143
Berger, P. L., 6

Berry, L., 167
Best, R., 166
Billis, D., 161
Birrell, D., 121, 122
Bones, B., 81
Bosanquet, N., 155
Brenton, M., 3, 93, 158, 169
Brett, C., 139
Brigitte, B., 103
Britain, 24-25, 148; and Northern Ireland, 124, 125, 126-127, 128; pluralism in delivery, 156-162; pluralism in finance, 162-168; Thatcher era, 151-155; welfare alternatives, 149-151; welfare state, 13, 148-149
Brox, O., 89
Bundesarbeitsgemeinschaft, 41
Bureaucracy, 6, 7, 33, 60, 149
Burke, E., 5
Burkeman, S., 165

C

CARITAS (Germany), 41, 43, 44
Catholic church: CARITAS (Germany), 41, 43, 44; and education, 65-66; and politics, 65-66, 69; and public agencies, 208; as special-purpose provider, 110; and subsidiarity, 5-6, 33-34, 36, 37, 69; and taxation, 51-52
Central Community Relations Unit (CCRU; Northern Ireland), 132
Centralization, 178, 183, 187, 200
Cesareo, V., 207
Charities: A Framework for the Future, 142
Charities Aid Foundation, 152, 163, 164, 166
Charity, 12, 13, 88, 148, 163, 164-168, 221, 222-223, 224, 229
Charity Commission, 165
Child care, 45, 48
Church-state relations, 15, 36-37, 110
Civil law, 35-36
Clarke, M., 152
Collaborative model, 19-20, 27-28. *See also* Cooperation, government-third-sector

Collective goods, 7, 62, 100-103, 111-112
Colozzi, I., 201, 202, 206
Commercial nonprofits, 104
Community development, 133-138
Community relations, 128-133
Community Relations Council (CRC; Northern Ireland), 133
Competition, 159
Competitive paradigm, 5-8; different functions, 11; finance vs. delivery of services, 11-12; ideology, 8-9; impact of history, 12-15; level of analysis, 9-11; national traditions, 15
Confessional organizations, 66-67
Conflict, government-third-sector, 5-8
Conservatism, 6, 66, 69, 89, 127, 150, 151-152
Consumer democracy, 87, 92
Contracting, for services, 157-158, 210-211, 234
Cooperation, government-third-sector, 8-9, 12-15; France, 228-236; Germany, 37-38; Italy, 204; Netherlands, 60; Northern Ireland, 133-138; Norway, 82, 84-87, 93-94
Corrigan, P., 149, 159
Couwenberg, S., 69
Crick, B., 71

D

Daalder, H., 65
Dahl, R. A., 59, 68, 70
Dahrendorf, R., 169
Darby, J., 121, 123
Davis, B., 161
De Ambrogio, U., 206, 208, 210, 211
Decentralization, 15-16, 23, 87, 90, 92, 101, 152, 200, 220
de Hoog, R. H., 20, 157, 158
Delivery, of services, 11-12, 16-20, 153, 178; pluralism in, 156-162, 188-190
DeLorean, J., 130
Demand diversity, 69, 101-104, 178, 187, 192

Index

Dente, B., 200
Department of the Environment, 154
Dependency, 150, 168
Deutscher Paritätischer Wohlfahrtsverband (Germany), 43-44
Deutscher Verein, 37
Deutsches Rotes Kreuz (Germany), 44
Diakonisches Werk (Germany), 43, 44
Diessenbacher, H., 33, 43
DiMaggio, P., 54
Directory of Social Change, 165
Dome organizations (Netherlands), 60
Douglas, J., 53
Dowson, S., 157
Dual model, 17, 19

E

Ecclesiastical law, 36
Education, 45, 48-49, 50, 65-66, 184-185
Edwards, J., 167
Efficiency, 60, 61-62
Efficiency Scrutiny (Britain), 155, 168, 170
Eisenstadt, S. N., 181, 182, 183
Elackman, T., 143
Elderly care, 48, 50, 223, 231
Employment, third-sector, 41, 45, 48, 106
Engberg, J., 85
Erikson, R., 76
Esping-Anderson, G., 15
European Community (EC), 95, 137, 139
Extension ladder theory, 13

F

Family, 5, 32-33
Federal Consortium of Free Welfare (Germany), 41
Federalism, 34-35
Ferrera, M., 211
Field of service analysis, 4
Figurehead associations, 216
Filer Commission, 2
Financing, of services: changing, 178, 186, 189; contract funding, 160, 210-211; vs. delivery, 11-12; in government-third-sector models, 16-20; pluralism in, 162-168, 189, 190-192; stability of, 225
Fine, L., 183
Fiscal welfare, 92
Fitzduff, M., 132
Flexibility, 62, 225
Flora, P., 211
Forse, M., 217, 225
Foster, R., 132
Foundations Association in Israel, 189
France, 26-27; associations, 215-219; associations vs. public institutions, 224-226; background, 221-224; Decentralization Act, 220; government-third-sector cooperation, 228-236; local welfare, 219-221, 222-224, 227-236; rural associations, 228-231; urban associations, 231-236; welfare state, 222
Frazer, H., 132
Free expression and claim associations, 233-234
Free-rider problem, 7, 62, 113-114
Free welfare associations (Germany), 38, 39, 40, 41-50
Frey, R. L., 103
Fuglum, P., 81
Functionalist approach, 205
Functions, third sector, 3-4, 11
Funding organizations, 189

G

Galnoor, I., 183
Geiser, K., 105, 106
Germany, 20-21, 31-32; background, 33-41; federalism, 34-35; free welfare associations, 38, 39, 40, 41-50; government-third-sector cooperation, 37-38; legal system, 35-36; subsidiarity, 32-41; subsidiarity and third-party government, 50-54; third-party government, 32, 50-54
Gidron, B., 25, 188

Giolitti, G., 198
Gladstone, F., 149, 169
Glazer, N., 6
Gloppen, S., 92
"Golden age," of volunteerism, 7, 12, 76
Government: and competitive paradigm, 5-8; financing of service, 11-12, 17-19; functions, 11; level of analysis, 9-10; local, 107-109, 123, 129, 153-154, 200, 220-221; models of, relations with third sector, 16-20, 77-78; politics, 70-72; regulation, 67; special-purpose, units, 109-111; subsidization, 114-116; third-party, 32, 50-54, 140, 141; welfare state, 1, 6-7, 14, 16, 28-29
Griffiths, H., 129
Grindheim, J. E., 93, 95
Grossman, B., 157, 158, 160

H

Hadley, R., 7
Halfpenny, P., 166
Hall, S., 168
Hansmann, H., 53
Harris, M., 161
Haseltine, M., 143
Hatch, S., 7, 150
Health care: Germany, 45, 50; Israel, 185, 190-191; Italy, 199-200; Netherlands, 59-60, 61, 63-65, 71, 72
Heidenheimer, A. J., 211
Heinze, R. G., 43, 50, 51
Herzog, R., 37
Hestetun, P. A., 88, 95
Hippe, J. M., 92
Hirschman, A. O., 162
History, government-third-sector, 12-15. *See also* individual countries
Holistic social system, 184
Home Office, 155, 168
Hood, C., 58, 122, 142
Horlacher, F., 113
House of associations (France), 233
Hurd, D., 138

I

Ideology, 6-7, 8-9
Immigration (Israel), 178, 179, 185-186, 189-190
Incentives, to voluntarism, 113-116
Individual choice, 161-162
Individual initiative, 1
Individual organization analysis, 4
Individualism, 5, 33
Informationsstelle des Zurcher Sozialwesens, 106
International Fund for Ireland (IFI), 121-122, 133-134, 139, 138-140
Internationalization, 93, 95
Ireland, Northern, 24, 120-123; background, 123-126; community development, 133-138; community relations, 128-133; government and voluntary sector, 126-127; government-third-sector cooperation, 133-138; international support, 138-140; voluntary organizations, 133-138
Ireland, Republic of, 24, 123, 130, 139
Irish Republican Army (IRA), 124, 140, 142
Israel, 25, 179-180; conceptual framework, 177-178; formative era, 182-187; nonprofit financing, 189, 190-192; nonprofit growth, 188-190; pluralistic era, 188-192; Yishuv (prestate) period, 180-182
Israeli Association of Community Centers, 191
Italy, 26, 196-197; background, 197-201; government-third-sector cooperation, 204; interagency relationships, 206-209; "new" voluntarism, 202-205; professionalism, 204-205, 208; reseach limitations, 205-206; social activism, 203-204; voluntary associations, 201-202; welfare state, 199-201

J

Jaffe, E. D., 185
James, E., 53, 176-177

Index

Janowitz, M., 7
Jenkins, S., 193
Jewish Agency, 187, 189
Jones, R., 160
Jones, T., 149, 159

K

Kantonales Steueramt, 105
Kolberg, J. E., 88
Kramer, R. M., 2, 20, 60, 127, 142, 149, 157, 158, 160, 169, 183, 184, 186, 187, 203, 205, 208
Kuhnle, S., 13, 16, 22, 23, 76, 88, 92, 95
Kunz, C., 160

L

Lair, J., 150
Langton, S., 211
Law of Popitz, 107
Lawson, N., 150
Leat, D., 165, 167
Legal system, 15, 35-36
Leu, R. E., 103
Liberalism, 6-7
Lindblom, C. E., 59
Linder, B., 75
Lingas, L. G., 89
Lipset, S. M., 138, 141
Lloyd, J., 149, 159
Local government, 107-109, 123, 129, 153-154, 200, 220-221. *See also* Government
Local welfare, 219-221, 222-224
Lochen, Y., 89
Locke, J., 5
Loney, M., 149
Lorentzen, H., 16, 90
Lyell, L., 138

M

MacDonagh, O., 123
McDowell, R. B., 123
McGinley, A., 143
Management associations, 234
Market: failure, 7, 100-101; mechanism, 16, 150, 156-157, 159-162

Market Opinion Research International (MORI), 124
Marsland, D., 150
Maxwell, S., 159, 161
Media, public, 62, 72
Midre, G., 89
Migration, 107-109
Mill, J. S., 5
Mills, C. W., 100
Ministry of Social Affairs, 218
Mizrahi-Tchernonog, V., 10, 26, 28
Mocroft, I., 150
Models, of government–third-sector relations, 16-20, 77-78
Monopoly powers, 39, 68, 158
Monthly Bulletin of Statistics, 179, 191
Munnike, H. F., 59
Murie, A., 121, 122

N

National associations (France), 229-231
National Council for Voluntary Organizations, 160
National Institute of Statistics and Economic Surveys, 217, 220
National traditions, 15-16
Neoliberalism, 200
Netherlands, 21-22, 57-58; background, 65-67; concept of nongovernmental organizations, 58-61; dome organizations, 60; education, 65-66; ethics and nongovernmental organizations, 68-72; government–third-sector cooperation, 60; health care, 59-60, 61, 63-65, 71, 72; politics and nongovernmental organizations, 65-68, 70-72; social diversity, 69; technical rationale for nongovernmental organizations, 61-65
Neuhaus, R. J., 6
New Israel Fund, 189
New Right, 150, 151-152. *See also* Conservatism
Nisbet, R. A., 6, 75
Nongovernmental organizations (NGOs): concept of, 58-61; and

ethics, 68-72; and politics, 65-68, 70-72; subsidization, 115-116; technical rationale for, 61-65
Nonprofit federalism, 141
Nonprofit sector, 3, 197. *See also* Third sector
Northern Ireland Council for Voluntary Action, 121
Northern Ireland Voluntary Trust (NIVT), 121, 133, 134-137
Norway, 22-23, 75-77; alcoholic-care organizations, 80-82; background, 77-84, 88-89; government-third-sector cooperation, 82, 84-87, 93-94; handicap organizations, 82-84; public health organizations, 79-80; public vs. private responsibility, 79; renewed interest in third sector, 90-91; types of third-sector organizations, 78-79
NOU (Norwegian Public Reports), 89, 90, 92

O

O'Brien, C. C., 143
Occupational welfare, 92
"Oeffentliche Finanzen der Schweiz," 115
Offe, C., 68, 90
Olk, T., 43, 50, 51
Olsen, J. P., 87
Onrheim, G., 95
Organization for Economic Development and Cooperation (OECD), 90
Ostrander, S. A., 211
Oyen, E., 89

P

Paci, M., 13, 90
Paragovernmental organizations (PGOs), 58, 123, 141, 142
Parallel bars theory, 13
Parallel-track model, 19
Paramunicipal associations, 235-236
Pasquinelli, S., 9, 26, 206, 208, 210, 211
Passaris, S., 218
Paternalism, 71-72, 183
Patten, J., 155
Pedersen, A. W., 92
Perlmutter, F., 159
Peterson, J., 167
Pinker, R., 7
Plaschke, J., 34
Pluralism, 149-150, 153, 170-171, 188; in delivery, 156-162, 188-190; in finance, 162-168, 189, 190-192
"Political Vetting," 138
Pope Leo XIII, 34
Pope Pius XI, 34
Posnett, J., 166
Powell, W. W., 197
Preference-guided society, 149
Private goods, 111-112
Private sector. *See* Third sector
Privatization, 1, 10, 159
Professionalism, 62, 204-205, 208, 225
Protestant churches: Diakonisches Werk, 43; and education, 65-66; and politics, 65-66, 69; as special-purpose providers, 110; and subsidiarity, 36; and taxation, 51-52
Public goods, 7, 62, 100-103, 111-112
Public law, 35-36
Public nonprofits, 104
Public policy, 70-72, 85-86
Purchase-of-service contracts, 157-158

Q

Quality, 64-65
Quasi-nongovernmental organizations (quangos; Netherlands), 58

R

Raaum, J., 95
Raffi, G., 218
Ranci, C., 206, 207, 208, 210, 211
Rankin, M., 166
Reagan, R., 5, 9
Red Cross, 44, 80

Index

Regulation, 67, 153
Rein, M., 159
Relay associations, 216
Religion, 178, 181. *See also* Catholic church; Church-state relations; Protestant churches
Representational function, 4, 11
Responsiveness, 201
Ringen, S., 89
Rolston, W., 139
Rose, R., 127
Rosen, B., 191
Rossi, G., 201, 202, 206, 207
Rotter, R., 184
Rush, M., 128

S

Sachse, C., 43
Salamon, L. M., 2, 4, 5, 9, 12, 13, 14, 20, 32, 52, 53, 61, 75, 109, 122, 140, 149, 155, 164, 167, 168, 169
Sands, B., 130
Saxon-Harrold, S., 121
Schendelen, M., 66
Schmitter, P. C., 60, 67, 68, 72
Scholten, I., 60
Schuppert, G. F., 58
Scott, D., 158
Sector level analysis, 4
Seibel, W., 15, 54
Seip, A., 76, 95
Self-help, 87, 150, 151, 197
Selle, P., 13, 16, 22, 23, 88, 93, 95, 96
Service function, 4, 11
Shamay, N., 184
Sinn Fein (Northern Ireland), 124-125, 130, 138, 140, 143
Smolka, G., 165
Social activism, 203-204
Social Democrats, 39, 43, 69-70, 91, 124, 125
Social pressure, 116
Social utility, 205
Socialists, 66, 180-181
Special-interest organizations, 79, 82, 85, 104
Spencer, K., 160

Spiegelhalter, F., 41, 50
Spieker, M., 33
Sporri, D., 105, 106
Stability, 225-226
Stanley, J., 138
State. *See* Government
Statistical Abstracts of Israel, 179
Stewart, J., 152
Stortingsmelding, 90
Subsidiarity, 5-6, 21, 32-33, 69; application of, 37-38; origins of, 33-37; resistance to, 38-41; and third-party government, 50-54
Subsidization, 114-116
Svasand, L., 96
Sweden, 76
Switzerland, 23, 101-102; incentives to voluntarism, 113-116; migration, 107-109; size of third sector, 104-106; social diversity, 103-104; special-purpose governmental units, 109-111; supplementary activities, 12-113
System of National Accounts (SNA), 104

T

Tax deductibility, 116
Tax exemption, 114-115, 159
Taylor, M., 9, 14, 24-25, 28, 153, 166
Tennstedt, F., 43
Thatcher, M., 9, 24
Third-party government, 32, 50-54, 140, 141
Third sector: and competitive paradigm, 5-8; defined, 3-4; finance vs. delivery of services, 11-12; functions, 3-4, 11; and history, 12-15; and ideology, 6-7, 8-9; level of analysis, 4, 9-11; models of, relations with government, 16-20, 77-78; and national traditions, 15-16; renewed interest in, 1-2, 90-91; types of, organizations, 104, 111. *See also* individual countries
Thränhardt, D., 43, 50
Tiebout, C., 108

Titmuss, R. M., 92
Tomlinson, W., 139

U

Unell, J., 165
Unemployed, 223-224
United Kingdom. *See* Britain; Ireland, Northern
United States: origins of welfare state, 12-13; profit/nonprofit competition, 112-113; third-party government in, and Germany, 51-52; third-sector contribution to GNP, 105-106

V

Value guardian role, 208-209
Van Til, J., 211
Volkswirtschaft, Die, 103, 105
Voluntarism, 196-197. *See also* Third sector
Voluntary associations (France), 228-229, 233
Voluntary failure, 140

W

Waerness, K., 89
Wagner, A., 23, 104, 105
Ware, A., 148
Warner, A., 13
Webb, B., 13
Webb, S., 13
Weingrod, A., 183
Weisbrod, B. A., 7, 53, 101, 102, 104, 105, 106, 107, 113, 114, 117
Welfare: Britain, 13, 148-155; dependency, 150; France, 219-224; Germany, 38, 39, 40, 41-50; Israel, 185; Italy, 199-201; Norway, 88-90; pluralism, 149-150, 153; social/fiscal/occupational, 92; state, 1, 6-7, 12-14, 16, 28-29
Williamson, A. P., 24, 121
Wolfenden Committee, 149
Wolfenden Report, 13
Wood, F., 184, 194

Y

Yanay, U., 190, 191
Young, J., 149, 159

Z

Zentralwohlfahrtsstelle der Juden in Deutschland (Germany), 43
Zero-sum competition, 5
Zurcher Gemeindefinanzen, 109, 110
Zweckverbande (Switzerland), 109